The Words of
Our Father

Debi Dickson Wagner

ISBN 978-1-64670-085-1 (Paperback)
ISBN 978-1-64670-086-8 (Hardcover)
ISBN 978-1-64670-087-5 (Digital)

Author Photos—Alanha Lucas, Capture the Dream Photography
Watercolor, Front Cover/Chapter Headings—Norma Jean Sass

Visit our Website at:
http://covenantbooks.com/books/?book=the-wordsof-our-father

Covenant Books, Inc.
11661 Hwy 707
Murrells Inlet, SC 29576
www.covenantbooks.com

Lovingly dedicated to my precious grandchildren, Renly, Isabelle, Remy, Ryker, Blaine, Kiersten, Michael, Joel, Jacob, Ellen, Devin, and others as yet unborn. May you claim our family inheritance of faith, hope, and love and pass it on to my great-grandchildren, my great-great-grandchildren, and beyond.

Truly, nothing else matters.

Artistic Symbolism

F*eathers* symbolize the virtues of hope, faith, and charity. They also represent freedom and the heavens by facilitating flight.

It Couldn't Be Done

Edgar Albert Guest

Somebody said that it couldn't be done
    But he with a chuckle replied
That "maybe it couldn't," but he would be one
    Who wouldn't say so till he'd tried.
So he buckled right in with the trace of a grin
    On his face. If he worried he hid it.
He started to sing as he tackled the thing
    That couldn't be done, and he did it!

Somebody scoffed: "Oh, you'll never do that;
    At least no one ever has done it;"
But he took off his coat and he took off his hat
    And the first thing we knew he'd begun it.
With a lift of his chin and a bit of a grin,
    Without any doubting or quiddit,
He started to sing as he tackled the thing
    That couldn't be done, and he did it.

There are thousands to tell you it cannot be done,
    There are thousands to prophesy failure,
There are thousands to point out to you one by one,
    The dangers that wait to assail you.
But just buckle in with a bit of a grin,
    Just take off your coat and go to it;
Just start in to sing as you tackle the thing
    That "cannot be done," and you'll do it.

Contents

Prologue

At first glance you might believe that this book is about life after death. In actuality it is about *love* after death. To fully comprehend how love can transcend into the afterlife, you have to understand the depth and power of love in this life.

Like many couples my parents vowed publicly to love each other until "death do us part." However, privately, my parents made a deeper vow to love each other even beyond death. We children often heard them proclaim that they would wait for each other in heaven. A promise, laughingly touted, lovingly made, and brought to fulfillment by the depth of their love, which knew no bounds.

This is the story of their love and how my father sent a message, fourteen years after his own death, to support my mother during her transition to the afterlife, where he was waiting patiently—or rather impatiently—for her to join him at the pearly gate, as promised. They walked the journey of love in this world and into the next, faithfully following the example that Christ laid out: "And the greatest of these is love" (Proverbs 3:16).

Somebody Said that It Couldn't Be Done…yet Love Can Do Anything

I t happened in an instant. One minute my sister, Molly, and I were walking across the convention center cafeteria to put our trays away; and the next minute, our lives would be forever altered. Our ways of thinking would be stretched beyond the boundaries of what we always thought we knew but didn't. Our priorities and lifestyles would be analyzed, questioned, and redesigned. What is really important anyway? How can we make amends for injuries inflicted? How do we let go of our grudges and move forward into peace? What does it mean to love selflessly? Our father knew.

We heard his voice—more accurately we felt it, but with the awareness and recognition that comes from having spent every moment in his presence since our lives were breathed into consciousness. It was undeniably the voice of our father, who had passed away fourteen years earlier. We stopped solidly in the middle of the cafeteria, still holding our lunch trays, riveted in place.

I would have talked myself out of what I knew I had heard had I not turned toward my sister. Her face was ashen and she stood eerily still. I knew that she was hearing him too. That reality could not be denied, and we were both transfixed to the voice. We stood dead still and waited for confirmation of what we knew was real in a very unreal sort of way. We waited, we listened, we yearned for our father to continue. We wanted to be with him, to dispel the notion that we had somehow fallen into some other version of reality while we completely lost our grip on this one.

The hustle and bustle of the cafeteria and the sounds of general unruliness faded away as we clung intently to his voice. How comforting and unreal it was to hear that voice after all these years. A voice we thought had been lost to us forever. All the love and admiration we felt for Dad bubbled up with confusion, yearning, and homesickness for a time long past.

Our father spoke volumes with measured words in the short time we stood there, giving our rapt attention to every syllable, every nuance, every glimpse of the man we knew so well. When it was over, we felt queasy and weak in the knees. We could not form the words to confirm the encounter to ourselves or each other. Our heads felt light, and our vision was obscured. We were walking through a cloud without direction or purpose.

It was both surprising and humbling to learn that the impetus for this reunion was not really centered around Molly and me. We were merely the conduit for a more far-reaching message, a message about forgiveness and love eternal. We paled in the shadow of a love much greater than a father feels for his children, no matter how strong that bond.

So egocentricity would not rule the day. From the first sentence our father spoke to the last, he had an agenda. Through later reflection, we slowly gleaned—by the tone and urgency—just what was pushing this exchange. For yes, it was an exchange. However awkward and ineffectual, we also spoke, asked questions, and probed for clarifications as best we could. There were limits to the things he would and would not share and limits to how well we could and could not understand his answers.

It was not a leisurely conversation, for he knew what we did not, that our time with him was limited. In hindsight, we wished we would have chosen our initial, hastily constructed questions more wisely. As it turned out, the first time we talked was really more about Dad trying hard to press through our shock and disbelief. Our emotions surged so high that we could not think clearly. We were euphoric, both light-headed and light hearted.

In a handful of moments, he was trying to help us regain our equilibrium and convince us of the legitimacy of his presence. He attempted to invoke both urgency and love while at the same time impress upon us the time limitations. His task was nearly insurmountable as he had to deal with our scattered and sometimes incoherent questions clouded with our earthly priorities and understandings. Not only did he want us to receive and understand his urgent messages, but he wanted to inspire us to act on his behalf. Yes, our father's mission was thorny, and we were the thorns.

And then, without fanfare or farewells, we sensed that our time with Dad was over. He left us so abruptly, with so many questions still unasked and unanswered. Understandably, we were in shock, yet we yearned for so much more. It is beyond my comprehension how we had the presence of mind to ask to meet with him again the next day. We received assurance that a second opportunity to be with our father would take place. Our intensity was defused, and we could part without creating a sobbing scene—no small blessing considering we were still standing in the middle of the cafeteria in clear view of all of our fellow conference-goers.

Our eyes and our ears released him as our senses returned to the here and now. We were surprised to see that no one else was paying the slightest bit of attention to us. They acted as if the most monumental thing had not even transpired. It was at that moment that we knew it was profound and enduring love that prompted our father to return. My sister and I had shared an experience too surreal to capture or contain. It was beyond words. We had been in the presence of a miracle, and truly, what do you do with that knowledge?

We dispensed with all other plans for the evening and barricaded ourselves in our room at the retreat center, where we were attending a Heart Centered Therapy workshop led so expertly by Alaya Chikly, the founder. While my sister and I had taken numerous classes separately, September 2009 was the first time we had attended together. As we were to later understand, this was but one reason that Dad chose this moment to reach out to us after so many silent years.

In the quiet of our room, Molly and I debriefed; everything began to tumble out of us in jumbled disarray. It was Molly who first ascertained that we had indeed shared the same vision and heard the same words. Now what? What does this mean? It didn't feel clear. What did we actually hear? What did he really want from us, for us? We both felt certain that there was an agenda beyond what we had grasped during the first visit, but what could it possibly be? We had snippets of thoughts, and we clearly felt his intensity, but the overriding focus had not registered amid our tangled emotions.

To dispel any confusion and to preserve the accuracy of our jangled short-term memory, we each scripted what we remembered from the exchange. When we merged the two accounts, a clearer picture emerged.

"Oh, I'd forgotten he said that."

"Now I think I remember he worded it this way."

We mulled over each precious utterance with an enormous amount of love. It was disjointed at best, and we longed for the presence of mind in the moment to have captured the words more precisely, to have paid closer attention to the nuances of what he said with and without words.

It was late into the evening before we realized that we had an opportunity before us to be more focused during Dad's next visit. We spent the rest of the night generating questions. We didn't know how much time we would have or how possessive Dad would be of the time. We laboriously created an expansive list, ranging from silly to spiritual and everything in between. We wrote some questions specific to our lives and our futures, some that were blatantly self-serving. We couldn't know or understand the bounds of his capabilities, willingness, or desires to appease our curiosities or indulge our own petty human interests.

We had hoped to rewrite and prioritize the list, but weariness prevailed, and we dozed off into fitful bouts of sleep. Our bodies were still processing the previous day's encounter when the wake-up call jangled us into awareness.

We held on to the hope and the promise that with the new dawn would rise a new opportunity to reconnect with the one man we had known so fully on earth and who had influenced our lives so significantly. We hardly dared believe that we were going to get a second chance to talk with Dad after so many years apart. Our love for him welled up in our hearts; we were spellbound.

Eager as we were to get back to our Heart Centered Therapy workshop, we were also acutely aware that today would be no ordinary day. We were going to get to talk to our father…again. What a blessing! We wondered how and when the connection would take place. By late afternoon, both of those questions would be answered, but a whole host of new ones would appear on the horizon—some answered clearly, others not so much. Ambiguity and uncertainty were becoming our close companions.

The reality is that none of us ever really have all the answers to all the questions swirling around us as we journey through life. We all live in a self-imposed level of understanding, ever-changing and evolving as we learn, grow, and struggle to unravel the essence of our lives along with the mysteries beyond. My sister and I were pretty clueless as to the magnitude of the lessons our father would unfurl before us on this day.

The pattern was familiar; after all, hadn't we been learning lessons from our father our whole life? He had avidly tutored us in the ways of the world long before we ventured from the safety and security of our family home. Yet the framework for this particular lesson was beyond anything that we'd ever conceptualized. He was gone. Dead. Yet how could we still depend on him for insight, wisdom, advice? We were about to find out what was important and what was not!

It was late afternoon. Molly and I were walking by a cozy sitting area in the hallway when Dad made his presence known. While we were still in utter disbelief and awe, this time, we were prepared.

I pulled out a notebook and began scribbling every word that was exchanged as fast as my wobbly, uncertain hand could move.

While he was speaking, we heard his voice not with our ears exactly, but with our hearts. The sounds appeared in us. Our sight was not nearly as reliable. We rarely saw him fully or clearly but caught glimpses here and there. We saw his chin once when he threw back his head and laughed. We saw his hands reach forward in a familiar gesture he used to illuminate his point. We really felt him more than we saw him. I've never had this feeling before or since, and I think it was his pointed perseverance, spurred by the knowledge that he had limited time, that nudged this encounter into existence. He was purposeful.

While we weren't able to parade out our huge array of illuminated questions about life and death, we did manage to slip in quite a few of them, ranging from the practical to the downright hilarious. Dad was always a light-hearted pragmatist, so we thought he'd approve. In hindsight, I'm not sure he did this time. I think our questions sometimes led him away from the purpose of the visit and proved to be frustrating for him. Hmm, fairly reminiscent of our teenage years. I wonder if that felt familiar for him too.

During this second visit, we were surprised at times by how much he had changed and how his priorities and focus had evolved. Sometimes, it felt like he could not quite connect to why we would ask a particular question, because his world was so far removed from our very practical one. Our concerns were not always his concerns. We both tried, but the chasm was too great at times, and we had to sometimes give up pursuing a question or asking for clarification. Our father had his own ideas about how he wanted to proceed.

The one aspect that remained true and pure was the undying love that our father had and has for our mother. But I'm getting ahead of myself. Let me just say that we were enthralled and endeared by how we still recognized him and how much still remained of the man we loved, the man we still love. All in all, our father was still our father.

What sifted out of our dialogue was the intensity of his love; clearly Mom was the main impetus for his return, not us. It wasn't long into our conversation with Dad that Molly and I respectfully took a backseat (with some reluctance) to our parents' center stage love story that had spanned nearly six decades, nurtured six children, endured countless heartaches and joys, and continued beyond the boundaries of death.

There was no denying his focus and passion as Dad repeatedly brought the conversation back to Mom. As much as our father loved us, the reason for his return was not about us. We were his vehicle to comfort, warn, and vow his faithfulness to the woman who brought him the greatest joys of this life and the life beyond. His earnest and heartfelt words to our mother, then eighty-seven years young, invoked the true depth and breadth of love and romance. The true essence of our father's message can only be fully understood and appreciated within the context of the loving life he had shared with our mother for over fifty years.

This book is about the messages that were so incredibly important and pressing that our father returned to ensure that his words were delivered to our mother. Messages about love, fidelity, greed, strength, courage, living, dying, forgiveness, pride, faith, love, and more. Through his messages, our father orchestrated a final Christmas gift for the woman he loved beyond the boundaries of life itself. A gift born of love, delivered at the family gathering only a few short months before Mom was called to join him in heaven.

Most of the names, places, and events in this book have not been changed. They are as accurate and factual as I know them to be. Everything in this book has either been related to me by my parents or I experienced myself. I have asked for divine guidance, of course, but this is not a fictitious tale.

And so begins my humble telling of the greatest love story I have ever witnessed.

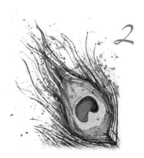

He Tried...and They Met

His Perspective

His eyes landed on her the instant he strolled into the roller skating rink, and he was intrigued. He felt a vibration, a feeling that alerted him to the fact that this would be no ordinary evening. He couldn't take his eyes off her. For starters, she was the best skater he had ever seen in all his twenty-odd years. She was graceful, fluid, and confident on her skates backwards, forwards, spinning, rexing. She obviously had spent some time on skates, and the sight of her mesmerized him. Of course, some of that could be the fact that she was beautiful too, in a fresh, wholesome kind of way. Her face was like chiffon, soft, flowing, flawless, with a hue of opalescence. Her thin, well-painted lips marked the spot where a smile lingered for no apparent reason, except that she was just happy.

Her legs were long and toned from hours of practice on her skates, and she floated across the floor like dandelion fluff across the fields. The exertion had caused a small clump of soft blondish-brown hair to escape the confinement she had placed upon it. She brushed at it absently with a hand that was dainty and pale, hiding the evidence of hard work, perseverance, and a strength that had not yet been revealed to him.

Kenneth Dickson was no slouch on skates, but in her presence, he felt off his game. He usually skated at the larger roller skating rink in Swanton, Ohio; but tonight, for no perceivable reason that he could think of, he drove over to Assumption, Ohio, another twenty miles away. To be honest, it had been some time since he'd had the luxury of going roller-skating. Heck, going anywhere for that matter. He'd been working every day in the fields to get his parents' crops planted and growing. Jesse and Leola Dickson were grateful for their son's loyalty, without which they would most assuredly have perished long ago. Their life had been wrought with difficulties, too numerous to ponder right now on what promised to be an enchanted evening, if he had anything to say about it.

Kenny, himself, had plans—big plans. He was determined to change the destiny of his life. So he enrolled in college and devoted every free minute to the study of dentistry. He also knew that he wanted someone special in his life someday. Someone wholesome and happy, someone who understood that hard work was an important component of life, but which was pathetically meaningless without love and family, faith and fun. He wanted a woman to be his partner and his soulmate. Somehow, the search for such a lofty ideal had left him lonely and disillusioned. He had all but given up. It was such a pivotal decision. He had vowed long ago that his own children would never experience the hunger and hardships that had engulfed his childhood, and he would not rush into picking out their mother. For the time being, he had decided to devote himself to the work at hand.

Besides, he had an enemy nipping at his heels. Time. He didn't know how much he had left. He could feel the pressures of the outside world closing in all around. It was 1942, and World War II was scarring the earth with many young men already drafted. He knew his turn was coming, so the last thing he wanted was to meet a girl, any girl.

Ah, but this girl was different. Besides her dazzling skating ability, she had a gentle smile and a twinkle in her beautiful green eyes. She smiled easily and confidently. He guessed her age to be about twenty-two. He watched her as covertly as he could. He noticed with interest that she seemed to listen, and in Kenny's experience, that was a rare find in a woman. The women he knew all seemed to prattle endlessly without really saying anything of importance. He was embarrassed to admit that he mostly found himself impatient and generally disinterested in their presence.

Joking was a different matter. Joking required intelligence and wit and timing. He had always been a bit of a wisecracker and loved a good belly laugh. Apparently, so did she as he watched her throw her head back with wild abandon and laugh at something one of the gentlemen in her presence had just offered.

For the past several years, he had longed to meet a woman of substance, someone who could not only carry a conversation, but would take the time to understand his viewpoints and his dreams. He was intelligent, and he admired that trait in others. It was hard to tell from this distance if that beautiful lady shared his quest for knowledge and valued education. He wanted someone who could be an equal partner with him along life's journey. Unfortunately, the timing could have been better, but fate is not a force to be denied.

Heads turned as Kenny glided on his skates toward the circular sea of gyrating patrons, but he really didn't notice. He was singularly focused on her. There were so many things he wondered, but her beauty and grace had been ascertained with his first glance in her direction. Now, to find a way to meet her. He hatched a plan. He situated himself next to the rink entrance in hopes that it would be a strategic spot to catch a word with her when she exited the floor.

Across the skating rink, the ladies definitely noticed him, but he had no time for any of them. Compared to her, they were obvious in their veiled attempts to capture his attention, and Kenny was having none of it.

When he looked at *her*, she cleanly sparkled with natural exuberance, and her eyes twinkled with intellect. She was deeply engaged in the conversations around her as she skated, stopping periodically to make a point or clarify a statement. She had not even seen him (or so it appeared).

Had he only known then that Noreen Irwin was keenly aware of his presence but was much too much of a lady to let it show. Her eyes were fixed demurely on the friends around her. Kenny made a calculated adjustment in his position, nearly blocking the exit off the rink, so there would be no margin of error. He just had to meet her. The lights swirled overhead to the rhythmic music, catching and reflecting bits of fairy dust.

Magic may have been in the air; he couldn't speak to that, but what he did know was that he needed a plan to get the ball rolling. He had thought that this position would allow him access to her as she exited the floor, but things didn't seem to be working out. "What was taking her so long? Would she ever take a break?" he stewed. He was already planning a witty line to capture her attention and amuse her.

As he waited and watched, watched and waited, he noticed with interest that her facial expressions changed from serious to laughter and then back again. When she spoke, she looked the fellows straight in the eye with sincerity and appeared to give them her rapt attention. She was engaging in her mannerisms. Sometimes, she even skated backward to facilitate more direct communication and interaction with her various skating partners. And oh, how she laughed at their jokes and smiled at their cleverness, which was beginning to rankle Kenny to no end. She was obviously not going to cooperate with this plan; he needed another.

He wondered what it would be like to be on the receiving end of those sparkling green eyes. His eyes casually rolled across her wavy shoulder-length, light-brown hair as the revolving lights cast shadows on her, creating a halo-like effect. He was embarrassed to admit it to himself, but she really looked like an angel.

She was tall and thin and impeccably dressed in a wholesome, respectable sort of way. She was wearing a swirly blue skirt, the shade of a robin's egg, and a pale-yellow sweater that made her clear complexion glow with health and vigor. Her appearance was so relaxed and unassuming that it appeared as if it had all come together effortlessly. Ah yes, she was most assuredly a no-nonsense natural beauty, or so he thought.

It was then that Kenny's eyes landed on a wee bit of whimsy belying the fact that Noreen had, indeed, put forth some specific effort and thought into her appearance that evening. Upon her skates were two enormous-sized yarn pom-poms, handmade specifically to match the blue and yellow colors in her clothing. Kenny laughed at the attention to detail and realized that she was a dichotomy of contrasts. He wondered whatever possessed her to think that she needed any additional adornment, and he smiled. She was clearly the most beautiful and fetching woman he had ever seen. He had to meet her.

The pom-poms prompted Kenny to look more closely to see if he could detect any of the preening and pretentiousness he had seen in so many other girls. There was nothing in her demeanor to suggest that she was overindulged. In fact, quite the opposite. Her skin was fairly glistening from the exertion of her intensive skating, and she didn't seem to care. So many girls would have been off to the powder room at that point, but not this one—darn it all, for he was still waiting for her to exit the floor so he could execute his well-planned strategy.

She seemed forthright. Yes, that was it. It was as if her very presence was making a clear and matter-of-fact statement that life was indeed hard work, but could be lightened by smiles, simple pleasures, and a positive outlook. He was captivated, to say the least.

All this from blue-and-yellow skate pom-poms? Surely not! Yet he had this sense of deep knowing, a sixth sense or intuition, if he believed in that sort of thing. The evening had just taken a decidedly compelling twist, and he was not about to squander the opportunity by lingering in rumination. Kenny was too much of a pragmatist, and he had no time to waste. He had to figure out a way to meet her; he just had to, that's all. And so it began. With a sharp intake of breath, the girl who reminded him of blue birds singing threw back her head and laughed. Her gaze flitted in his direction without focus or purpose. He was invisible.

Her Perspective

Noreen had noticed the handsome stranger, all right, the moment he entered the skating rink. He was tall and muscled with a chiseled jawline. His shoulders were broad, and his hips were thin. He strutted in confidently, self-assured on long, nimble legs. He had an easy smile and eyes that danced with mirth that was privy only to him. His hair was perfectly arranged with just the right amount of effort to appear carefree. His face was thin with a strong Roman nose, and he looked like an actor in a perfectly cast movie.

For only a moment, she wished she could behave like so many of the other girls, already flocking toward him, endeavoring to engage him in conversation. Noreen noticed how he politely disengaged from each young lady that approached him as he made his way across the rink. With sheer strength of will, she tried not to stare. Oh, it was difficult. She noticed the brilliant smile that he flashed easily and often. When he laughed, his pale blue eyes scrunched up with delight, and he laughed a lot with strangers he passed, with random ladies trying to catch his eye, with the clerk at the counter where he rented skates.

Hmmm, rented skates—that was not a good sign. Noreen had spent a great deal of her free time practicing on her skates, she had several pairs. The owner of the rink had taken her under his wing and tutored her to be his partner as a marketing technique to build excitement for the sport. Since she lived so close to the rink, had a natural grace and beauty, and, most importantly, the discipline it took to practice, practice, practice. They were friends—partners really, nothing more. Not that he wouldn't have liked a shot with her and not that he hadn't tried, but she had made her sentiments clear, and he was not about to press her and risk losing her as a business asset. He would do nothing to make her feel uncomfortable or awkward around him. They made a good skating duo, had even competed at skating tournaments, won some too. She really classed up the joint, and it was just a bonus that she was also fun to be around.

She had brought boyfriends around from time to time but, apparently, nothing serious. She once confided to him that skating at the rink was always more fun without the tediousness of making someone else feel comfortable. She just wanted to skate without all the dating nonsense that got in the way. Noreen had an abundance of dating rules, and most of the boys bristled or stumbled, if they even made it that far. For starters, they needed to pick her up at the front door and meet her mother. She would only double date with her sister, Sue Ellen, which became cumbersome over time. She set and obeyed her own curfew and expected her dates to respect her wishes.

Noreen just held herself to a higher standard than most girls. Her biggest rule was she would not chase boys, any boy. Unfortunately, that included this one too. Of course, she wondered, if the rules about boys would also dictate her actions with men as well. How funny to make that distinction. Noreen had learned that it was actions, not age, that marked the entrance to manhood. How sad that most of her male skating companions that evening had not yet made the leap. They were entertaining, to be sure, but superficial. They really hadn't lived, had no life experiences, and had nothing of substance to discuss.

Boys, men—yes, the rule about not chasing them would hold. It would not be bent. Noreen decided that if the mystery man wanted to meet her—and she hoped he would—he was going to have to work at it. She would not make it easy because, well, she wasn't. Yes, Noreen was confident and proud. She would never lower herself to clamor over the boys (or reluctantly, men) the way the other girls did, though she had to admit it worked for them sometimes.

She knew her skating would eventually catch his eye, at least she hoped it would. It took self-discipline and patience to put her desires on the back burner and concentrate on her skating. If this man did not want to meet her, then so be it. His loss. The thought of that possibility brought a catch in her throat. Wow, what a strong reaction to a virtual stranger. Her senses were on high alert, and she knew that she needed to proceed with caution—grave caution. This man was too handsome for his own good, too handsome for her tastes really. She just didn't want to battle a flock of female adorers for his attention. Plus, her experience had taught her that the most handsome men knew it, and she hated their egotistical self-centeredness spawning from a life where everything came too easily.

Noreen did not move fast in relationships. She knew that love—real love—took time. She was not about to rush into anything or anyone for any reason. Her mom's words of warning reverberated often in her head, "Marry in haste, repent in leisure."

Noreen had resolve and discipline, plus firmly planted faith. She trusted that God had plans for her future, and she was not going to fall victim to a fling of fancy, even with this new man so deftly invading her local skating haunt. She found herself suddenly nervous and knew full well the reason. She was inexplicably drawn to him, even though she resolutely refused to head in his direction. She would stay on the skate floor all evening to avoid making the first move if she had to, wouldn't she? That would remain to be seen.

Noreen cast a furtive glance in Kenny's direction and wondered why he had not asked anyone to skate. There were certainly plenty of agreeable ladies orbiting him. Perhaps he couldn't skate well. After all, he didn't have his own skates like nearly all the boys she skated with on a regular basis. Oh, that would be a disappointment since she dearly loved the feel of flying across the floor in her partner's arms jumping, spinning, turning, and dancing. Maybe he was painfully shy or, worse, immature, like many of the boys she had been laughing and skating with tonight. Ugh, maybe he was vain or conceited.

There was just no way to answer any of her questions from merely his appearance, but there was something about him that was different. How she wished she could share her dreams and ideals with someone who really understood life, who understood her—a mature man. For Noreen was bright and articulate, a real thinking woman, and she wanted a partner who was interesting. She was tired of the typical array of suitors. In truth, they bored her, though no one would suspect it from her kind and polite demeanor.

Noreen Irwin continued skating song after song with one fellow after another. Every time she thought about making her way to the exit where she knew he was standing, looking all carefree and non-chalant, someone else would ask her to skate. She felt God's hand holding her back, for surely she wanted to give in and make the first move to be closer to him.

But Noreen had rules for a reason—actually many of them. For example, she never turned down an invitation to skate, no matter who was asking. She knew how much courage it took for young men to step forward and put their egos on the line, so she decided long ago that a skate was not a lifelong commitment, and it was her very small way of inserting kindness and compassion into the world. A skate was not a date; it was just a skate. She reassured herself that regardless of how incipient the companionship might be, she dearly loved to skate, and this kindness truly was a small price to pay. Noreen respected each person and searched for their goodness. She made it her goal to try to recognize Christ in everyone she met. She viewed the world as delightful and found joy in each day.

However, on this night, with this very alluring man present, she wished she knew how to be more callous or abrupt or perhaps even downright rude. At this rate, she would never have the opportunity to skate off the floor and glide past the stranger with the pale-blue eyes, if she even dared to do so anyway.

Noreen had a shy streak, a social insecurity that she tried to challenge, but more often than not she hid the discomfort behind kindness. She was a wonderful listener, humble and sweet, unless her Irish temper flared. She avoided the limelight when she could, but would take a stand when necessary. She knew she should take lessons from her father, such a natural and exuberant social butterfly. As the evening wore on, Noreen noticed, with a prick of disappointment, that the man who had captured her imagination had finally asked a young woman to begin as his partner for the snowball skate.

The couples lined up in a circle and skated directly behind the couple ahead. When the music stopped, each man skated forward to the next woman and skated with her until the music stopped again, something like musical chairs. By the end of the song, every man would have skated with every woman. "Could he really be that clever, or was it just coincidence?" she wondered. Her experience taught her that most men simply went along willy-nilly and would hardly put forth the brain power to plan out a meeting strategy. Surely, she's reading far too much into this sudden development, or was she? Well, time would tell, all too quickly.

Noreen couldn't help but notice that the man had positioned himself only two couples behind her. "Was that just an accident?" She also noticed, with a gleeful smile, that he was very adept on his skates. "Oh, this would be fun."

Now Noreen suspected, but did not know that Kenny had a plan of pursuit. When he reached Noreen, she turned expectantly. His hand sought hers, electricity flowing between them. When the song ended, Ken simply refused to skate forward to the next partner. His actions caused considerable confusion with the other skaters, and several shot him disapproving glares, but he pretended to be oblivious, and so did she. Ken's natural gift of gab kept Noreen smiling as the young couple shared their very first "us against the world" moment.

For the remainder of the evening, Kenny devoted himself to the task of monopolizing Noreen's attention. He never left her side. There was a connection, electric and magical. They were mutually mesmerized, and the sparkle of new, fresh love materialized unbidden and uninterrupted.

But He with a Chuckle…Survived

Life was hard. That's what he learned. That's what he knew to be true. And the truth of that knowledge was reinforced day after day, after long grueling day. For Kenneth Dickson was born to poor sharecroppers and struggled for survival both physically and emotionally. The challenges were many, the joys were few.

Leola and Jesse Dickson were not thrilled by the news that they were expecting, again. The situation became even more untenable when they discovered they were having twins. Without pregnancy, Leola was a dumpling of a woman, with wide hips and plenty of jiggle. Her graying hair and sallow skin showed the effects of too much sun, too little sleep, and too much stress, giving her the appearance of a much older woman.

Jesse hardly had time to notice; so engrossed was he in trying to keep a roof over their heads and oftentimes failing. He was lean and diminutive, not quite five and a half feet, with arms that were more sinewy than bulky. His skin was darkly tanned, the color of an overripe apple, deeply weathered with grooves that gave a path for the sweat rivulets to follow as he toiled in the fields from morning to night. He was a hardy man, a good worker.

He regularly worried. "How will we manage?" It was hard enough to feed the three children already in their home, and now two more would be arriving. "I'm just weary, bone weary," Leola told her husband one evening after the children had fallen asleep. Every day brought the same challenges: securing food, working the earth, struggling to keep the hearth fed, repairing the dilapidated shed of a house. More importantly, he had to find a way to feed the animals and the children. It always came down to the children.

The Dicksons knew that their home lacked the necessary elements for children to thrive, and they mourned their situation, their shortcomings. Most days were so demanding that they found themselves too exhausted for the niceties, the frills, like food, warmth, shelter that were commonplace in many homes. Their hearth rarely held a raging fire, and their table never had enough sustenance to keep the growling at bay. Most nights found them all collapsing into exhausted sleep despite the gnawing of nearly empty stomachs.

The demands would be greater with newborn babies in the house, and Leola couldn't imagine where she could possibly find the energy and the resources to care for twins and still work in the field beside her husband. The winters were so harsh in Huron, South Dakota. Adults were marginally able to handle a scantily heated house, but certainly not newborns. Her only consolation was that if she was able to carry them full term, it would be almost Easter and the weather might be milder by then. Not warm exactly, but less fierce for sure.

Jesse secretly worried that the babies would be girls. He already had two of those, Beulah and Dorothy Pearl. It's not that he had anything against girls, but boys would be so much more useful, and he could surely use their help, someday. If they were boys; if they lived. Jesse knew that he depended too much on the labor of his only son, Clifford. He was wearing the boy weary. They were all overworked, but that was their life. There were no other options. They had to work to eat, and even then, it was slim pickin's. He didn't share his thoughts with his wife; he knew better. She had enough to deal with, and whether they were boys or girls, it would all work out. He needed faith, to hold on to something.

It was the first day of spring, when the buds should be bursting forth with new life and promise. Instead, yet another blizzard rocked the prairie, and the wind whistled through the clapboard house where Leola was struggling with labor pains. The hours and hours of labor felt more like days and days to Leola. Birthing twins was challenging, and they had hired a midwife, who they really couldn't afford, but they loved those babies and wanted them to arrive safely. They'd figure out a way to pay the bill; they always did, somehow. The twin boys, Kenneth and Curtis, were welcomed into the world on March 21, 1922—too early, too cold, but pink and healthy and beautiful. The entire household celebrated their healthy birth. Jesse gave a secret sigh of relief—boys not girls.

The twins grew up fast, and they grew up strong; there was no alternative. As sharecroppers, the Dickson family moved around often. The children attended a different school every year. The demands of farming pushed the twins into the fields when other boys their age were still wearing knickers and chasing butterflies. Since Ken was always a head taller than Curt, most people just assumed that he was older. Well, he was, by about five minutes.

Ken's height served another useful purpose; it gave him an advantage when push came to scrapping, as it often did. With each new school, Ken knew he would have to prove himself and establish the pecking order in no uncertain terms. Inevitably, some young bloke would make fun of Curtis, being a smaller, easier target.

"Well, look at them holey shoes."

"Can't see the bib overalls for all the patches."

That was Ken's cue, and he never hesitated. He knew what he had to do. He would cut loose and deck the lad with such ferociousness that everyone gave them a wide berth after that. If he performed well, there usually was not a curtain call.

Life was hard. Leola knew this. Jesse knew this. They were teaching their children this lesson day by painful day without words. They hoped their lot would get better, but with each passing year, what was left of their pitiful optimism waned. It seemed impossible to keep the bitterness at bay. It was difficult to focus on their precious few blessings when, mostly, they all went to bed hungry and cold. The nights were the hardest as thoughts and regrets had a way of sneaking into their consciousness. As they readied for sleep on that fateful night, they had no way of knowing that mourning would soon join the ranks and take up residence as a nighttime plague.

The waling began well after midnight. Leola was jolted awake with the realization that one of her children was in jeopardy. The moaning was so ethereal that at first hearing, she could not identify which child was hurting. She just knew in her bones it was serious. She nudged her husband awake, regretfully. He was so exhausted, and she hated to disturb his much-needed rest; but she needed him, his strength, his levelheadedness. She needed his courage.

Together they hurried to the children's sleeping loft and found Clifford rolled up in ball, weeping and flailing his arms. He had a fever, that was clear, but what else ailed him?

"Clifford, Clifford, what is it? Talk to us." He couldn't speak. Jesse set out immediately to fetch the doctor who had delivered the twins and would be totally paid off if the next harvest cooperated, that is until this visit was added to the tab. It was a ten-mile ride by horseback, and he prayed that the doctor would be home. The winter had been strenuous on everyone in the vicinity, and the rural doctor was already spread mighty thin.

In his absence Leola began to panic. Clifford couldn't focus his eyes or communicate coherently. His moans breathed shivers of helplessness in his mother. This was her baby, her firstborn. She pressed a cold cloth to his brow and whispered soothing words in an attempt to keep Clifford calm. And then suddenly, as if on cue, the commotion subsided. Leola thought, *Perhaps his fever has broken, finally.*

What she could not see and could not anticipate was that something far more catastrophic was broken. Clifford stopped breathing and died unceremoniously of appendicitis in the arms of his mother. Tears swam in her eyes as she kissed his sweat-laden forehead and felt the enormity of his death. This death of her son left her bereft, from which she would never, ever be able to recover, no matter how many years passed. Her soul was branded with the worst type of agony that only a mother who has lost a child can fully understand.

Ken stood in the doorframe and watched the agony play across his mother's face. He tried to tell himself that it would be the last time he would stand witness to such a loss, but it wasn't.

When Jesse returned with the doctor, there was nothing left for him to do but pronounce Clifford dead. Jesse was as inconsolable as Leola, for the same and additional reasons. The death of Clifford in 1934 was an incalculable blow to the already struggling family. Besides missing his presence, his smiles, his love, there was a practical loss as well. Clifford was the oldest, the strongest, and he knew how to farm. Like all the Dicksons, he had grown up on hard work, and his labor would be infinitely missed.

This knife that pierced Leola's heart brought the feelings of hopelessness to the surface where it mingled with anger and bitterness. Each night, she slept like a heavy stone embedded at the bottom of the creek. The anguish swirled above her, but she could not reach the surface. No one should bury their child, it's against the natural order of things, but when it happens the nightmare never ends. "My future will be forever haunted," she promised herself and wept with an endless grief that took up residence in her soul.

She missed her son more than words could say. There were days when she couldn't help herself and she wailed at God. Better God than the children, though truth be told, she did plenty of that too. She was in pain. It felt like death was playing Russian roulette with her sanity. Her pejoratives reigned through the household, unbidden and unstoppable. "Why couldn't things work out for us just once, just once? Why am I surrounded by sorrow and heartache and agony every day of my life? Is there no end to the pain of this world?" There was precious little time for thoughtful reflection on loss and love, so both suffered.

The children mourned the death of their brother quietly, internally while their mother's grief submerged the family. They felt helpless in its wake. Young Ken watched as his Dad bravely trudged forward, resolutely and stoically. His grief was a private affair. When it became too unbearable, he would step out into the desolate night to feel the impact of the grit-laden wind as it slapped his cheek like an angry woman, forcing him to focus on the here and now—his farm, the family that surrounded him, and the wife whom he loved despite the befuddled behavior that had become her mantle or perhaps yoke. Somedays it felt more like a noose.

Jesse's example would be the rock to which Ken would one day cling when his own son would be wrenched from his life. Thankfully, the future remained hidden, and Ken did what each of the other family members did, wearily plodded onward, day by day, finding comfort and strength from each other and from their faith that Clifford was resting comfortably in the loving lap of Christ Jesus.

The remaining Dickson children worked extra hard, picking up the slack left by Clifford's death. They seized every opportunity to ease their parents' burdens. The girls learned how to make soap from a neighbor and took on the task of laundry. The twins caught crickets and parlayed their catch into fresh fish for the table whenever they could. They caught and sold extra crickets to the neighbors and became known as the Cricket Crew.

Everywhere they walked, the boys stayed alert for anything that could be utilized by the family. They purposefully wandered the bumpy, gravely backroads looking for ears of corn that had bounced out of harvest-laden trucks heading to the granary. They gathered mushrooms and wild carrots. They collected pine cones, branches, leaves, and even, sometimes, dung to serve as kindling. They used their slingshots to bring home small game and soon learned how to use a shotgun so they could extend their menu options to include deer, wild boar, and turkeys. The health and well-being of their dispirited family was dependent on every member's contributions. They could not afford the luxury of wallowing for long. They did what every poor family does: they survived, any way they could.

Farming has a definite rhythm as it ebbs and flows from season to season. Ken's favorite time was the heat of the summer when all the crops were planted and all that was left to do was pray for ample rain. The spring garden exploded with produce, which meant less time foraging for food and more time for less sensible endeavors. The long, lazier days of summer included plenty of breaks for creek swimming, county fairs, and baseball.

Ken was intrigued by many things, but it was baseball that held his passion. He watched every game within walking distance and practiced with Curt whenever he could. He was graceful, athletic, and competitive. He so wanted to be a baseball player, and he really thought he had a chance at a career, if only he could get noticed. He wondered how he'd ever accomplish that in South Dakota. Why there wasn't even a semi-professional team anywhere near them. This goal would take some work for sure. He kept this secret dream from his parents, because they had enough to worry about. They had already lost one son, one laborer. They would not be keen about losing another, for any reason.

The growing season was short in the Dakotas, so their success hinged on perfect spring weather—a rare occurrence indeed. There were years when the rains would wash away the seeds or be absent altogether, causing the ground to smolder and crack into concrete-like ruts. Ground fires were plentiful, and the Dicksons had lost their crops, their squatter home, and everything in it on more than one occasion. They praised God for sparing what was left of their family, and they moved on, yet again, to greener pastures—or so they hoped every time. They moved so often that the whole family felt plumb out of kilter, what with the packing and unpacking, getting acclimated to new surroundings and trying to fit into a new community without really trusting that it would last for long. They were nomads in no man's land.

Like many men of the era, Jesse could be a stubborn man. Many a night, Leola begged him to let her return to teaching, but to no avail. "No wife of mine is going to leave my home and parade around town working. You will not give fodder to them gossipy folks that I'm havin' trouble supportin' my family. I won't allow it, no way, no how. End of subject. You are needed here." His pride was at stake. He would rather die than live in shame. But for the grace of God,

Jesse would never know just how close he would come to making this statement a reality.

Leola's Life

Leola's birth on July 26, 1883, was a blessed celebration in the Lloyd family. They cherished their children and had the means to support them, since they owned a substantial chunk of prime Ohio farmland. They weren't exactly wealthy, but all the children finished school, and most went to college. Leola, specifically, became a teacher. They had more than enough of everything to live comfortably, and they could provide a few advantages to their children.

It never occurred to Leola that the comfortable life to which she was accustomed in her youth could be shattered beyond repair. She had always been protected, coveted by her parents. They had showered her with indulgences most girls never enjoyed: an extensive wardrobe, piano lessons, and a college degree. On her eighteenth birthday, they organized a party for all her friends and surprised her with a Wurlitzer piano, newly manufactured in their home state of Ohio.

The unexpected death of her parents dealt a fierce blow to Leola, one from which recovery was unlikely. The last will and testament was very clear: everything went to the firstborn son—everything. Although the terminology in the will was customary for the time, nevertheless, Leola tried to reason with her brother Jacob, and when that didn't work, she resorted to begging. She thought it would be the last time she would have to belittle herself and fall on her brother's mercy, but it wasn't. This scene would replay in the not too distant future with nearly the same result.

Had her older brother Jacob been the sort of person who held compassion as a virtue; he would have allowed Leola to stay on and help him work the farm. As it was, he was not that sort of person, and Leola was sent packing, penniless and forlorn, although he did allow her precious piano to exit with her.

Leola had few options and chose, for better or worse, to piggy-back her dreams with those of her sweetheart, Jesse Dickson. They were married quietly on February 3, 1909, and took up residence in an inexpensive boarding house near the Lloyd farm. Jesse didn't have much in the way of material belongings, but he was smart and ambitious, and she was certain it was only a matter of time before they built their own family empire—well, maybe just a well-run farm would be sufficient, but for sure it needed to be bigger than the farm Jacob inherited. And she would see to it that it was!

At that time, the land prices in Ohio were well beyond the young couples' grasp. They struggled to save enough money to launch their dream, but saving proved to be more challenging than they expected. Leola's teaching salary barely covered the necessities, and Jesse picked up odd jobs—farm hand, grocer, blacksmith—but brought little in the way of serious money into the household.

It didn't take long for the glow surrounding their nuptials to tarnish. Leola grew increasingly disillusioned, embarrassed in front of her family and friends. She wanted to escape their stares and prove to everybody that she was somebody, a successful somebody. She wanted to hold her head high again, but the weight on her shoulders made that impossible. She was so weary of catching snippets of cruel, gossipy words from the neighbors, her so-called friends, and worst of all, her brother who made her feel discombobulated with her life's trajectory.

One day, Jesse came home from fixing fence posts for a neighbor to share his own small nugget of gossip, "And they were saying that land there is practically free. Sometimes, it *is* completely free. They are trying to get folks out there to tame the land and settle the prairies. Maybe we should think about this."

There was no thinking necessary for Leola. Here was her chance to escape the magnifying glass she was living under. Nothing would thrill her more than to get away from the smirking comments her brother threw her way. In less than a week, they'd packed up their paltry possessions, Leola's piano and Jesse's fiddle, and headed to South Dakota in search of fortune and adventure.

Her parting words to Jacob were perhaps a bit harsh, and certainly premature, but she didn't care. "Go ahead and be greedy, I don't need you or your money—I mean Dad's money. One day you will be begging me for help, and I will turn my back on you."

The power of those words lay between them, nearly killing the flame of family that had once blazed warm and bright. But the ominous significance of the statement would not be realized for many years to come. The twists that lay ahead could not be predicted. Had she only known, her common sense would have warned her to bite her tongue. But alas, she extracted her measure of vengeance, and it felt mighty good.

The adventure in South Dakota soon found Leola and Jesse fighting for their very existence. The land was harsh and the living conditions untenable. Rain was sporadic, and winter temperatures could reach forty-five below zero. The babies arrived in rapid succession, and the responsibilities multiplied. Leola longed to give her children the advantages that she had enjoyed back in Ohio, but that seemed so far away she could hardly recall what they were, save one. Education!

Although her teaching career, prior to marriage, had been brief, it had spawned a strong value for education. Before their marriage, it never occurred to her that her husband would be so obstinate about having a working wife. Now, she had no choice but to give in on that point. Instead, she stayed home and helped him work the farm. The chores were never ending. But no matter where she and Jesse lived or how badly they needed the children's labor, she would never, ever tolerate them neglecting their studies. School was non-negotiable and dropping out unthinkable. That was her bottom line.

For the Dickson children, the trek from the farm to school was often an arduous journey. The snow and rain would leach up through the holes in the soles of their shoes, that's if they had any shoes that fit. Many winters, they walked barefoot through the snow or wrapped cloth around their feet to protect against frostbite. Many of the other students arrived to school by buggy or horseback, and the Dickson children couldn't help but notice the disparity. The lesson from Mother was clear: a proper education would be their saving grace.

Leola was the main reason that all the children did well at school and grew up speaking proper grammar with ease and flair. She corrected every improper utterance and asked them to reconstruct and repeat every grammatically incorrect sentence. They memorized poetry and multiplication tables. They read every book they could get their hands on, over and again. They learned to think before they spoke, and they learned self-control. This passion for learning would serve Ken well for one day, he would pass on his love of learning to his own children.

School also offered a reprieve from the grueling work in the fields, and Ken applied his quick wit to his studies as well as to entertaining his classmates, much to his teachers' chagrin. Self-preservation had taught Ken to be funny. "If you can make the kids laugh, they just accept you faster…if not, knuckle sandwich."

He loved words and how they could evoke a response, laughter from the students, frowns from the teachers. Kenneth had a broad sense of humor and delighted in jokes, limericks, hyperbole, puns, colloquialisms, funny poems, and phrases. One of his favorite childhood poems, author unknown, was:

> One bright day in the middle of the night,
> two dead boys got up to fight.
> Back to back they faced each other,
> drew their swords and shot each other.
> If you don't believe this lie I just told you,
> ask the blind man. He saw it too.

He was a master of childish humor to be sure. As he matured, so did his utterings. One of his favorites was the first stanza to a much longer poem by Edgar Albert Guest, called "It Couldn't Be Done" that he adapted and repeated to fit his youthful mood and vocal cadence:

> Somebody said that it couldn't be done, but he
> with a chuckle replied, that maybe it couldn't,
> but he would be one who wouldn't say so 'til he
> tried. So, he buckled right in with a bit of a grin
> on his chin, and if he worried, he hid it and he
> tackled the thing everyone said couldn't be done
> and he did it!

Learning was fun, school was fun, people were fun. That's how Ken felt about all things academic and social. He dreamed of going to college, a dream he would carry for many, many years into the future.

When Leola and Jesse Dickson finally secured a piece of land of their very own, they were sure their hardships were over. Perhaps college for the children would be possible? Like so many others of Scotch-Irish descent, they had never owned the dirt that extracted their labor from sunup to sunset. Jesse boasted in a letter to Leola's family back in Ohio, "Now things will go our way. We have made our mark. We are now landowners too. We started with nothing, but now, we have something, and we did it all without your help, without my wife's rightful family inheritance." Leola too felt the giddy pleasure of pride in their good fortune, in their shrewd handling of government paperwork, property titles and securing the necessary start-up funds from the land bank.

"Yes, siree, we are on our way," Jesse spoke out loudly. "Finally, we've got something all our own to be proud of." In her exuberance, Leola, didn't even mention the dangling preposition tumbling from her dear husband's lips. For once, she agreed with him!

Ah, if it could only be that easy. They had changed their status from sharecroppers, where they worked someone else's land for a portion of the profit, to homesteaders, where they literally claimed free land, or nearly free land, directly from the government and kept the profit from their own crops. They were also, however, responsible for the losses, a point which Jesse and Leola blithely glazed over in their excitement and pride of land ownership. The bank was all too happy to loan the seed money, betting on being repaid when the crops came in…if the crops came in. Unfortunately, their newfound optimism was to be short-lived. Fate was plotting against them, and it was only a matter of time before the Dicksons found themselves deeply indebted and in terrible trouble.

"Pride cometh before the fall" (Proverbs 16:18).

The plains stretched from Canada to Southern Texas, from the Missouri River to the Rocky Mountains. Though the weather was notoriously tumultuous, the soil was protected predominantly by the roots of the buffalo grasses, which reached down sometimes five feet, forming rich, interlocking sod. The natural prairie, unmolested by mankind, had found a way to lock the sporadic moisture into the earth and nourish it during the long periods of drought.

The soil had proven to be uniquely suitable for bison and beef, maybe too suitable. Ever-increasing numbers of settlers brought ever-increasing herds of cattle, which wrought demands on the land at such a dizzying pace that buffalo grass rejuvenation could not keep pace. Vast acreage was overgrazed and left abandoned as the settlers continued their nomadic trek across the open plains. Farmers joined the raid on the land by plowing under the grasses to make room for crops that were highly marketable, particularly wheat.

At thrashing time, the neighbors all pitched in to help each other harvest the wheat. They would spend two to three weeks at one farm and then move on to the next. They slept in hay mows or attics, on barn floors and wagons—anyplace really to rest their exhausted bodies. They reveled in Sundays, a day of rest, save for the obligatory trek to church.

The women would feed several dozen men every day, an arduous and expensive task with no refrigeration. They generally ate ducks, chickens, or pheasants, either fresh or canned.

On one particular farm, Jesse and the thrashing crew were thrilled to be served freshly slaughtered lamb the first day they arrived. As the days turned to weeks and the mutton was still being served, the crew grew disgruntled. So much so that they hatched a plan. If lamb was the proffered fare, they would respectfully bow their heads and allow the ringleader to offer up the blessing.

When the mutton was delivered to the dinner table, the prayer spoke volumes.

> Oh Lord our God, look down from above
> upon this leg of mutton. It once was sweet
> and fit to eat, but now **BY GOD** it's **ROTTEN!**"

The next meal they had duck.

As far as farming went, it seemed like utopia, for a while. Land was cheap, if not free, and crops grew easily in the rich soil. Wheat prices soared. Everywhere across the center of the United States, the land was turned and tilled to make way for crops. The harvest prices held strong during the late 1920s and promised boon years ahead, even when the rest of the country was reeling from the effects of the Great Depression.

In hindsight, it was just a classic bubble—short-lived and ultimately prosperous for those few with impeccable insight and perfect timing. Unfortunately, Leola and Jesse had neither and would not be included in the brief, windfall profits of crop production. Their timing was off, their optimism premature. They caught the tail end of the profit bubble and tumbled down hard.

The fragile ecosystem, which had evolved over millions of years, was all but destroyed by excessive farming, grazing, and agricultural indifference or perhaps ignorance. Dandies from the cities—or suitcase farmers as they were called—arrived by the trainload to catch a piece of the glimmering profits. They would secure the land, plant the wheat, and return back to their cities until harvest. Overzealous farmers and human greed shared a portion of the blame for the demise of the great prairie land, but Mother Nature played her own part in the catastrophe that was brewing.

As with many things in life, timing is everything. A crescendo of events shook the land in one of the most memorable events in human history, the dust bowl. Over nearly a decade, the hard-won lessons would be taught and learned by not just the perpetrators and the developers but also by the innocent, God-fearing farmers like the Dicksons, who toiled long hours to carve out a better life for their family. A heavy toll was extracted in human suffering and broken spirits. With little to fall back on, the poor farmers suffered the most.

The wind blew so hard that the dirt would literally pelt the Dickson family through the walls of their dug-out sod shanty, which stood just two and half feet above the ground. With the profits from his first harvest, Jesse had proudly enlarged the sod house so his family would have a more proper home. He had added a back room to their prairie home with an above-ground entrance large enough to double as their kitchen. The clapboard addition, built on higher elevation, was damp and frigid when the fierce winds whipped across the prairie and slammed into the walls.

On the rare day when the dust would settle, so to speak, they could barely find the sod portion of their house as it was buried well over the windows, nearly to the roof. The family would set about the task of shoveling out the rooms in the half-buried dug-out home, and each storm would undo their efforts in less than a day.

Finally, the family of six resigned themselves to existence in just the one room built above ground level. Now the family sat huddled together in one ten-by-twelve-foot room, week after week, year after year, trying to avoid the punishing winds that drove out all semblance of life. They covered the walls inside with tar paper and quilts, but still, it penetrated into their home. They clung together with nothing but time to kill. Leola once counted twenty-two days with no break in the storms. The sun was blocked out nearly all the time, and the howl of the wind increased their sense of hopelessness.

Prayers upon prayers were catapulted toward heaven but somehow missed their mark. One parched day followed another without the nurturance so necessary for survival. It seemed that the earth's shell would crumble into powder at the slighted provocation and just when it seemed the most hopeless, a drop of rain fell and then another, both quickly gobbled up by the dehydrated soil. Within minutes the sky cracked open with a mighty groan and released the angry torrent with such ferocity that it bounced off the hardened earth and ran in rushing rivulets toward the lowest elevation. Before the inhabitants could grab their pots and pans to chase down the escaping droplets, the earth claimed the water for itself as the last raindrops were siphoned into the cracks and crevices. Dejectedly the farmers trudged back to their homes, hoping that the brief rain at least might inspire the ground to spring back to life. Their hope was tragically misplaced.

One blessing or perhaps curse from the children's perspective was Leola's teaching degree. She insisted that the forced incarceration include academics. When they had toiled over their studies sufficiently, a music break was allowed. Jesse played the fiddle, Leola the piano; and together, they helped the fidgety prisoners to pass the time singing every hymn they could remember. Everyone turned a deaf ear to the scratchy squeals that escaped the piano as the sand made its presence known between the keys, among the wires. The family sing-alongs were one of the few bright spots in their existence.

The other bright spot was Christmas. Oh, how Leola loved Christmas. She had an unexpected knack for making the holiday special. The popcorn and cranberry garland gave way to paper chains as supplies dwindled, but still, the merriment was fostered. The traditional hymns turned to Christmas carols as they decorated every corner of their tiny bungalow. Somehow, Leola scraped together enough ingredients to delight the children with cut-out cookies. The sparse presents were handmade but heartfelt and helped to set the tone for profuse holiday spirit when there was precious little else to bring them joy.

No one wanted to endure the blast outside, but the animals had to be fed and water fetched; lives had to be lived—*braved* was more like it. Leola protected her brood like a mother hen. She couldn't survive another death—she just couldn't. Before she allowed anyone to leave the house, she would wrap them in cloth from head to foot and donned a wet feed sack over their heads to keep the sand out of their faces and lungs. She strapped a dinner bell to their waistband to signal in case they were lost in the dense, darkness that blocked the rays of the sun and caused perpetual nighttime. This was no way to live, no way to raise a family, but what choices did they have?

"Quit wiggling, Curtis, let me tie this scarf on you over the cheesecloth. The wind will blister your skin in the blink of an eye. You have to be covered. Old Henry two farms over lost an eye, and that's not happening to any son of mine." So, she was steadfast in her ministrations and covered their faces with the thin gauze-like material to break the impact of the flying sand and soil, twigs and pebbles. The ferocity of the dust bowl, sometimes thirty feet high, was unimaginable and relentless, claiming victims at every turn. She vowed silently to herself and to God that her family would not be counted among the dead or maimed.

Church observance, which had been a mainstay in their marriage, was all but abandoned due to the onslaught of the elements. It just wasn't safe to travel.

For as far as the eye could see, there was a steady wall of dust angling toward them. Storm after storm buffeted the prairie. There was no way to escape it; the wind and dust followed them everywhere, even inside. It was dark and desolate, with almost an eerie, evil feel to it. Every God-fearing Baptist in the territory painted too obvious comparisons with biblically based plagues and plights and smites.

Had God really turned his vengeance on this land, on them? Was their pride responsible? Their greed? Was He punishing them for some long-forgotten sin? Was there no escaping His wrath? Was this the God of Abraham, Isaac, and Jacob? Was He really a vengeful God, as claimed by the Old Testament? Where was mercy, forgiveness, love? Oh, their faith was being sorely tested. It was not their belief in God that wavered, for there was no hesitancy on that score. Instead, they questioned His compassion, His mercy, as the storms raged on and on and on.

A mountain's worth of topsoil blew clean off the fields and tumbled across the dry, flat wasteland that was South Dakota. What little vegetation remained was devoured by hordes of grasshoppers and rabbits. Both, when captured, helped to sustain the Dickson family through those hungry years. They brought a few of the chickens, the rooster, and several ducks inside and fenced off a tiny corner of the back room to protect them so that eggs could be collected without dire effort.

With a great show of restraint, two dozen of the precious eggs were left untouched to incubate, thus ensuring the continuance of their brood. Within several months, they had amassed a bevy of yellow angora-like chicks that delighted the boys and offered hours of enjoyment plus the promise of future eggs.

Surprising everyone, the weather broke one fine April Sunday morning, and the family happily trotted off to church where they gathered with other neighbors, equally as hungry for some scripture, civilization, and socialization. Several new babies had arrived since the congregation last gathered, so the sermon centered around new birth, baptism, hope, and promise.

The twins were mesmerized by the babies' immersion and seemed to grasp the concept of salvation, so much so that upon returning home, they unceremoniously "baptized" every last one of the little yellow chicks in the horse trough with much too much gusto. The adorable hatchlings met with an ill-fated death, and the woe-begotten chastisement fell heavy on Kenny and Curtis.

The in-betweeners, time between the storms, were cherished snippets to catch a breath, mentally regroup, and reset supplies for the next onslaught that was surely coming. During these respites, the twins' job was to gather up the dried-out cow dung and corn cobs in a tub and place it by the back door to be used to stoke the fire inside. They loved the job because it afforded them a bit of freedom outside the house. They would rush inside at the sight of the next storm coursing pell-mell across the fields. The massive storms could rise up a mile high and two hundred miles wide, effectively making them impossible to outrun.

Many a child caught out in the open during a storm would be lost forever. Death by suffocation. Leola guarded her children's whereabouts, which the rambunctious twins found even more suffocating than the storms themselves. They wanted to run and tumble and frolic like all young boys do, but that was a luxury beyond their grasp.

Like many parents of the day, Leola and Jesse didn't understand the long-term health consequences of the dust bowl. The Red Cross declared a medical crisis with dust pneumonia being the largest offender. Penicillin had not been invented, so there was no cure for the ailment. Emergency hospital wards were hastily set up in church basements, school gymnasiums—wherever space was available. Health records showed an increase in measles, strep throat, and eye infections since hygiene was likewise compromised.

People weren't the only ones afflicted by the weather. One by one, Jesse and Leola watched their livestock, purchased with bank notes, die out. The horses survived only because Jesse finally developed a system of wrapping their heads with cheesecloth, removing it only to feed them. But feeding the horses became more of a challenge every day, and they wondered how long they could persevere in this Godforsaken land.

Water provided another level of difficulty altogether. The Dicksons had mortgaged the land to build the windmill that sustained their animals, garden, and family. The incessant wind and blowing debris bludgeoned it virtually useless. Jesse made numerous attempts to resurrect the structure, but the fix rarely lasted more than a day or two. Long enough to refill the pots, pans, tubs, and troughs, but not long enough.

Life was miserable. There was dirt everywhere. Where skin rubbed together—under the arms, behind the knees—the grittiness caused bleeding. Since wounds could not be kept clean, infection spread, and was a very real and present threat. Sand and dust took up residence in eyes, ears, throats, noses, teeth, hair, plus every drawer, every container of food, every engine, every bed, every dish, every trough—everywhere! Leola's precious piano became thoroughly dilapidated. Even the drinking water well filled with topsoil and contaminated what precious droplets remained after months and months of drought.

The fields, which had sparingly produced crops in good times, were now cleanly stripped of the life-giving topsoil. Farming was becoming extinct, but the locals just didn't want to face it. Each year, they would hope and pray for better results, a better crop. But there was to be no reprieve from the lean and bitter years that had engulfed them.

When the storms paused momentarily to regroup, Leola walked the early morning fields to free herself from the vision of her husband's boots, yawning in impotence under their creaking bed. She knew the dusters—as the locals called the storms—would renew their efforts with a vengeance soon enough, pelting and attacking the boots and the dreams of all who remained in that desolate land, year after year after year with no end in sight. She could not figure out a way to unlock the cold vise that had created gridlock in their life.

No doubt about it, South Dakota was in trouble. The Dicksons were in trouble. They were flat broke, in debt, and that was enough to break the spirit of any self-respecting, hardworking homesteader, almost. The land that they had waited so long to acquire was worthless. They had notes due at the bank, and there were still four hungry children, alive and clamoring. South Dakota offered no opportunity for poor farmers with no other means to feed their family and simply no way to eke out a living. The dust bowls raged on with no end in sight, with despair vehemently pounding at the door.

Once the exodus began, with families attempting to relocate back east or wherever they might have welcoming relatives, the stories ran rampant. Tales circulated about carloads of people stranded in ditches, engines choked out from dust clogs, and trucks hopelessly lost because driving was nearly impossible with the zero visibility brought on by the swirling dust. Many cars were plagued with electrical difficulties due to the massive amounts of kinetic energy in the air prior to a duster.

However, change too was in the air. Despite the fear and uncertainty, there was a steady stream of families leaving the area, just giving up. Jesse and Leola knew that they just couldn't continue this way, but quitting was not in their makeup. Their little family had endured so many, many hardships, how could they uproot and walk away from the only life they knew, no matter how challenging? Who could promise that a life elsewhere would be any better? They paused and discussed and waited too long to be able to sell their property as they watched the value vaporize before their tear-brimmed eyes.

Leola made one final, halfhearted pitch to return to teaching, knowing before she spoke the words that her plea would be rebuked by her husband. According to her expectation and with a ferocity that was reserved for this subject alone, he shouted with finality, "I will **NOT** allow this, not ever."

A part of Leola was relieved really. Since Clifford's death, she just didn't have the heart or the fortitude to prepare lesson plans, face the students with a cheery smile every day, and keep up with her many, many chores at home. Besides, there were very few children left in the area; and most days, they couldn't even get to the schoolhouse.

Leola felt cursed and abandoned. She worried that Satan had taken hold of her family and her circumstance, and she needed to wrap her family in God's protection. She turned in fervent prayer as her Baptist roots had taught her, "Heavenly Father, I humbly bow in worship and praise before you. I cover myself with the blood of Jesus Christ and claim the protection of the blood for my family, my finances, my home, my spirit, soul and body. I surrender myself completely in every area of my life to you. Take care of everything. I take stand against all the workings of the devil that would try and hinder me and my family from best serving you. I address myself only in the true and living God, who has all the power and control over everything. Satan, I command you and all of your demon forces of darkness, in the name of Jesus Christ to leave my presence."

Once her self-prescribed exorcism was complete, she approached her husband. They talked and thought and planned and prayed together. They wondered if Leola's brother, Jacob, living so comfortably in Ohio, might be open to their return. Since he had inherited her childhood family farm, they had hardly spoken. Leola remembered anew the pain and betrayal she felt when the will had been read and Leola had received nothing, simply because she was a daughter, not a son.

"Certainly, they'll help us. After all, they *are* still family," she whispered to her husband late one night. With a tad bit of cajoling, the decision was made, mostly because there were no other reasonable options.

Leola stood alone in her kitchen for the last time and swallowed her remorse. She regretted abandoning her dust-infested, but beloved, piano, though she had little choice. Likewise, they left the farm implements, the tractor, and the furniture behind. The wagon could not support the space or the weight, and the horses did not deserve the extra burden. They needed the room for the children, and something had to go. Mattresses were hastily spread along the bottom of the wagon bed to ease the journey. Blankets, cooking implements, and foodstuffs made the cut as well.

The Dicksons walked away—ran away really—from Huron, South Dakota, shook the dust from their shoes, and never looked back. The ashen skies heralded their defeat as they packed up their pride and their inconsequential possessions and drove the team of horses a thousand miles to reunite and reconnect with family, such as it was.

Necessity is a mighty strong motivator while against all odds and all manner of obstacles; the Dicksons persevered. The scorched soil watched as they made their escape. They traveled from barn to barn, throwing themselves at the mercy of strangers along the journey. They were met mostly with some semblance of kindness, compassion, and understanding, just enough to satisfy their Christian duty, but not too much. Some storms forced them to dally longer than the hospitality held out.

They stayed packed, ready to resume their journey at a minute's notice, day or night. Their crisscross, irregular, and perilous path was akin to the underground railroad a century earlier. They were wholly dependent on strangers, and their future was as uncertain as the emancipated slaves arriving in Detroit. Would there be jobs? Would they find shelter? How would they feed themselves? How would their presence be perceived by the locals? Would they be safe, healthy, happy? Would they finally find home?

Experiences are as varied as the individuals involved, and that's how the stories of life are woven, one thread at a time. As could be predicted, this ragtag band of nomads was not a welcomed sight when they arrived at the family farm in northern Ohio. Jacob and his family grudgingly offered just enough assistance to keep the Dicksons from starving, but not enough to encourage them to stay on longer.

Leola was demoralized by their indifference to her family's circumstance. She felt the sting of betrayal, of selfishness, of coldheartedness, and her heart beat with anger and pent-up regret. Oh, how she wished she had resisted the urge to deliver a tongue-lashing to her curmudgeonly brother when she left for South Dakota. She had hoped her brother had forgotten her lapse in judgement, but clearly, he had not, and her apology did little to warm the cockles of his heart. She wished she had other options, other opportunities, but there were none. She languished at his mercy, and he showed her little.

While it wasn't an easy transition and Leola grew more sullen with each passing day, in some ways, the change brought waves of hope. With everyone pulling together, working odd jobs, saving every penny they earned, they were able to purchase the first farmland they had ever truly owned outright. No mortgage, no debt, never again.

The small farm was located in southwest Michigan, just outside of the village of Waldron. The area was inconveniently located to everything, so trips to market were arduous and time consuming. To secure supplies and tractor parts required a day's investment. But the land prices were shockingly low, the soil rich, and the sellers motivated to move on to a more populated area.

Waldron was a close-knit community, where everyone knew everyone and neighbors helped each other. The flat, rich land was partitioned off by fence rows with plentiful trees that protected the topsoil, protected the crops, protected the family's future. They were safe.

Finally, no more sharecropping, no more viciously cold temperatures, though Michigan did have its fair share of ice and snow, nothing could compare to the Dakotas. They had endured such extremes at the mercy of climate, pestilence, and all manners of discomfort. It felt almost eerie to be settled comfortably into a place they could call home. A place where dust and wind were not constant companions. Leola should have been happy, but there had been so many calamities getting to this juncture, it was hard for her to draw up her faith and step forward and trust that their good fortune could be anything but futile and fleeting. But the children—ah, the children were resilient, and they flourished in their new community.

The girls were in high school with the twins heading that way, by the time their parents had finally set down roots, real roots—something they had never known and had yearned for all of their short lives. They enrolled in school in the nearby town of Hudson, Michigan, in 1934. They stayed put, and it felt good, real good. They even made friends without wondering when they'd have to leave them. It was a relief not to have to defend himself as the new kid at every turn. Kenny was fun loving and affable; popularity suited him well.

Within a few short years, Ken and Curt were surrounded by buddies and babes. Dating came easily for Ken, but money was definitely an issue, so he usually avoided it. Instead, he frequented the nearby roller skating rink because it was inexpensive, and he got to hold hands with lots of girls. At this tender age of fifteen, he would never be able to imagine that in an equally small town, less than an hour away, the woman he was destined to marry was, even then, practicing and honing her roller-skating skills. But at this occasion in time, of course, he had no idea that skating would become pivotal to his future.

Pete Murphy was one of the boys Ken got to know casually at school. They played ball together and went fishing or swimming whenever they could squeeze time away from their families and the mountain of chores. Pete was a big bloke with broad shoulders, a full head of hair, and thick dark sideburns. His confidence showed in both his long–legged swagger and the easy wit that fell from his sarcastic, pouty lips. No one ever knew for sure if he was kidding or not. Pete had a car, and he often took Kenny along with him to the skating rink, where both boys grew adept on their skates and taunted each other to excel. Neither boy could anticipate how their future lives would one day be irrevocably entwined and that something as simple as roller skating would turn the hands of fate favorably in their direction.

The Dickson children could freely participate in school activities. The boxing team seemed like a natural fit for Kenny. He had practiced that skill so excessively, out of sheer necessity through his traveling years, as a means of survival, of acceptance. He also enjoyed football. However, it was still baseball that really caught his fancy. His long, muscled legs had served him well running back and forth to school and all around the farm. He had never walked anywhere, always ran. He had strong arms from hefting bales of straw, which made him a natural when he stepped up to bat or threw a fast pitch.

Kenny loved to practice ball and would race through his chores and his homework to carve out some time for baseball. The coaches were impressed with his dedication, and as he entered high school, they began specialized training to better prepare him for a potential future as a professional ball player. For as long as he could remember, this was the dream that had kept him going, given him hope, brought him through the hard days, the sad days, the bad days.

The local paper heralded Ken's baseball talents, and the townspeople flocked to watch the young upstart clobber a ball into smithereens. His baseball notoriety eventually spread to the Minor Leagues, and he was scouted for several teams. When he finally got his big break and was offered a contract, he shocked everyone, including himself, when he regretfully declined. As affirming as the offer was, he just knew that after all his family had endured, he needed to stay close and help his parents keep up with the farm. Ken was a loyal, loving, and dutiful son—traits that would follow him into his marriage one day and create the foundation for a happier life, a more joyful life. A life he had been dreaming about forever. A life filled with security, peace, and promise. A life with Noreen, whom he hadn't—as yet—met.

But She Would Be One…to Thrive

Noreen Rita Irwin, was breathed into life on November 13, 1921, to Howard and Anna Irwin. Her birth was celebrated by a huge circle of extended family, aunts, uncles, cousins, grandparents, and neighbors and fellow parishioners from Our Lady of Assumption Catholic Church. Everyone marveled at the miracle of life that was baby Noreen.

Her earliest memory was emblazoned on her soul, not a memory exactly but a sensation that vibrated her being. She had just come home from the hospital and was peacefully sleeping in her cradle, an unembellished family heirloom that had rocked many an Irwin baby into blissful slumber. Noreen Rita Irwin awakened to find both her parents, Howard and Anna, standing over their firstborn child with unabashed awe and profound love. While Noreen could not actually decipher what they were whispering so lovingly to each other, she could feel their sentiments, sense their intense love for her and for each other. She knew, she just knew that they were exclaiming over her beauty, her temperament, her perfection.

The realization touched her at a primal level, and with all the willpower she could muster from her three-day-old body, she willed herself to remember that feeling of being totally cherished forever. This memory imprinted on Noreen and forged the foundation for all her future endeavors, her goodness, her self-confidence, her peaceful-ness, and most of all, her capacity to love and be loved.

Anna held the tiny gift and was mesmerized by her spit bubbles and the unexpected smile that curled her lips, probably by reflex, but she cherished it just the same. Her arms surrounded the precious bundle with reverence and love, breathing in the sweet, warm scent of perfection. She placed a hand on top of her perfectly formed head and felt the rhythm of her life beating in the fontanel.

What little Noreen did not know, could not possibly grasp, was that she would be one of the lucky ones who would one day find a man, a good man, who would love her forever with the same inten-sity as she had felt in that moment.

Noreen's parents' social circle was far-reaching, mainly because her Dad, Howard, was quite the charmer. Friends would stop by reg-ularly for a solid dose of laughter and a touch of spirits, the alcohol kind. Prohibition was still in effect, but in the close-knit community of Assumption, Ohio, the residents didn't really care.

They were called Blind Pigs, which really meant drinking behind closed doors with friends you trusted. More than anything, Howard loved to chat with neighbors over a frosty pint. It was good-natured and friendly, even seemed harmless in the beginning. As is often the case, time would prove otherwise.

A tear strolled down Anna's round, cheerful face that was nearly always enlivened by a smile, except today. Today her eyes were red rimmed from crying way too many tears for a situation that was becoming untenable.

"It wasn't supposed to be this way…he promised it wouldn't," Anna bemused to herself. "What have I gotten myself into?" To be sure, Howard loved his wife. She had elicited a promise from him that he would give up drinking before she would even consider mar-rying him. The promise was barely off his Irish lips, the wedding consummated, before it was broken time and again.

Howard was beguiling, and Anna had definitely fallen under his spell. She loved the way his cheeks scrunched up and his eyes nearly disappeared when he smiled. His mouth did the same, but she learned too late that the words that fell so casually from his lips could not always be trusted. He was not particularly tall, just under six feet with thin, unmuscled shoulders and an easy, carefree gait. She loved the way his hair fell into his face and the way his slender, uncalloused hand absently brushed it away.

She remembered the first words he ever spoke to her, "How's sha cutt'n'?" which was the Irish equivalent of "Hello, how are you today?" She exploded into laughter and laughed right up to this moment when somber thoughts became her point of convergence.

On more than one occasion, she watched as his own ill-conceived words had come back to bite him, and he responded with a shrug of his shoulders and "Aw grippers, I'm just a daft ejit as bent as a nine bob note." Little did she realize that it was more truthful than not, for he *was* a bit of an idiot and a wee bit dishonest...in a lovable sort of way!

Howard was a farmer—or at least he tried to fulfill that obligation. Truth be told, he hated everything about it. It was such a solitary occupation, devoid of variety and gaiety and social interactions. He farmed because he felt he had to in order to please his wife, his parents, and his in-laws. Both families had set the young couple up with land as well as equipment, an enviable position for most newlyweds, but Howard wasn't burgeoning with enthusiasm. Eighty fertile acres, a sweet deal if you liked to farm, which Howard didn't.

It's so true that when you don't like something, you don't really apply yourself and you do poorly, which makes you like it even less. So it was with Howard and farming. He knew he had a wife and a precious new baby girl to provide for, but each day, he found it harder and harder to go in the fields.

And so he procrastinated. He lolled around the house, playing with little Noreen until late morning. He quit early in the afternoon when his friends and neighbors stopped by for a short visit that usually lasted well past supper time and into the wee hours of the morning. The next morning, Howard would often sleep in late. He missed the prime planting season that year, and his crops had difficulty reaching maturity before the crisp, cutting fall temperatures landed on them with a thud.

The early peaceful tendencies exhibited by Noreen proved, with time, to be true indicators of her temperament as her personality unfolded into toddlerhood. Her second earliest memory, after feeling her parents' adulation, was sensing the harried pace that is a natural part of every budding family, but far worse when laced with financial uncertainty and malcontent. Noreen could sense her mother's stress as she worked tirelessly to carry the bulk of the family burden day after day, while Howard kibitzed with his friends.

In just over a year, fourteen months to be exact, another baby was welcomed into the Irwin home. This time, a boy, Eldin, received the adoration and boundless love of the family. As the luck of the Irish would have it, red hair sprouted across the newborn's head. His small green eyes nearly disappeared when he released an impish grin, giving him the illusion of being a leprechaun. The two children grew close, never experiencing the strain of sibling rivalry or jealousy in any of its forms. They were raised together almost like twins.

When Noreen was learning to read as a first grader, Eldin was so excited that he insisted she read to him over and over. He eagerly squinted up at his big sister, listening intently to lesson after lesson until he soon learned to read right along with Noreen. By the time he reached second grade, he was so far ahead of his classmates, he was promoted to third grade. What could have been grounds for unbridled jealousy, two different-aged siblings in the same classroom, wasn't. Noreen welcomed Eldin with open arms, and the other students followed her example.

Throughout their school career, academics came so easy to Eldin, but Noreen had to apply herself. Each night she toiled over homework while he raced through it to free himself up to research one interest or another. How does an airplane fly? What is the gestation period for a sloth? Does a square root have any practical applications? His rapt attention to learning would eventually win him the coveted distinction of valedictorian of their graduating class, even though he was only sixteen.

Time marched on, and Anna increasingly found her station in life to be riddled with difficulties. For as surely as she loved her husband, the practical aspect of living with a man who drank too much and worked too little was placing a strain on their budding family. The cracks in their relationship were becoming more and more visible with each passing day. The seeds of dissatisfaction had taken root and were widening the cracks, making their presence known. Anna's cache for forgiveness was crumbling as she struggled in daily prayer to patch it up.

When thinking back on her decision to marry, Anna remembered thinking that she didn't really need him to take care of her; she just needed him to want to and *that* he did. With every good intention bubbling out of his good-natured Irish heart, he clearly wanted to be the man that she wanted him to be, but he wasn't.

She was trapped in a predicament of her own making, for which there was no easy solution. Anna was a woman of strong faith and fierce determination, especially when the future of her precious children was at stake, and she felt it was. In the early days of her marriage, she had promised God that if he blessed them with children that she would raise them to His glory. But that was before she fully understood the challenges she would face with Howard's lackluster participation. She had vowed to raise the children in the Church and to introduce them to Jesus Christ on a personal, heartfelt level.

"How am I going to hold true to my promises?" she wondered in prayer. "I barely have time for urgent necessities like cooking and laundry when the fieldwork calls out to me too. I need help. I need a plan, a concrete plan."

Prayer became the order of the day, each day, all day long. Anna bombarded heaven with pleading and promises. Gradually, she felt her irritation and worry subside ever so slightly. Her newfound tranquility broke down the worry walls just in time for another adorable baby to join the family. Sue Ellen was born on November 9, 1925; and like all their children, they loved her immensely. They recognized her for the blessing she was—an affirmation from God that He would help them, some way, somehow.

Anna stopped focusing so entirely on the negative aspects of her situation and started counting her blessings, literally. Her children were top on her list, and Howard was there too—sort of.

She had really wanted God to step in and fix Howard. Remake him, so to speak, into the man she thought he was, hoped he would be. There was precious little progress in that prayer, but something did start to shift in her thinking. For instance, she began to notice just how often Howard kissed the children, played with them, cherished them. Their youngest baby, Sue Ellen, chortled uncontrollably at Howard's silly antics. In those moments, she fairly glowed with forgiveness, happy satisfaction, and love for him, for their family.

So Anna started praying a different sort of prayer, and from it grew the determination to instill in her children not only love for their father but tolerance for his shortcomings as well. She would teach them—model for them—how to love and forgive Howard despite his weaknesses, despite his drinking. For she loved them—truly and completely loved them all.

She had a new mission, and she gave God all the credit. She wanted her love, Christ's love, to reach down through the generations, through her children to her grandchildren and great-grandchildren, even her great-great-grandchildren someday. She wanted them all to inherit that love and the kingdom of heaven. That would be her legacy, that would be her burden.

All that was well and good, but...they still needed a way to financially sustain their family. So it became evident that Anna was not nearly as enamored with the status quo and pushed Howard one last time to invest his efforts into farming the land. She didn't know what else to do. They had to make a living somehow, and she couldn't do it alone.

The bedazzling personality traits that had drawn her to Howard in the first place were now wearing thin, and she chafed under the uncertainty of their financial woes. Maybe with a bit more nudging... maybe.

Instead of harping and hounding at poor Howard, she encouraged and trusted. Trusted that he would be diligent at his farming chores. Trusted that he would not fritter the day away chatting with everyone he encountered. Trusted that the crop prices would hold even though their meager harvest was delivered to the granary, to be weighed and sold, so much later than the crops of the other more dedicated farmers. She trusted that God would let her in on the plan for their future. Trusted that her efforts in the fields would be enough to sustain them. Trusted that they would somehow pull out of the financial gloom that surrounded them. Her trust was sorely misplaced as she waited patiently, and sometimes impatiently, for God's time to catch up to her time.

After a long day in the field, Anna would barricade herself in the kitchen with the children. She loved to cook and bake surrounded by her children. Well, surrounded was a stretch. Noreen was an avid participant, but truthfully, Sue Ellen couldn't have cared less. She much preferred playing with her toys or romping in the backyard. She was active and carefree. On the opposite end of the spectrum, Eldin's nose stayed firmly planted in a book nearly every waking moment.

"It brings me peace and contentment and makes me feel energized," she told Noreen one day as she was whipping up an enormous batch of banana bread so there'd be plenty to share with the neighbors. "No matter how bone weary I am, I can always find energy and happiness in the kitchen. I'm proud of the meals I make for my family, and I love to share it with everyone around. It's one way I show love, I think."

Noreen tilted her head quizzically and asked, "Is that why you feed all of Daddy's friends too?" Anna had never considered the why of it all. She fed them because they were there, laughing and lolling about. She was just being polite, neighborly. Was there more to it? Was the fact that she was good at it and enjoyed it reason enough?

For the first time, she realized that she never resented cooking for whoever might happen to show up at their table. The one caveat was that feeding the masses was getting expensive and time consuming. It was hard to help Howard in the fields when there was a house full of children and an ever-changing cornucopia of company. Her plan to trust and gently nudge Howard into becoming a more efficient farmer had not materialized. Apparently, it was not God's time. The minute she got distracted with cooking or cleaning or child rearing, Howard retracted his lackluster farming efforts and slipped away. At least he was predictable, too predictable.

More often than not, Anna found Howard drinking shoulder to shoulder with his friends when he should have been in the fields with his shoulder to the plow. Finally, Anna came to grips with the fact that farming was much too much for Howard. Even with Anna toiling tirelessly at his side, pushing him on, progress on the farm was meager. More often than she wanted to admit, she worked the fields without him, mostly when he was recovering from one of his headaches, which seemed to plague him on a regular basis most generally on the morning after.

Her plan was clearly not working. Nothing she did could make it work. Whatever did God have in mind? She hoped he'd fill her in on the plan sooner rather than later, for her patience and endurance were stretching painfully thin.

One Sunday, while kneeling in their regular pew at Our Lady of Assumption Catholic Church, a realization began to slowly envelope Anna. After a mountain of prayers, clarity finally blew away the confusion and led her to face the facts. Howard was never going to be a successful farmer, and she just couldn't do all of the farming, all the housework, raise the children, and take care of the cooking and cleaning all on her own.

Howard was in his glory when he was in a room full of people. He loved to talk and joke with anyone within earshot and she loved to cook and bake. So her plan, hatched at first out of desperation, grew into much more. She walked out of Mass that day with a new insight.

She had to own it. Part of the reason for their dire financial situation was that she was too generous, too giving. Specifically, she was doing all the work for both of them. Additionally, she fed too many of Howard's friends, and her family just couldn't afford that anymore.

So in order to make ends meet, she started charging their neighbors and friends when they'd stop over for a drink and charge them a bit more if they stayed for dinner. "Things are hard right now, and I just can't give ya a pour without collecting a little something to cover the cost."

Howard was aghast at first. "I don't want anyone to call me Scabby. I would hate our three gollybeans to think that of their Pa."

"Howard Irwin, you are the most generous man I know, too generous." She thought it might discourage him from inviting them or them from staying. She thought charging a bit might defuse or discourage the situation and that perhaps she might find fewer feet under their table each night. But Howard got over it, and all the neighbors seemed to understand, and they continued to frequent the Irwin household, much to Anna's chagrin.

The next step on the path to blind faith was that Anna rented out their land to real farmers who had a passion and a knack for turning the earth into harvests of profit. Anna and Howard convinced themselves to be content with a reasonable percentage of the crops, certainly an easier proposition for Howard to accept than Anna, who was full of ambition and energy. Next they focused all their attention and efforts on doing the things that made them happy; they followed their own passions.

She and Howard planted a garden, just a garden. Small enough that it could be tended by Howard in the early afternoons, which clearly were his most productive three hours. Then they set up a vegetable stand to sell off the excess. Howard manned the booth and chatted up the customers to his heart's content. It was a perfect secluded place to catch a snooze and a bit of booze between patrons without retribution. During the hot summer months, they sold cups of homemade ice cream and steaming mugs of cocoa when the weather turned chilly.

The Irwin home was conveniently situated on a stretch of highway halfway between two established towns. Folks regularly traveled old Territorial Road and often stopped by the Irwins' to borrow the outhouse, water their horses, and pause for a rest beneath the shade of the oaks and maples that lined the driveway. Anna saw an opportunity and grabbed it, firmly with both fists. She sold the travelers sandwiches and baked goods and sun tea. To her own surprise, she was successful beyond her imagination. Everyone loved her cooking. With her newfound career and newly acquired confidence, she slowly expanded the menu. She was working her passion and finding joy in the process.

Anna clearly and decisively capitalized on Howard's strengths too. He was a captivating host. He was full of blarney and did his Irish heritage proud. He could spin a yarn and dazzle anyone with his wit. That was what he was good at, and that was what he loved. Likewise, Anna loved to cook and bake. As they allowed their natural God-given inclinations and talents to guide them, the Irwin Restaurant was born.

Without apology or regret, Anna became a working mother. When Prohibition ended, they openly and unabashedly served beer, wine, and hard liquor. They prided themselves on being a wholesome family establishment, not realizing that that opinion was not always held by others in the community. Some of the churchgoers boycotted the newly opened restaurant, with alcohol being the suspected culprit. But the Irwin Restaurant offered something for everyone and many of the teetotalers chose, instead, to ignore the subtle imbibing at nearby tables in exchange for Anna's fine cooking.

Good food and friendly service helped their reputation spread, and soon it became a destination location. Anna's cooking, the abundance of alcohol, and Howard's charming anecdotes coupled with warm hospitality catapulted the restaurant to a sort of local fame status.

As soon as Noreen could walk steady on her feet and carry a tray, she worked with her parents at the restaurant, carrying items to the tables, circulating among the guests, and thriving on the praise and attention she received. As she grew older, her responsibility included helping out with her younger siblings, Eldin and Sue Ellen. She kept them occupied and quiet so they did not disturb the diners, no easy task.

"Noreen, please take them into the back room and get them ready for bed."

"Noreen, I need you to put the laundry on the clothesline."

"Noreen, could you please get the mail and make up the beds."

She learned early how to handle the basic household chores because her mother was so busy with the various tasks of running the restaurant. There were no ill feelings, no regrets, no angst over the situation. This was just what was expected of family members. Everyone worked, everyone helped. Some more than others, obviously.

This close association with her family helped to define the very essence of Noreen. She grew to love her siblings with the pride and protection of a surrogate parent. She longed for the day when she could fill her own home with love and children. Noreen never imagined that her own childbearing dream would only materialize with extraordinary effort. Her own entry into motherhood would be wrought with years of struggle, anguish and heartache. But in the meantime, she relished the closeness of her siblings and the opportunity to help her parents.

The days were long, and the nights were short. Noreen, Eldin and Sue Ellen grew up surrounded by strangers and learned to coexist peacefully.

"Shh, lower your voices."

"Love each other."

"That's not how we behave."

They were never allowed to argue or raise their voices. They learned to play quietly with each other and to move throughout their home, masquerading as a restaurant, without fanfare.

As is often the case, the baby of the family always remains, well, the baby. So it was with Sue Ellen. What little was expected of her was often left undone, hastily completed, or blatantly ignored until it got to the point that Noreen chipped in to protect her harried mother. Perhaps Sue Ellen took more after her father and sought the more fun and frolicking lifestyle. It was the one bone of contention that brewed between the sisters, bristling just below the surface, and forgiveness was nowhere to be found.

"Don't you know that when you shirk your responsibility it falls on someone else's shoulders, like Mom's or mine?"

"Well really, who would choose to be Martha?" she retorted. "Oh, that's right you, oh holy one! Heck, if you want to work your entire summer away, month after smoldering month, six days a week from sunrise to sunset, I'm sure not gonna stop you. That's not the portion I choose."

The biblical story of Martha and Mary was often thrown up in Noreen's face as justification for her sister to choose the more enjoyable path. Noreen had no comeback. Each time she stepped in to cover her sister's chores when Sue Ellen was nowhere to be found, the deep seed of resentment took root more solidly in the depth of Noreen's loving heart. It lurked there undetected, unchecked, unforgiven until far, far into the future when a familiar voice, from beyond the grave, identified the sin and sent directions to irradiate it.

However, the sisters had no way of knowing that this experience of working together and helping others would provide the foundation for another opportunity in the far-off future, when God would beckon them to a different yet similar calling. Ah, but that's jumping ahead far too far. There were lifetimes to live and loves to share. Let's be content at this point in the knowledge that neither of the Irwin girls could anticipate the tasks that the Lord had in store for them.

As the children grew, Howard was especially generous and doted on them shamelessly. On a whim, he would send them off to the movies or the roller rink without thought to the extra burden it would place on Anna. Somehow, they managed. He would wink at her with his Irish charm across the room, and she would coyly smile back. Against all odds, strange as it was, they had found their niche. Surely this was God's will for their lives; and their family was thriving, despite the drinking, despite the restrictive nature of restaurant life, despite sibling rivalry or misunderstandings.

The restaurant was closed on Sunday, because it was church day and family day. Regardless of how late the customers dallied the night before, every member of the Irwin family marched off to Mass together on Sunday morning, and that included Howard, despite how much he imbibed the previous night or how woefully he protested.

Many a Sunday morning, he awoke with a warped field of vision, knocked askew from too many pints shared with too many friends. Howard was predictably irritable, and nothing ever seemed to flow smoothly as the family hustled about to get to church on time. Inevitably, there was last-minute drama—a lost shoe, missing keys, or a misplaced coat—and it was always Noreen's fault. After all, she was the oldest, the one who kept the house in order, picked up after the family members, and tried to keep their lives organized; but it seemed that no matter how conscientious she was, something always went wrong.

"Noreen, where'd you put my tie. I know I had it hangin' on this shirt tucked away so spritely behind the door where I always keep it."

"Really, Dad, I didn't touch it," Noreen would reply bewildered and distraught. Why did this keep happening and why was every-thing her fault?

"Ya need to be more careful, lass. Keep things where they belong so we can skitter around this place and get this troupe out of here on time."

"Here it is, Daddy!" Sue Ellen shouted. "I found your tie" or "your keys" or "your shoe".

"Ah, you are a dear, sweet posy, my baby beauty. Always helpin' your old Pa to stay out of hot water with your Ma. Now, skedaddle out to the car, and tell her I'll be right there."

Noreen slinked out of the room determined to avoid a simi-lar drama the following week, but somehow, the same scene would replay again and again, despite her renewed efforts. Had Noreen been the suspicious type, which she wasn't, she might have delved more deeply into the mysterious Sunday morning vanishings. She might have noticed that she was the knave, playing cross stage to her sister's hero role. Instead, Noreen tried harder to stay on top of all the details that made family life run more smoothly.

Sunday afternoon was always spent visiting the grandparents or other relatives, going on picnics in the park, or simply catching up on neglected reading or simple tasks at home. It was family time, and no amount of hangover or tiredness or the unavoidable morning-after syndrome would exempt Howard. His only respite was a well-placed Sunday afternoon nap. That was the price he paid for his addiction, and to him, it was worth it.

On this particular Sunday afternoon, the Irwin family—minus Howard, who was home nursing his hangover with a nap—was enjoying a community potluck at the local roller skating rink where Noreen was taking lessons. Eldin left early with his buddies while Anna and her daughters stayed to help clean up. Squealing tires and frenzied screaming seized their attention as several carloads returned to the rink all in a whirlwind, every horn engaged.

Anna went flying outside just in time to see Eldin's friends bolt out of their cars shouting, "Anna, hurry home. There's a fire, and Eldin ran in to get his dad out. The volunteer firefighters are there now."

"It's real bad."

With quivering hands, Noreen, who hated to drive, maneuvered their 1919 Ford Model T Coupe—a jalopy really—down the potholed dirt road toward the paved one that led to their home, their restaurant, their livelihood. "Tin Lizzie" bumped and rattled, sputtered, and spouted bringing them minute by minute closer to the disaster awaiting them.

By the time they skidded into the driveway, Anna's face was ashen white with fear as she gripped her daughters' hands. "Split up, find them," she admonished her daughters. Before they could comply, their brother came stumbling out of the smoke-laden structure, carrying their inebriated father in his arms. As it turned out, all the rushing was in vain, for Eldin—with love and bravery—had taken care of everything that mattered. The women threw their arms around the two men blackened with soot, giving praise to God for sparing them both.

The fire blazed out of control, and the firefighters themselves stood by helplessly, watching the structure collapse to the ground. Anna and her church friends prayed on their knees in the water-soaked grass, but to no avail. She scrutinized the fire chief as he approached them, shoulders slumped.

"I'm sorry, folks. I really am. My wife and I always enjoyed eating here." He had an oversized paunch, a walrus mustache above quivering lips. His eyes, though sincere, were red and gelatinous from peering through the smoke, the heat, and the flames. It had been a rough fire to collar, and he had given it his best, but there was no hope. Anna patted his arm, smiled, and turned away. There were just no words for her sorrow.

The cause of the fire was never established, and the result was temporarily devastating. The family clung to each other in shock and despair, unchecked tears streaming down their sooty faces. One by one, the firefighters, the neighbors, the friends, the patrons, slipped away, leaving only the Irwin family to face the finality of their situation.

With heavy feet and heartsick expressions, they stoically trudged back to the homes of relatives where they salved their wounded spirits and clung to those who loved them most of all. In that moment, they could have, should have, would have found comfort in the Bible verse, Roman 8:28. "All things turn to good for those who love the Lord." But as it was, they wallowed in their grief and felt the full impact of the unexpected blow.

That night, Howard and Anna held each other tenderly and cried tears of anguish for their loss. They wept for the Lord to intervene and show them how to get through this hardship. So immersed were they in their pain, they could not yet envision how much better their life would be after weathering this storm. God's plan was far-sighted, but they were blinded by their tears.

The following months were exhausting and nerve-racking. The insurance company paid out less than expected, claiming one exemption and another, leaving the rebuilding in jeopardy and the fate of the family in the hands of God and his workers on earth. The family relied heavily on the generosity and kindness of their extended community to rebuild their home, their lives.

"But can we really accept this charity from the people we know? I need to think about this, pray about this." And that's just what she did night after night, sleeping in someone else's house.

At last the tension and uncertainty broke. Anna awoke one night for no apparent reason with an idea of how to proceed. She stepped outside as the smoldering dawn poured over the countryside and the brilliant orange and yellow streaks cut the darkness with the newness of another day. She gave heartfelt thanks for prayers that had just been answered, so adeptly, so lovingly by her Father in heaven.

Howard could be convinced; she was sure he could. She planned the conversation and waited ever so cleverly until he awoke naturally, for the hangover affects would be less and he would be more amenable. With a bit of finesse, she persuaded Howard to rebuild two distinct structures, which effectively separated the restaurant portion from their home. This would create more of a safe haven for the family, a privacy niche where they could relax away from the prying eyes of the restaurant patrons. Anna believed that God had led her to this idea because He knew that if she and the children were to have any part of Howard's time, there had to be distance between him and the temptation of entertaining every guest who frequented the restaurant. Anna stepped back in awe at the wonders God was producing.

The question still remained, could they accept the proffered help from neighbors and friends and family? On the one hand, they really needed the help; but on the other, they were used to being self-sufficient.

When the wrestling match in her mind played itself out, Anna responded with, "If God sends them, we won't turn them away. We will welcome their generosity and feed them soundly."

With the meager proceeds from the insurance company, the sale of some of their acreage and much-donated labor, the Irwin rebuilding project was underway. It was a long, slow, tedious process. At one point, it was obvious that a bank note would be needed. While

Anna was the capable, responsible one behind the restaurant business, bankers still wanted to loan to men.

So Anna conscripted Howard into his Sunday best and marched him into the bank to sit beside her and do what he did best, charm the pants off that city slicker. The banker sat stiffly in his chair as they approached the loan officer's station. He was spiffily clad in a cravat, black-and-white patent leather wingtips, and a gold-encased glass monocle. His hair was meticulously parted with a strong dose of Brylcreem to keep it in place. He looked important and imposing.

Anna sat quietly with her eyes demurely downcast and stared at her hands, tightly clasped, in the lap of her best, freshly ironed, housedress. Unexpectedly, she felt a wave of pride and respect bubble up as she listened to her husband, clearly enjoying the challenge. Less than ten minutes into the application process, Howard had worked his magic, and the two gents were guffawing and slapping their knees in merriment. The Irwins left with check in hand, and the building project continued.

It always seems to happen when the parents aren't looking, children grow up, too fast—way too fast. Noreen, now a high school graduate, decided to give up her secretarial classes, and take a job in town to help support the family until the restaurant could be rebuilt.

Ironically, without her restaurant duties, she found herself with more unscheduled time than she had ever experienced in her life. She had always enjoyed roller skating but now there was time to perfect her precision skating, counters, brackets, rockers, and her favorite, the serpentine. She became adept at figure skating, artistic freestyle skating, and creative solo dance, but her favorite was precision synchronized skating because it involved coordination with a group.

Without slowing down one iota, Noreen could lower herself down to the floor with great agility, extending one leg forward and resting her bottom oh so gently on the heel beneath her. She skittered across the floor, weaving between the other skaters like a race car maneuvering between orange cones. As her skills grew, it became increasingly more difficult to assemble synchronized skaters who could perform at her level. To advance her skills, she moved into paired skating and generally found herself coupled with the instructor or the best skater in the house for the Keats Foxtrot or the Flirtation Waltz.

Despite the difficulties facing her family, Noreen enjoyed the increased practice time. She halfheartedly offered to work a second job and earn more money, but her parents pressed her to participate more fully in the frivolity of youth that had been in short supply during her restaurant servitude. The newfound freedom was heady and oh so appreciated. She adored the rush of air on her damp skin as her lithe body spun through the air and landed gracefully on a single wheel before engaging the rest into a perfect circle or teardrop. She was having fun, and so were her siblings, well most of them.

In between college classes, Eldin agreed to help his dad and all his drinking buddies to clear away the rubble so the rebuilding could begin. Eldin was not especially handy with back-breaking work his shoulders were too skinny, his hands too uncalloused, but persevered because his family needed him. He enrolled in night classes and secretly vowed to avoid menial tasks in his future life at all costs. "I will use my brain and not my brawn," he swore. Fortunately, he was exceptionally bright, and his tool-and-die training came relatively easy for him and helped him fulfill his promise to work smarter, not harder. He pursued a journeyman's card in electronics and expanded his skills to include television repair, plastic Mold-A-Matic machines, and appliance sales. Over the course of his lifetime, he applied for over two dozen patents for his inventions. He was smart and ambitious, a winning combination.

Eldin loved skating almost as much as Noreen; he just had less focused time for it. He was a serious sort of fellow, but fate or faith or plain old luck has a way of making things happen. One illustrious evening, Eldin found his mind, as usual, distracted by one invention or another as he glided across the keenly polished walnut floors of the skating rink where he and his two sisters were enjoying a night out. In the middle of a half spin twist, with his head otherwise occupied, he collided into one of the patrons, who landed solidly on her well-shaped fanny.

He stopped dead still on his skates, stared in awe, and noticed—he really noticed. She was lovely! Raven black hair and snapping brown eyes that were avidly searching for the clumsy culprit who had up-ended her. When her eyes landed on his green apologetic ones, she softened. His crimson hair was mussed and droplets of sweat moistened his upper lip which was locked in an awkward grin. She thought to herself, "He's adorable." Faster than a breath, he was at her side, apologizing, helping her up, holding her steady in his arms. A tingle of energy shot through his analytical brain and brushed away the logic, mathematics, patents he had been formulating. What he felt made no sense, but he felt it, deeply. Just like that, he was in love with Rosie Hinkle and the two became inseparable.

Sue Ellen, however, was the happiest of all when the daily toil of restaurant work came to a screeching halt—well, not work exactly, but it was avoiding the work that was so exhausting. Finally, she could concentrate more fully on her social life, her skating, and her school events. Noreen would pick her up when she got off work on her way to the skating rink, and the shared experience was good for their sisterhood. "This is so much fun," Sue Ellen exclaimed time and time again. Life returned to some semblance of normalcy, only better.

That summer, Noreen mastered backward triple toe loop jumps on her skates. The rink owner had arranged for private tutoring sessions to help her master the maneuver, and she practiced her heart out to succeed. They registered for competitions and started bringing home the trophies. It was an exciting hobby, and Noreen enjoyed the challenge of it all. The skating rink was rising in notoriety and was often in the news in towns as far away as Toledo and Ann Arbor.

The love affair between Eldin and Rosie tickled Noreen immensely. He was relaxed and happy in a way she had never seen him before. Rosie brought peace and contentment to his rushing brain and quieted his thoughts of inventions, equations, and the like. In her presence, he became present in his life.

Noreen had dated lots of fellas but had never come close to the intensity of the love Eldin and Rosie shared. Noreen felt like she was marking time and lost interest in dating altogether. She wanted the all-encompassing love that she witnessed in her brother, and she made a whispered promise to wait for him, whoever he was, wherever he was. She would not, could not settle for less.

Noreen remained diligent with her practice and laughingly said, "I'm a nose-to-the-grindstone kinda girl." This trait would prove invaluable and unavoidably alluring to Kenneth, who would soon step into Noreen's life like a fresh-blown breeze across the prairie. Neither Noreen nor Kenneth could anticipate the joys and the challenges that would come calling. Would they answer or ignore the call of love? Would they even recognize the possibilities placed before them or blithely skate on by? Only God could know for sure.

With a Bit of a Grin on Their Chins... They Loved

There were some inherent difficulties in courting a good girl with many rules, Kenny soon learned. To begin with, she refused to go out with him unless he found a date for her younger sister, Sue Ellen, as well. That presented a challenge as so many of Ken's friends had already been drafted into the military.

After much contemplation, an old high school buddy from Hudson, Michigan—Peter Murphy—came to mind. Pete was agreeable to the double date, and the couples went to the highly acclaimed musical, Yankee Doodle Dandy, chosen, of course, by the ladies. The movie brought out an avid discussion. The sisters loved the song and dance, but the men were attracted to the rags to riches story line; a partially fictional story of George M. Cohan, AKA the man who owned Broadway. Tough guy James Cagney stole the show and later received an Oscar for Best Actor. As the highest-grossing film of 1942, it helped promote patriotism and build support for the war effort at home, a topic of interest to everyone in the country. However on this enchanted evening, the couples pushed the war worries aside and fell headlong into the blissfulness of love. Noreen's sister, Sue Ellen Irwin, was spirited and carefree and that suited Pete just fine.

In many ways, Noreen and Kenny were very much alike. Noreen was interested in world events and was intrigued by politics. She also had spirited opinions, which Kenny found refreshing, if not a bit daunting. He had to be quick on his toes to keep up with her. They found they had an uncanny number of things in common including a strong faith life, work ethic, love of family, and sense of integrity, but there were differences too. That kept things interesting for sure. After the movies or skating or just to get away from family for a bit, they would go out for ice cream.

"I'd like a double dip of chocolate ice cream please."

"Oh, the same for me, only vanilla," she echoed.

"Noreen! Who orders vanilla? Is that even a flavor?" he chortled, simply for the sake of livening things up. Ken had a strong personality, enjoyed a good ribbing, especially when someone else was on the receiving end.

Noreen, however, had a shy streak in new social settings. Ken just jumped headfirst into any conversation, never at a loss for words. He also dove headlong into any body of water he could find, regardless of the temperature. So many years spent swimming in creeks and rivers and lakes all around hardened him to the discomfort.

"It only stings for a minute," he crowed.

The day he discovered that Noreen did not swim at all was etched forever in his mind. It was worse, she didn't really even like to be in the water, regardless of the temperature. Ken shuffled his feet with downcast eyes and released her hand from his when the swimming conversation surfaced.

"Well, this is it. We're over! I can never date a woman who doesn't swim," he exclaimed with a big show of emotion bubbling to the surface.

Noreen was aghast. How in the world could something so seemingly petty hold that much significance? Her Irish temper, usually kept well in check, began to flair; but it was then that she noticed the wee little crinkle on the outer edges of his eyes, belying the well-concealed fact that he was teasing her, yet again. Would she ever get used to his sense of humor? The man was incorrigible and adorable, both at the same time.

That summer and the accompanying fall, Kenny and Noreen grew close, very close. Love is strange that way; it sort of crept in, took them by surprise, and erupted into fireworks in every corner of their souls. They talked of a future together and how that might develop. They wanted children, of course, and they wanted to stand side by side in the raising of them.

Nothing worthwhile is ever easy, and so it was with their relationship. Somehow, they had overcome the debacle from the swimming and vanilla ice cream revelations, only to be blindsided by a much more serious conversation. Like Eleanor Roosevelt used to say, "It's the struggle that makes us stronger and likewise makes us appreciate the accomplishment all the more."

The discussion of religion had never surfaced as an issue between them. Kenny had accompanied her to Mass often, and they each assumed that their deeply held faith was in sync.

Kenny's family had gone to many different kinds of churches and had attended services in various denominations in lots of different communities. In fact, they had been nearly everything except Catholic, and Ken's mother, Leola, wanted to keep it that way. At that point in history, Catholics had been widely misunderstood and persecuted. Crosses were sometimes burned in their yards. Some parents did not want their children to even date a Catholic. Leola was one of them. She wanted to save Kenny from the hardships of Catholicism. She knew that it was not an easy path.

But Noreen's family had been Catholic for centuries. It was the one thing that was consistently inherited from generation to generation. Noreen had attended Catholic schools for most of her growing-up years. Her parents had nurtured her and insisted that she attend church faithfully. Somewhere in the midst of the obligation, Noreen developed a deep reverence for her faith. It was as much a part of her as the air she breathed.

Noreen believed—actually, *knew*—that the Lord had led her to this family, to this faith for a purpose. Her faith had to come first in her life; that was a promise she had made long ago at her Confirmation ceremony when she placed the tiny gold cross around her neck as a reminder of her commitment. When she was baptized as an infant like all good Catholics, the decision to walk this path was made for her. Confirmation was a revisiting of the baptismal vows once she reached the age of reason. There had been years of parental modeling and religious education that prepared her for the big decision to follow in the footsteps of her ancestors.

When she was at Mass, she felt closer to God than anywhere else in her life. She loved the holy feel of the traditions. It was important to her that she could trace the history of the Catholic church back to Peter, when upon that rock her Church was built (Matt. 16:18). So much history reverberated within those ancient walls where reverence and faithfulness clung to the stained-glass windows and permeated the pews. The ornate, vaulted ceilings bore witness to thousands of christenings, countless marriages and innumerable funerals, standing witness to the hopefulness and sanctity of life's journey.

Sin is a constant in our world, no matter how much we hate it. "All have sinned and fallen short of the Lord" (Romans 3:23). Noreen would have liked to believe that Peter had led the first Church without incident, perfectly; but of course, that was not the case. Why, Peter couldn't even walk flawlessly with Christ right next to him. Nowhere is this illuminated more clearly than in the Gospel of John, where an incident takes place in the Garden of Gethsemane. Peter, the Rock, impulsively cuts off the ear of the servant Malchus, trying to protect Jesus. The servant and the rest of the lynch mob had come to arrest Jesus, an arrest that would ultimately lead to his crucifixion and subsequent resurrection. A death that would break the bonds of sin.

Peter had innocently thought he should fight for Jesus. But Jesus had other plans. "Put your sword away, Peter." Jesus then heals the ear of his enemy in the same way as he heals everyone's sin. Yes, Peter sinned even as he walked shoulder to shoulder beside Jesus. He continued to sin even as he led the new Catholic Church into being as the first Pope. He took twists and turns that sometimes led believers astray, but always Christ was there to guide him back, to forgive him, to inspire him, to love him, and those sheep he brought into the flock. Not because they deserved Christ's love, but because he gave it freely.

Noreen thought about the modern Catholic Church in all of its imperfections, and she knew that sin would always be there. Sin is everywhere, and everyone sins. Sin is even present in the men and women who have been vetted to carry out the work of the Church. They are flawed, they sin, intentionally and unintentionally; but with Christ, there is always redemption, always a second chance, always a healing. Jesus is the author of forgiveness and offers it to everyone, freely. He brings about change and welcomes repentant sinners home.

Noreen started thinking about her sister and felt a prickling sensation around her heart. Had she ever really forgiven her? It was easier to say it than it was to do it. In Noreen's way of thinking, Sue Ellen never pulled her fair share of the load at home, and that had rankled her for far too long. She had buried so many hard feelings.

Life is strange. You often don't know where you are going until you arrive. When Noreen found Kenny, she just knew it was right, but when religion entered into their discussion, Noreen grew uncharacteristically quiet. How could she ever explain to Kenny how important her church was to her? How could she convey the deep sense of belonging to something bigger than herself, something that spans generations and has its roots with the Jewish chosen people? Her faith was at her very core, and it defined her as a person, as a woman. Her whole future hinged on the discussion that was inevitable, potentially explosive, and filled her with dread. Her strategy? Avoid! Avoid! Avoid!

Well, that worked really well...for a while. But eventually, Kenny sensed the reluctance and encouraged open dialogue. "Tell me what you feel? Why does this matter so much to you? What difference does it really make where we go to church, so long as we go... together?"

Noreen knew that Ken's background had been different than hers. She was afraid that he harbored some anti-Catholic sentiment. She had suspected accurately that his mother did. She just couldn't bear it if this came between them!

Finally, Noreen held her breath and settled for a simple conversation starter. "This is an integral part of me. It's who I am and what I believe. If you love me, then you automatically love my faith. The two are as inseparable as the sunlight that clings to the grass. This is me." Then she held her breath.

Ken enfolded his precious woman in his arms with a love that knew no bounds. With each breath he took, his feelings compounded. He did not want to be away from her for a moment. He couldn't imagine going to a different church apart from hers, and he would not separate her from her faith. He loved her that much!

When he told her how he was feeling, joy flooded into her very soul, and she exhaled all the fear and uncertainty she had been holding. With her next breath she instantly sent up a prayer of thanks to the One who made it all possible. Within the next few months, Ken learned more about the faith that was so important to her and finally made the decision to join the Catholic Church, despite his mother's vehement disapproval. He promised to raise their children in the Church and to bring them up in the ways of the Lord. What more could a mother want for her son, really? Well, Leola had a thought or two to share, and share she did.

"Good sons respect their mothers and listen to their counsel," she quoted at him through unsmiling lips. Although to be fair, Ken did that. Ken shot back, "But a man shall leave his mother..." (Matthew 19:5). He was beginning a new life with Noreen, and they would "raise up their children to the Lord" (Proverbs 22:6). Their house would not be divided, and they would cleave to each other as the Lord had designed it. Growing up, Leola had taught her son so many Bible verses and she did not appreciate him throwing them back at her, but she nonetheless held just a glimmer of respect and appreciation for his strength and persistence. "Over my dead body," she spat at him. He hoped it wouldn't come to that. Ken wouldn't put it past her to keel over just to spite him.

The discussion was lively, animated, and hurtful. His final words put it all into perspective. "Mom, I'm not asking, I'm informing." In the end, she stood there before him, strikingly alive. Her undying love for her son caused her to pause, a smile slowly replaced the scowl and she gave her blessing, albeit grudgingly. The happy couple took it, and off they flew to continue their courtship at a much-deeper level.

Noreen wanted to be accepted and loved by his family too, so she carved out time to work with them. When the gardens exploded with bounty, Noreen was there to help, and she always arrived with fresh baked goods, which easily won over Ken's father, Jesse, who's face, though wizened, held a perpetual smile at his good fortune in these later years. He loved when the young couple visited and the fact that, Noreen was a marvelous cook certainly didn't hurt. In between tasks, she chatted, asking questions about her beloved's boyhood and listened intently. Little by little, she thought maybe she was winning over Kenny's mother; but appearances can be deceiving, and that was definitely the case with Leola Dickson.

As the summer months turned to fall, Kenny longed for quiet time alone with Noreen. His dentistry classes kept him busy during the day, and homework threatened to claim his evenings. The best he could occasionally finagle was sitting in the yard behind her house with her parents and siblings just inside the door. As she went inside to fix lemonade, he ruminated over their relationship. It felt as if their hearts were already beating in synchronized rhythm and harmony. When she returned, he silently reached for her fragile hand and turned it over and over in his strong, muscular one as if he were trying to read the lines and predict their future. He felt her pulse beneath the skin, and his heart swelled with love and devotion; wordlessly, their lips met, melting together like a fork full of butter in a sizzling hot skillet. Ken knew he had to turn down the heat.

Ken broke the moment, intentionally, to protect her, him, their relationship. With his arms around her, he took a deep breath and focused his attention upward—anything to distract him from the yearning he felt for her. He loved her, respected her, needed her. Regardless of the personal cost, he would avoid anything that could possibly damage their relationship and that included moving too fast. He couldn't risk scaring her away. Therefore, he waited, patiently (mostly) for their love to blossom. So with strength and a burning hope for a not-too-distant someday, he changed the subject and spoke of what every good farmer knows, the weather.

"Mackerel sky, not twenty-four hours dry." Noreen laughed at the abruptness of this utterance, and then Kenny joined her. She saw right through him and loved him all the more for it.

"You just learn these things when you farm. It's important, and it matters, just like this!" and he kissed her nose.

"What?" she whispered, half joking, half insulted. "I don't know too many dentists whose livelihood depends on predicting the weather."

"Not true! My sister Beula can tell when the rain is coming because her back molar starts to throb. True story!"

"That's not what I meant and you know it."

Theirs was not the only budding love in the household as Sue Ellen and Pete continued to enjoy each other's company. Their relationship was strengthening with each passing date as well. As luck or fate or folly would have it, Pete was a terrific skater too and the couples spent many evenings skating at one rink or the other. With Ken and Peter around, there was always laughter and plenty of teasing.

Noreen had gotten used to Ken's razzing, mostly. Since Noreen was six months older than he was, he used to joke about dating an older woman. Noreen would act indignant until she could suppress her laughter no longer. Her mother always told her to marry a man that makes her laugh. When Kenny was around, everyone laughed.

Well, maybe not everyone, once Noreen was riding on the back of Kenny's motorcycle, speeding down a rain-slicked highway, when his bike slipped and so did she…right off the back of the bike and onto the pavement. Finding herself firmly planted on the hard surface stunned her momentarily, just long enough to be jolted by a passerby who stopped to make sure she was not hurt. His draconian words brought her up sharply, "You should not get on the back of that bike ever again. It's just not safe to ride with him."

Noreen's response was swift and wordless as she leapt to her feet and mounted the bike securely behind her boyfriend. Away they sped, happy, unharmed, and in love.

As the next year unfolded, Kenny and Noreen had experienced the highest of highs and were on the precipice of being plunged into the lowest of lows and then back again. In the midst of their burgeoning love affair, World War II raged on. Kenny had been spared the draft, but his number was quite literally almost up. He wondered, "Should I just enlist and get it over with or ride out the numbers game of the draft?"

The biggest benefit if he signed up voluntarily was that he could choose his branch of service and have some say in his fate. The biggest drawback was that he would be giving up precious time with his newfound love. "I love my country, and I want to fight for the right to be free, but how can I leave you behind right now? You mean everything to me."

The decision to enlist was not reached lightly, and there were many tearful evenings of discussion before it was decided. Kenny and Noreen knew that the road ahead was fraught with uncertainties far beyond their control. Each wondered, in the quiet of their hearts, if their lives would endure or be forever altered.

The papers were signed, the commitment made. The deed was done. Kenneth put a hold on his dentistry studies. He applied and was accepted by the Naval Air Force to be trained as a fighter pilot. Their first separation was for boot camp. Noreen had never felt such intense longing, and Kenny ached to be with her. When he returned home for his first leave, he simply had to ask her to marry him. In reality, she didn't really need a ring to cement their intent, but the ever-romantic Ken would have it no other way. Down on one knee, he placed the question and the ring before her. "Will you marry me?"

It was a rhetorical question really. Their hearts had been committed long before, on the evening when their eyes met across the roller rink floor. How simple things were then in contrast to the complexity of their current situation. But love is optimistic and ever hopeful. Ken looked with adoration at the woman who always reminded him of gentle breezes frolicking through the wheat fields, lithe and fluid, magic in motion. He reached for her hand, and she willingly gave it to him, joined as one forever.

And then way too quickly, he was gone. He was a full-fledged sailor attending aviation classes, reveling with his unit, loyally following every order given. He was not in control of his destiny. He moved from base to base, training to training, at various locations around the United States. His quick intellect and stellar work ethic served him well in the face of the myriad challenges of the naval pilot training. The pace was grueling.

In the darkness of exhaustion, just before sleep claimed him each night, he would conjure her up in his mind and smile at the image. Ken tried to write to her every day, but sometimes, fatigue got the better of him. Noreen, however, was unwavering in her daily letter writing and kept him abreast of all the local happenings, family news and friends' updates—simple reminders of an uncomplicated life. Their letters were full of encouragement and proclamations of love and plans for a future they both hoped would arrive soon.

The lid of the hope chest was propped open as Noreen and her mother began taking inventory. The box was filled with the most interesting smells, cedar and moth balls, which conjured visions of a future just beyond her grasp. Her thoughts skittered this way and that as Noreen tried to imagine a life with Kenny.

"I think you need a few more pillowcases for when we come to visit you in your new home someday," her mother imagined out loud. "Definitely!" Noreen giggled. Whenever they could squeak a minute away from the restaurant, they worked side by side embroidering the linens and collecting the necessary trappings for starting a home from scratch.

Sue Ellen was not the slightest bit interested in this practice of preparing to be a homemaker. "Heavens, I just want to enjoy Pete right now. That stuff will all take care of itself."

And then because she couldn't help herself, she aimed a bit of good-natured razzing toward Noreen. "Martha, Martha, Martha always has to be working, working, working. Well, not me!"

Noreen cringed, partly because she'd heard it all before, and it brought back memories she would rather avoid and partly because there was a sliver of truthfulness in her sister's barb. She also wished that Ken were here with her as Pete was for her sister. As the only son of a farmer, her sister's beau was exempt from service, which Sue Ellen saw as infinitely more entertaining.

Anna smiled lovingly at her two daughters—so different, yet both so strong and vibrant. She had raised them well, and she basked in their love for her and for each other. She listened to them prattle on about wedding dreams and what their houses might look like. They imagined where they might someday live and talked about their someday children. Anna hugged them both reassuringly and wished it all to be so for them, if only it were that easy.

Whenever Kenny was stationed nearby, Noreen tried to visit him. The Navy had so many rules and held regimented demands on his time, so she found herself alone most of the visit, but even a few hours together helped to forestall the emptiness that would engulf them when they parted. The Navy did not recognize her status as the fiancée. To them, she was a distraction; to Kenny, she was his salvation. But things would soon take a decided twist…of fate, of faith. In the blink of an eye, everything would change dramatically for the young couple.

One day, out of the wild, blue yonder, Kenny called Noreen from Chicago and asked her if she could plan their wedding in a week. A week! He had been granted an unexpected leave and was going to hitchhike home. Her heart was all aflutter. She would be his wife in a week! Yes, of course she could make it happen. Well, maybe not all by herself, but she knew that her mom and her sister, were there to help; and honestly, the important thing was the marriage itself, she thought dreamily, not the wedding.

Hastily made plans were completed in a flash, and Kenneth Lloyd Dickson and Noreen Rita Irwin were joined in Holy

Matrimony on August 23,1944, before a small group of family and friends, while Kenneth was home on a furlough. The wedding ceremony, held at Our Lady of Assumption Catholic Church in Noreen's hometown, was beautiful in its simplicity but rich in sentiment. Sue Ellen was the maid of honor, and Kenny's twin brother, Curtis, was the best man. The profound love between the beautiful bride and the handsome groom permeated the room, and all who witnessed the union were moved beyond words. Surely, here was a couple whose love could go the distance. But just how far would their love take them? The answer was known only by the wise author of their love; not surprisingly, God was not going to spoil the ending.

Alone in their honeymoon hotel suite, together for the first time as newlyweds, Noreen laughed and cried with Kenny about their future desires. They wanted children, of course, but first, there was so much uncertainty to overcome. The war for one. It loomed larger than life and threatened to eradicate the marriage vows they had so recently embraced.

Noreen was quivering in the face of the hardships ahead. Kenny knew what would fortify them as he reached for her hand, now resplendent in a simple gold band snuggled up next to the tiny engagement ring, both sparkling in the moonlight. They held hands and prayed. Verbally, Ken petitioned God to give them at least fifty long years together. Fifty! It would be 1994 in fifty years. It seemed impossibly far off into the distance. Noreen was just hoping God would help them get through the next year. "Wasn't he always the optimist?" she laughed to herself. To him, she replied, "Are you sure you can stand me that long?" His response was immediate and fierce with a kiss so passionate neither of them could breathe. Their hearts pounded with passion, waiting to be revealed, fully over time. With no words spoken, he communicated to his beloved the depth of his love. To himself, he thought, "Even fifty years is not enough, not nearly enough!"

Like all couples, the years unfold as they are meant to unfold. The unexpected turn was that Kenny and Noreen would be allowed to extend their love well beyond the bounds of their earthly existence. Their newly formed union would one day expel the myth that love and marriage end with death. For the truth is, love never dies. It lives on and on, only to be revealed in its complexity in the fullness of time. Who could have predicted that life (and death) would require Noreen to wait a virtual lifetime here on earth before she would thoroughly understand the magnitude of their love as it was proclaimed on their wedding day? Eternal vows, eternal devotion, eternal faithfulness on the rippling sea of love.

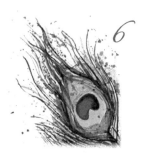

They Tackled the Thing…
and They Married

Isn't it interesting that something so monumental as Holy Matrimony can have such a minute effect on the day-to-day existence of two people? Kenneth went back to the Naval Base and resumed his studies, his naval maneuvers, his responsibilities. Noreen also continued with her normal tasks, her job, her family, her church. Their longing never subsided, but they learned to live with the ache. Marriage hadn't really changed anything, except the comfort from knowing that they were forever bound to each other. For fifty years, that's what he promised, and she was going to hold him to that particular promise!

Each evening the Irwin family would get down on their knees in the middle of the living room and pray for the safe return of Kenneth to their family. The prayers of the Dickson family were equally as fervent. The prayer was always the same, "Please, Lord, somehow, some way, protect Kenneth from being shipped overseas when his training is finished." In the privacy of her thoughts, Noreen feared that if he went overseas, he would never return to her.

Rationally, of course, this prayer made no sense. Why in the world would the Navy train a fighter pilot only to clip his wings and keep him grounded? But despite the odds, the prayers were launched again and again in an unending pattern of pleading to God for mercy, for a miracle. Faith—it all boils down to faith, then hope and finally love.

Kenneth struggled to complete his pilot training and felt the warmth and security that comes from being encased in prayers of love. Finally, a glimmer appeared on the horizon, for Noreen, with her new status as wife, was allowed to stay with her bridegroom when she visited him. When eventually, the most difficult part of his training was complete, they relocated to married housing and lived on base. What a joy! For the first time since their marriage months previously, Noreen and Kenneth shared a life. Noreen got a job at the commissary, and Kenneth would pop by to see her throughout the day as his classes would allow. They were giddy with love, and those days marked the calm before the ultimate storm, which began to brew overhead and overseas.

After much dedicated study, Kenneth graduated from flight school. It was a day of both celebration and foreboding. For as this chapter ended, another far more-challenging one would begin. Kenneth and Noreen knew that the Navy would soon deliver the ship-out notices. The biggest worry was that he would be sent overseas into armed combat in enemy airspace. Even though prayers were ceaselessly offered to the contrary, it seemed that the assignment was eminent.

The wide-eyed innocence and optimism of youth was overpoweringly prevalent. "Don't borrow trouble," Noreen whispered to herself and to Kenny. They blithely ignored the dangers around them and concentrated on their love, their hopes, and their faith. They refused to face the horrors of war as it pertained to them until it was forced upon them. And so the newlyweds celebrated in innocuous bliss and smiled really more than they should have, considering the situation.

The translucent curtain fluttered with the breeze from the open bedroom window. Noreen lay perfectly still for fear of disrupting this moment of contentment, feeling him there, present and alive, with her. If only they could stay in bed and shut the world out of their lives. Ken sensed her pensive mood, stirred, and pulled her close to him. She nestled under his arm, resting her palm on his chest, rising and falling with the rhythm of life, strong and steady.

When the alarm clock sounded in their tiny cubicle of an apartment on that fateful morning, little did they realize that the end of the day would arrive much more somberly than it had begun. The start of the day gave no indication, no clue that there was anything out of the ordinary smoldering just behind the balmy breeze, just beyond the brilliant blue sky alive with the gentle soaring of birds and planes, sharing the sky as wayward companions. The breaking dawn hid the evidence of the havoc that would soon be unleashed upon the unsuspecting newlyweds.

Noreen was the first to rise as Ken fell back to sleep. She deftly made breakfast for them and sat down with a cup of hot black coffee and a homemade yeast roll traditionally called a long john, a recipe she was practicing with all the perseverance she had once devoted to roller skating. Those days seemed eons past. The coffee girded her to face the day, which she expected to be extra busy since they were shorthanded at the commissary. The routines of her day would be broken only by an occasional kiss from her husband, stealing a precious moment to connect with his beautiful new wife. Ah, those kisses made it all worthwhile. Just to be in his arms and feel the culmination of their love manifested into the daily regime of Naval life, yet surviving, thriving.

The coldness of the military contrasted sharply with the warmth of their love. Strict, regimented, unyielding—impersonal, yes, but they were together at least some of the time, sharing late-night chats and early morning drowsiness. How they both adored married life and selfishly cherished every minute they had together. How greedy they had become. They could not carve out enough time to satisfy their love.

Over and over, Noreen repeated, "Count your blessings, count your blessings." A trait she had unknowingly absorbed from her mother. Still, they both yearned for simpler days and more relaxed time together. Little did they suspect that these feelings of being denied ample access to each other and the stress-laden frenetic pace of military living would help shape their future vocations one day.

But this day, the military briefings and maneuvers would exact an inordinate amount of Ken's time, and the long hours that Noreen faced at the commissary meant that simple was nowhere to be found. That calamitous morning, Ken only had time for a quick cup of coffee and grabbed a yeast roll for the trek across the base. He so loved her cooking, especially the baked goods, and her delectable yeast rolls were approaching perfection. He did count his blessings often and knew that he had been blessed beyond his wildest expectations. If only he could spend more time with his bride, but duty called, and he had to answer.

Fate is a tricky adversary, for just as Kenneth arrived unknowingly at his post—filled not only with yeast rolls but with love, satisfaction, and yes, pure joy at his lot in life—he would soon experience a twist more heinous than he could ever have anticipated when he passionately kissed his bride good-bye and headed out the door just minutes before.

For so long, he had been dreading what seemed like the inevitable. Now, each breath was marked by the ticking of the clock; and steady, even heartbeats, drew him closer to war. Since the very first day he had enlisted, it was not the fear that constantly prickled the edges of his heart, it was the facts. The fact that this unspoken enemy had the power to forever alter his existence or nonexistence on this planet. The fact that war was one of the few things that had the scope and capacity to separate Kenny from Noreen short-term, long-term, or forever. This fact could alter everything about his life as he knew it, and he was instantly filled with trepidation. The worst had happened. Ken had received his orders to ship out overseas.

"How will I ever survive this? How will she? How can I bear to tell her?"

As in every other moment of his life, he turned to prayer. He begged, pleaded, and cried inside, masking his emotions on the outside. The appearance of blithely walking through his day did little to forestall the agony in his soul. There were mountains of paperwork and numerous tasks to complete for the upcoming deployment. He found himself crisscrossing the base to pick up this record or that document. He exuded a brusqueness to the personnel that he did not mean and was so unlike him. On this day, everything about the Naval Air Force was incredibly irritating to him, so he busied himself to avoid the inevitable that would be waiting for him at home.

Kenneth did not sneak away for a quick kiss all that black, ominous day. He just could not face her. He had to find a way to tell her without belying the truth of how scared he was for their future. He could not bear to be parted from her for even a day, leave alone for months, perhaps years. It was with heavy feet that Kenneth returned home at the end of that life altering day. One look at his face and she knew, beyond a shadow of a doubt, there was trouble.

The day had been busy for her, and yet she found herself distractedly looking for him every few minutes. It just was not like him to stay away. He could almost always carve out a few minutes here or a few minutes there.

Noreen had resolutely refused to face the inevitability of this day, yet now, she could not deny it or escape it. Kenneth had received his orders, and he was to be shipped overseas within the next few weeks. Noreen and Ken made weeping calls to their families who promised to bombard heaven with prayer.

Noreen felt like she had been caught in a storm of emotions and couldn't find a peaceful place to examine them. Everything happened with such speed and precision. The Navy does this sort of thing routinely, and they had procedures in place. For her, unfortunately, there were no maneuvers that would help, no manuals, no protocol or rules of conduct; this was personal.

Sometimes it felt like the weight of the world was on their shoulders, yet they remained steadfast in their faithfulness to each other, to their country, and to God. They grudgingly made plans while sharing fears, whispering deep felt proclamations of love.

The long hours of separation while Ken prepared for deployment was a cruel training arena for what promised to be the worst challenge to their young marriage. When they were together, they put on brave faces; but in the darkness of the night, they clung to each other with tearstained pillows.

Both families (the Catholic Irwins and the Baptist Dicksons) prayed earnestly to the same God for the same thing. Protect Kenny. Keep him on U.S. soil. But each day brought them closer to the inevitable.

On the day she moved from the base, back to her childhood home, Noreen's dark and despondent mood was sharply contrasted by the bright and beautiful spring morning swirling all around her. She drove all day and into the ruddy darkness, watching the street-lights loom and then abate. She felt like her happiness and her life were slipping away from her. She just wanted to be surrounded by family, so she pressed the pedal and anxiously gripped the steering wheel as if she could control something. There was such a barrage of emotions flowing through her, over her, tumbling with such force that she couldn't capture a single one to scrutinize it.

The year was 1945. Kenneth was now living in the barracks with his unit where they trained without rest for days on end. He was so exhausted that he scarcely noticed the buds just beginning to pop on the trees and the warmth carried by the breezes across his sweating brow.

In the final analysis, regardless of his heart's longing, Kenneth was a soldier. He had sworn to do his duty, and nothing would prevent him from that end, even love. His strong work ethic that had been honed by his family during the long lean years of his boyhood was nothing compared to the trial he now faced. An even more grueling fight faced him, the fight for survival. There was so much at stake, and he knew it. His life and his marriage, while elemental to him personally, were sorely eclipsed by the enormity of the war effort. It was not just his way of life in jeopardy, all of America was being challenged. Kenneth threw himself into the preparations with the zest of a man who believed in the cause, because he did.

The hardships relegated to American soldiers, including being separated from loved ones, meant nothing if the American ideals and the established way of life were compromised. Ken knew what he had to do, he had to stand firm, strong and fight for a safety and freedom for his wife and his someday children. There was no question; he would do his duty well. His word was his bond, and his integrity as a man was at stake. There were no other honorable options, and Kenneth L. Dickson was an honorable man.

So the days turned into weeks with Ken struggling to further hone his battle skills. His flight log clearly squealed as entry after entry, maneuver after maneuver were painstakingly practiced. And quietly, lovingly in the background, a virtual barrage of prayers was assaulting heaven every minute, every day.

The Dicksons prayed silently, separately begging God to spare their son. They added Kenny's name to the prayer chain at church. The Irwins also prayed privately throughout the day, and each evening, the family members knelt in the middle of the living room floor and shared a communal Rosary. Seventy-two recited prayers, their voices uniting with earnest love, fidelity, and faith—always strong, strong faith. The families were not giving up; they were not giving in, if and until Kenneth's feet had left for the battle zone. Until that moment, there was hope and they prayed fervently for a different solution, not sure even what to pray, just knowing that they needed to petition God in perpetual prayer.

And pray they did, until their knees were sore and their voices hoarse. They believed in their hearts that God heard them and that their prayers would be answered as He saw fit. They recognized the utter hopelessness of their request yet called upon the Bible stories with constancy and faithfulness. Hadn't the man who ceaselessly pounded on his neighbors' door in the middle of the night for bread been rewarded out of sheer irritation? (Luke 11:8).

"Well, let God be irritated by our litany if he must," whispered Anna, "just please, please answer this prayer. Don't send our Kenny overseas. So many men never return and he is so needed here, so wanted here, so loved here." Surely God could turn all things to good (Romans 8:28). He said He would, and they claimed that promise.

When the final telephone call came, Noreen was on her knees with her family. As she raced to the phone and picked up the receiver, the sound of his voice made her heart leap into her throat with such force she thought she would surely choke. His words felt like a knife cutting her to the core as he explained that they were ready to board the Naval aircraft carrier that would be the vehicle to separate them physically for an indeterminate amount of time.

They professed their love, promised eternal fidelity, vowed to write daily, urged continued prayers, and finally, remorsefully, had to say good-bye to each other far too soon. For the next sailor was waiting impatiently and nervously in line, waiting his turn to make his final call to his loved ones who clearly must be feeling the same distress, the same longing for a different outcome.

Noreen returned to the family prayer circle and fell on her knees, wailing and weeping with renewed urgency to stop the horror that was swallowing her husband, threatening all that they had created. Their voices united with a frenetic pitch as they petitioned God again and again to let this cup pass them by as in the Garden of Gethsemane when Jesus prayed with the same fervor (John 18:10). All seemed hopeless, it *was* hopeless, yet they prayed on in faith, hope, and love.

They didn't rail at God. They didn't call him names or use profanity. They didn't throw things or kick the dog. They did not throw a temper tantrum. Instead, they redoubled their prayer efforts, begging and pleading as steadfast, faithful servants.

In just over an hour, their prayers were again interrupted by the ringing of the phone. Noreen did not leap to answer it as she did before, as she had been doing since she was forced to leave the base and return to her family. There was no one she wanted to talk with, no one who could salve her wounded heart. Nothing helped except prayer. So Noreen stayed praying and her sister, Sue Ellen, got up to answer the jangling and unwelcome intrusion.

From the other room, they heard her scream. With shock and disbelief, she squealed for Noreen and handed her the phone. By this time, all the family members in the Irwin household had squeezed into the parlor, rosaries in hand, to witness the spectacle that was unfolding before their eyes. A miracle in the making!

Kenneth's voice ignited the telephone line with an eagerness to reach Noreen. Unbelievably, he had good news, great news, miraculous news. Through tears of joy and love and disbelief, he relayed the story to his bride.

"When it was my turn to board the aircraft, there was a glitch. For some unknown reason, they could not find my paperwork anywhere. No paperwork, no deployment. They stamped my documents pending, and I stepped out of line, out of harm's way. Why me? I'll never know. Prayers? Oh, absolutely. But there are families everywhere praying today for this. How did we get so blessed? How did God hear our prayers?"

The Irwin family fell into each other's arms in quiet awe, for they knew, as clearly as they lived and loved, they were standing in the presence of a full-fledged miracle. Noreen's eyes widened as she watched tears stream down Eldin's face, unchecked, unashamed. Normally stoic, today Eldin allowed his sensitive side to emerge as he stuffed his hands awkwardly into his pockets. His shirt was tucked haphazardly into his dark trouser, his carrot-colored hair parted neatly on the side. Noreen could not remember having ever seen her brother cry, but here he was, standing beside her, loving her as had been his habit through all of their school years.

Their prayers had been answered in the eleventh hour when all reasonable hope should have been abandoned. Their faith had saved them, just like the thief who was crucified with Christ and asked to be remembered in heaven (Luke 23:42) only without the horrendous death scene they had all imaged as a potential outcome of deployment.

Noreen and Kenneth clung together, separated only by a thousand miles of phone cord. Their hearts were united, beating as one, living, loving, praising. This was to be the first of many miracles that lay in store for Kenneth and Noreen. They did not imagine in this glorious moment that their future would also include sorrow, injury, loss, and death.

Ah, but that day was not this day. Not today, for today the Lord had granted them a reprieve. "This is the day the Lord has made, let us rejoice and be glad" (Psalm 119:24). For today, their Lord and Savior had heard their plea and answered their prayer.

Now naturally, understandably, they all continued to worry. What if the papers were found? What if Kenny had only been delayed, not fully saved from the unspeakable demands of war? Prayers! They knew that it was the only answer, and they tripled their efforts, committing to hours of prayers until Kenneth was safely out of harm's way.

The prayers of every family in every household across the nation must have reached the ears of the Lord because within a matter of a few weeks, the war ended. Jubilation echoed around the world as mothers and wives, fathers and children, siblings and friends welcomed the news that their loved ones would be returning to them. Kenneth would remain in the military to complete his service time but would never be required to deploy to a combat zone. His future with Noreen was within his grasp.

The discharge day came earlier than expected, but not soon enough to satisfy Ken. His precious Noreen had planned to pick him up the following week, but here he was, standing on the curb with no ride in sight, but totally free. More importantly, his country remained free. The struggle to maintain freedom extracts a high price sometimes, and he had been willing, if need be, to sacrifice all that he held dear to protect all that he held dear. Instead, his feet were firmly planted on free soil where others before him had paid for that privilege. He was free at long last of the heavy cloud that had hovered since enlistment. The threat to his country was over, at least for this time.

He had to get home to her. But money was tight, of course. He donned his uniform, partly for warmth, but surely hoping some patriotic citizen would lend a hand or a car really. He stood at the edge of his new life and threw out his thumb. In the mid-forties, automobiles had not claimed their ubiquitous position in American society, so hitchhiking was commonplace. Cars were a luxury, and folks were generally happy to give a lift to a stranger, especially a man in uniform. Ken was counting on both to be true. He was heading home early to surprise his bride.

It was an odd sort of day, with unexpected bouts of unseasonable snow. In sharp contrast, the sun warmed his back as he stood by the side of the road, listening to the leaves scuttle across the pavement as if playing a game of chase before coming to rest in the ditch on the other side of the road where they were welcomed by a bevy of very hardy insects who called that area home. Home, he was going home. So distracted was he by the sights and sounds of the world all around, he didn't even notice a sleek, new Bermuda-green Studebaker had pulled up in answer to his thumb.

"Where you headed, soldier?" the professional-looking, overdimensioned man inside the car asked Kenny.

"Home, sir. I'm headed home."

"Then climb in, I'm headed that way." Ken noticed that a Rosary swung from the rearview mirror and reflected the brilliant sun heralding this luminous day, the beginning of a brave new adventure. Life!

The two men hit it off easily, talking about sports, the war, the economy, life, love and faith. The day, which had once been sunny and bearable, took a turn toward bitter cold, dreary, and overcast with more than a little fluff cluttering up the freeway. While the main roads had been plowed, the roads less traveled possessed a singular set of tracks, eked out by the previous traveler, a barely drivable serpentine-inspired track down the middle of the road. The drive was arduous.

Had Ken thought about it at all, he would have recognized that he was not a middle-of-the-road kinda guy. He was decisive and confident, not easily led astray by larger-than-life, well-dressed, flashy strangers or anyone else for that matter. Yet despite his constitution, here he was, listening and even considering changing his life goals, his values, perhaps even his future as they drove straight down the middle of the unplowed road.

The miles flew by despite the slipping and sliding, and Kenny rambled on about his dreams, trying to reconcile it in his mind. There were so many decisions before him. The stranger listened with kindness and compassion, understanding the ambivalence and uncertainty that awaited all the nation's military men returning home, returning to normalcy, returning to peace. Ken was one of the lucky ones as he was also returning to love.

It was an impulse really, or was it? The stranger looked over at Ken and said, "Son, the Lord's been good to me. I own a string of factories spread all across the Midwest with my headquarters in Chicago. We've been swamped building machinery for the war effort, couldn't keep up."

He paused, took a deep breath, smiled ingratiatingly, and continued, "I could sure use a good man like you to help me retool the factories for peace-time needs. I don't have a son, and I need a right-hand man to learn the business and help me nail down the profit line in this changing economy. You're smart, you're grounded, you're faithful, and I think we could take the world by storm."

It was flattering, of course, really helped with the old self-esteem. It would be a sweet deal, for sure. Was this oh so timely offer a hint from God? Kenny had to ponder; he had to pray. So much was riding on the decisions he would be making right now. The waning months of 1945 placed a premium on home and hearth. So many loved ones had been denied the luxury of both. He recognized how blessed he was to be returning to a world where love, family, home and God were treasured beyond all else.

Truly, what were his priorities? Did this new possibility really fit with them? How would it affect his wife, the love of his life? And then his heart and his thoughts turned to her.

Kenny could almost feel the happiness, the peace, the love that always surrounded his thoughts of Noreen, the most beautiful woman in the world, to him. The life he wanted was oh so close to becoming a reality. He wanted a normal life with her more than anything else he had ever desired. He would give up anything, everything, to create a home, a family where love would reign supreme.

He longed for the security and comfort he had never experienced as a child. He would build his life differently.

But there are so many options in life, as any young person knows. The future is defined by the choices made. It's easy to become one of the daring young men on the flying trapeze of ambitions, but is that what's best for his life, for Noreen's, for their someday children? Life is not a circus, though sometimes it feels that way; although unfortunately, life provides no safety nets.

Kenneth thought about his pre-war desire to become a dentist, and he knew that it would require long hours of study with little time to devote to Noreen. Truly, after everything they'd been through, that just seemed unthinkable. He thought about continuing his pilot training in the civilian sector, but there were so many unemployed pilots just out of the war gobbling up the airline jobs, and a pilot's life meant travel and time away from home, time away from loved ones. Home and love were what he craved.

And now, there was this new twist. Should he follow this path? He listened intently for miles on end as the man explained his vision for his empire and outlined the role that Ken would play in the burgeoning organization. It was exhilarating. Ken could imagine the adrenaline rush as together, they closed deal after deal, traveling around the world meeting with heads of industry. In this job, he could make a real mark in the world. He thought about the practical contributions to the country, providing jobs for returning servicemen, products for new families. He thought about the safety and security that stable employment could provide for his own wife, his own life. And then the most relevant question hit him.

Where was his passion? That was an easy question, Noreen, of course. He had to make a living, surely, but he wanted something that bound them together. He dreamily imagined what it would be like to wake up to coffee and yeast rolls with her head on the pillow beside his and hear the pitter-patter of little feet. He wanted to be able to see her throughout the day. He wanted a life free from the rigmarole, demands, and stress that had surrounded them during the war years. He wanted to work hard and see the fruits of his labor. He was tired of falling in line and kowtowing to the military brass. He wanted to be his own man and follow his own priorities.

With mixed feelings and not just a little regret, Ken turned down the job offer with the same melancholy he had experienced when he chose not to pursue a career in baseball. He turned away from the road that lead to certain wealth, position, and power. A position that would provide all the creature comforts that he had never had in his own life thus far. A career that would guarantee that his children would never be hungry, cold, or overworked. He chose instead, a road well-traveled. He chose it for all the right reasons, and that made all the difference.

As the miles to home diminished, Ken's heart began to speak more clearly than ever before. Ken listened intently to the voice within him. He sat in silence and prayed for the wisdom to know that he had made the best choice, the blessed choice. He prayed for God's hand to guide him toward the career path that would meet his needs, satisfy his passion, and support his family. Suddenly, he just knew what he wanted to do. He had reached a career decision, a life affirming decision.

Life offers many job opportunities, but the choice is always made with free will. Resting his head against the burgundy plush upholstery, he felt content with his choice. His would be a more peaceful career, one that allotted him all of the aforementioned pre-requisites: to be his own boss, to keep a relaxed schedule, to carve out ample time to spend with Noreen, and to create a home that welcomed God with children at the center of it.

He chose farming because he had years of experience, because he liked to watch things grow, because he loved to walk his land, because he just wanted to be home with the people he loved. But mostly, he chose farming for her, because he deeply and completely adored her. He yearned for a home like he had never had growing up. He wanted to work with Noreen to create a loving family. He just wanted a simple life filled with love. Was that too much to ask? He was going to put everything he had into this farming venture and find out. He would create a new farming reality, one without the angst that was so entrenched in his past. The past was past; Ken was only looking forward. He was looking forward to her.

Ken knew that the foundation of a happy life was to build it with all things good. In the eyes of the world, he was giving up a chance at the "good life," a finally secure life. But truly, what are the good things in life? It's certainly not about money or things, for they ring hollow and empty compared to the building blocks of love, laughter, family, and faith. He recognized that farming would not offer any of the fringe benefits of a professional career, but he had learned the hard way that life could be cut short and love was really all that mattered. He was not about to ever lose that—no way, no how. He would work the land together with those he loved and live his days simply, praising the Lord and marveling at the world around him.

That's just what he did, and many years into the future, long after his death, Ken would revisit this decision and speak to his children about the value of money, looking back on this moment and this choice from the other side.

And just like that, his mind snapped to attention. In the distance, he could see it. Like a desert wanderer coming upon a water hole. It sprang into view like a mirage. It seemed surreal. After all this time away, he was finally home. Noreen, the center of his world, was surely in that house. How surprised she would be!

When the car pulled into the driveway, faces peered out through the windows. They weren't expecting company, and they didn't recognize the fancy car. Their expressions changed from being mildly curious to being flabbergasted when Ken stepped out of the passenger seat, tall and lean and smiling ear to ear.

The house suddenly came to life. Noreen rushed into his waiting embrace and showered his face with kisses that tasted salty from the tears that were streaming down both of their faces. She inhaled the familiar scent of his Old Spice as she nuzzled his collar and ignored the commotion around them as family members screamed with delight, cried for joy, and hugged each other with gusto as the swirling snow made circles around their dancing feet.

The Dicksons were called, and they drove their buggy as fast as the horses could manage, considering the snowy conditions. Their farm truck was on the fritz again, but jubilation bubbled in their hearts as every mile brought them closer to their son.

Ken breathed in the love surrounding him. He was home, finally home, and he pledged to remain there, in her arms, forever. A promise that he was able to keep until God tapped him on the shoulder and said it was his turn to be deployed. Forced physical separation brought about by death was a much different type of deployment and one they would not have to think about this day or any day in the foreseeable future. There was much life to be lived, love to be shared before then.

When the emotions settled from disbelief into serenity, they sat for hours and days, sharing and connecting after their enforced estrangement. They held hands on the porch swing, snuggled underneath an afghan crocheted in hues of gold and brown. With a bit of trepidation, Ken talked about the man in the expensive car who had given him a ride and helped him solidify his dreams.

"I just want to be a farmer, Noreen, I really do."

Noreen, of course, was more than surprised to learn that Kenny had decided to give up his ambitious career dreams. The surprise on her face was evident, and she tried to mask it until she could examine her own feelings on the subject, but the conversation could not be averted.

She was not all that keen on being a farm wife. Truth be told, she hated the idea, but more importantly, she hated the idea that he felt he could make this monumental, life-altering decision for both of them. She felt her back bristling, and he noticed. She had to nip this behavior in the bud if she ever expected to have an equal say in their marriage.

"Waaait just a minute there! Last time I checked, I have a say in how we design our life too. I'm not so sure I want to live on a farm. It seems like there are easier ways to make a living. Let's talk about the options. This is something that we need to decide together."

So they discussed the pros and cons and examined all of the possibilities together. Ken spoke candidly about his feelings, and she began to understand his motivation. He had successfully kicked the arguments right out from underneath her. How could she say that she wanted him to be away from her and travel the globe with the tycoon or keep his nose buried in dentistry studies for years to come. She didn't exactly want a pilot for a husband either; they are away from home so much. She too just wanted to be with him.

She could find no fault with his reasoning. Kenny had lovingly articulated his priorities, his values, which she also held dear. She just had never imagined that they would willingly elect a life of hardship, physically and financially, yet here they were tiptoeing toward farming, together.

Alone with her thoughts, late at night, Noreen worried about her preparedness or lack thereof. While she had worked hard throughout her youth, she had experienced none of the desperation and dirt-floor poverty that had plagued Ken's family. Her mom had been a working mom, therefore had not passed on skills and knowledge that would be required of a farm wife. She could cook, of course, and clean, but there was so much more to living off the land and taking care of a family. Noreen was so naive, she could not even conjure up what those skills she was lacking might be…canning, soapmaking?

But she was smart and strong and persistent. Best of all, she had a "can do" attitude, and she was no stranger to hard work. Working in a restaurant was just a different kind of work. So was working in an office or in the commissary at the base. She would do what needed to be done because she wanted him to be happy in his work.

For not the first time, she considered her own career possibilities, but set them aside for want of a passion or a path to follow. There were few female role models for that sort of thing, and most men, including Ken, frowned on the idea of a working wife. She sighed and thought of her daughters whom she had yet to meet. She could mentor them differently. She could imbue them with more confidence and broader dreams than most woman of her generation were allotted. She could be the transition with one foot in the traditional past and one foot forging ahead into the unchartered future. "Now there's a worthy life goal," she whispered to no one in particular and felt her heart race with enthusiasm. "I guess that's my passion, just the thought of it makes me happy. I'll be a great mom."

So Noreen inhaled a deep breath, whispered a small prayer, before she put her arm lovingly through his and trudged forward into their unknown future, holding on for dear life to her positive, loving—although often independent—attitude. Whatever came, they would face it together. Whatever happened, God would walk with them and fortify them against the challenges that would inevitably come their way. They were not alone; they had each other, their extended families, and their faith.

They had chosen a path that was not less traveled, but rather well worn by the tractor wheels from many farmers who had plowed before them. The journey they chose allowed them to pause regularly to smell the flowers, count their blessings, to pray, to love, to raise a family; and in the end, that made all the difference.

They Buckled Right In...
and Laid the Foundation

She sat in the front seat of the truck with a setting of chicken hatchlings propped carefully on her lap, a parting gift from her parents. There were tears streaming down her face, his face, all the family faces. Noreen looked back at her waving family as Ken pulled out of the driveway heading toward their new life together, his prominently veined hands gripping the steering wheel to hold back the emotions that threatened to tumble out. He had a choice, tears or laughter. In characteristic fashion, he chose laughter.

"Well, this is where our fifty years begin," Ken smiled lovingly at his bride. They laughed tumultuously at how absurd that seemed. The bittersweet moment passed. They were young and healthy and had dodged the obstacle of war. Praise God!

It had been a busy few months negotiating priorities, searching for farmland, and packing up their paltry possessions. After much deliberation, they decided to settle around the corner from Kenny's parents, just outside the village of Waldron, Michigan. It seemed like a nice gesture. His mother still nursed a grudge that Kenny had joined the Catholic Church. Leola had accepted the fact that she couldn't change it, but she didn't have to be happy about it either.

Noreen hoped that just maybe, if they spent more time with her, Leola would come around. After all, a good marriage is about compromise. Noreen loved Ken with everything in her and wanted to give him this time with his mother. She could flex on this. It would be fine. That's the lie she told herself.

The farmland Kenny found was lush and fertile, yet still reasonably priced since Waldron was located quite a distance from any good-sized town. The gently sloping topography was interrupted by plenty of trees, fence rows and a smattering of cows. Ken recognized that he would be able to help with his parents' farm more easily from this vantage point. The downside was that the trek to the farmers' market in Detroit would be grueling. It also meant that visiting Noreen's parents, an hour away, would likewise be more difficult. Noreen was not keen on that notion, but in the end, the inconvenience was outweighed by the proximity to his family and the affordability of the acreage. She wanted to make Kenny as happy as he had made her, this year and for every year of their fifty-year contract.

It had been a pleasant, if not crowded experience living with her parents until they could get themselves settled into their own life. They had helped out at the restaurant when they could. It was fun in a way, just being together, feeling normal. So much laughter and merriment.

The couple soon noticed that gaiety and optimism were not as plentiful at Ken's parents' farm. Jesse and Leola had spent most of their lives silencing their hearts and souls, perhaps to escape the guttural screaming that stemmed from helplessness, hopelessness, and loss, so much loss. Perhaps with so many years of burying their feelings, they forgot how to fully express their emotions to themselves or to anyone else. They became proverbial strangers living under the same roof, but at least that roof didn't leak.

Age had not been kind to his parents, and the ruggedness and sadness of their lives showed in the deep creases on their faces and the aches and pains prominently making their existence known. Kenny did all he could to ease their burdens but found it increasingly more difficult now that he had his own farm to get going too.

It didn't matter. Whatever he and Noreen did, they could not interject happiness into his parents' lives. Happiness was a state of mind, and apparently, their minds could not focus on the positive aspects of their lives. There were plenty of reasons to be grateful—a son and wife nearby, enough to eat, a solid farmhouse, fertile acreage, a profitable farm, the dew on the morning glories, peace in their old age—but they just couldn't see it. The web of relationships that bound people together in love and harmony had been tattered by the weight of their woebegone past.

Jesse loved living within walking distance of his son and found a smidgeon of comfort whenever he could escape for an undisclosed visit, as much to avoid the negativity in his own home as to connect with the youngsters. More and more he found himself neglecting his own chores to give his son a hand with his.

"How about I help you get that old tractor up and running this afternoon?" "Do ya need a hand fixin' that silo chute?" "Why don't we get started on the stalls in that milking parlor?" Any excuse to get away from home was excuse enough.

Ken understood all this, knew all that his parents had endured, because well he had lived it too. He wanted to forget the past, but it came rushing back each time he darkened the doorway of his parents' house, sporting his scruffy, faded denim bib overalls with his chiseled jaw covered with stubble at the end of a long, hard day. Consequently, he found himself avoiding the visits more often than he should, and Leola noticed.

Her compressed lips sent snarky chirps in Ken's direction fairly regularly. "Ah, look what the cat dragged in! So, the prodigal son returns," she'd harangue in a not-so-passive-aggressive manner. "To what do we owe this rare pleasure?"

"Oh, Mom, it hasn't been that long. Been busy with the planting and the milking. Noreen and I are raising chickens and selling them all dressed out at the Detroit Farmers' Market. We get a better price from the city folks. Even the eggs sell for more. We're trying to get the new acres turned before we get too far into the season. There's just so much that's gotta get done and never enough time."

"That has to be done," she corrected him.

Farming is such a challenging life. He knew that from the beginning, and he chose it anyway; they chose it—well, mostly him. His dentistry dream had been solidly laid to rest, along with the offer from the business tycoon in the Bermuda green Studebaker. The commercial pilot option had likewise been discarded. They had made their choices, and looking back was futile. A lifetime of what-ifs and regrets can turn happy thoughts to bitter ones.

Leola was a living lesson on that, and Noreen took notes. "That is what comes from wallowing," she considered pensively. "Why doesn't she just forgive, forget, and move on? That will never be me. No matter what life throws at me, I won't live in negativity."

The resolve in her constitution was unwaveringly, strong, and expressly necessary to withstand the traumas of her own burgeoning life, as yet unrevealed. The stitching in life's tapestry unravels thread by thread with each passing day until it ceases to exist in this world, as we know it. What lies beyond is stitched by the hands of the Master and is not meant for us to hold.

The happy newlyweds settled into a comfortable rhythm and began the slow and tedious task of creating their life in the here and now. There was so much to do, woods to clear, fields to plow, crops to plant. But through it all, they remained true to their passion—well, almost always. Each morning they shared smiles and kisses over home-baked goods and freshly brewed coffee and held hands across the worn kitchen table, a hand-me-down from her mother. They carved out bits of time for each other throughout the day and prayed for rain—ah, glorious rain.

A rainy day was good for their crops and good for their marriage. Rain brought a reprieve from outside work, and they would revel in the day by snuggling in bed late into the morning and then putter around the house together. Yes, they grew to love the cleansing of the beautiful, fragrant Michigan rains. And when the rain stopped, everything smelled as fresh and dewy as their brand-new marriage.

Ken was happier than he had ever been before. Of course, there had been precious few truly joyous memories in his growing-up years, but Christmas, surprisingly, was one. Even though they didn't have much in the way of presents, his family always decorated robustly with whatever nature had to offer.

Christmas at the Dicksons had been an all-out adventure, so uncharacteristic, but such a welcomed change from the drudgery that claimed the rest of the year. They would spend a whole day traipsing through the woods to cut down the perfect tree and then invariably, they'd have to trim it up to fit into their tiny house. It always looked smaller in the woods for some reason. They would weave garland out of fresh greens and string popcorn with cranberries. The ceiling was adorned with colorful paper chains and cut-out paper snowflakes.

Leola, who wasn't particularly fond or adept at cooking, always rose to the occasion at Christmastime by spoiling her family with homemade cookies and pies and breads. She would squirrel away ingredients for months to bring forth the magic of the season.

When the holidays rolled around, Ken was surprised that Noreen was not all that enamored with the fanfare to which he had been accustomed. Noreen's family had a restaurant to contend with, and there was little energy to devote to decorating or frivolous Christmas trappings. There were presents of course, and midnight Mass; but beyond that, the celebration was sedate.

Ken just had to decorate; he couldn't help himself. Noreen didn't object exactly; she just didn't help either. It was all on him, and he was just fine with that. He'd string lights around the broken windows and wrap garland around rotted porch supports. He'd tape Christmas cards to the crumbling plastered walls and wire mistletoe to the dangling lightbulb in the middle of the living room.

Noreen would smile at Ken's holiday spirit, not really understanding it, but loving him despite it all. One exception was the manger scene figurines. They were near and dear to her heart and she displayed them carefully on the dresser top. She remembered how lovingly Ken had presented them to her when they were first dating and she cherished the memory. She had placed them in her hope chest when she was still living at home and dreaming of her future husband, hoping it would be him.

On their second Christmas together as an old married couple, Ken cobbled together a rough manger shanty from cast-off wood to surround the set. Although Ken was eager and industrious, carpentry was not his forte. Not wanting to bother his brother, the real carpenter, for such a tiny project, Ken stumbled away on his own. The end result clearly highlighted his shortcomings, which Noreen graciously overlooked. It was Noreen's most precious, perhaps the only Christmas decoration, that she loved. She felt it symbolized the importance of the season, the Holy Family. She looked forward to the day when she would have a family of her own. She smiled at the comparison.

The manger itself was nearly as ramshackle as their own farmhouse, desperately in need of remodeling. Both structures had holes in the boards that were patched with whatever material was handy. Kenny's version employed cardboard and duct tape, newly invented during the war to seal ammunition boxes. His manger sported a bent, rusty nail, which held the angel at the gable where a piece of roof had broken off. Their own roof was missing shingles and sometimes leaked if the wind swirled just right. The crudeness of the manger structure was endearing to Noreen, not just because it was built out of selflessness, but because it held an uncanny resemblance to the Christ child's birthplace, which was not new or sparkly or perfect, but real—just like their life, just like their home. What both structures held was love.

The couple's front door that had once been painted green, as ascertained by the few remaining specks of paint still stubbornly clinging to the weathered wood, sported a pine bough wreath adorned with cranberries; thanks to Ken's ministrations. He made one for his mother too, hoping to instill a little good cheer in her season as it was the first one without her husband. Jesse had died abruptly and unceremoniously earlier that year on March 22, 1946, and the holiday was bound to stir up old memories with fresh mourning.

Ken's guess was right on the mark. Leola compounded the grief over her husband with the memories of her son, Clifford, lost so many years prior. All the pain and anguish that had walked with her throughout her life claimed what little happiness she had tried to embrace during her first widowed Christmas.

Even Christmas decorations could not break through her bitterness, although Ken never gave up trying. He nudged Noreen to prepare a cookie platter to take to his mom, and they invited her to join them for Christmas dinner so she would not be alone. "Well, I suppose it's better than nothing," came her crotchety retort.

With time, Ken and Noreen found a compromise and celebrated the season in a manner that honored both of their preferences. Ken took charge of decorating everything except the manger—Noreen's job. Noreen cooked and baked and Ken brought home the Christmas tree. They always made it to midnight Mass together, holding hands throughout the service. The rhythm of their lives had been negotiated and established in a way that honored both of their beliefs, traditions, and desires.

The years slid by almost unnoticed, caught up with tasks and troubles, tasting (for Noreen was such a great cook) and teasing, "Only forty-seven more years to go!" They broke into giggles at how far away that seemed. They'd created a life that was comfortable and filled with love, not that there weren't some irksome moments and some irksome relatives.

Noreen had a level head, and not much rattled her; but there was one persistent thorn in her side—Kenny's mother. It seemed that no matter what Noreen did, she couldn't win Leola over. When Jesse, was alive, he kept her in check; but now it felt like her mother-in-law went actively out of her way to needle Noreen.

Leola made no secret of the fact that she wanted to be a grandmother. By this time, Ken's twin brother, Curtis, had three sons; but unfortunately, they lived so far away that she seldom saw them. Leola seemed to relish every opportunity to shine a light on the fact that Kenny and Noreen were still childless. Noreen held her head high, but her heart broke a little each time the subject surfaced, for she too wanted more than anything to bring a baby into their lives. But it just hadn't happened yet.

Men can be so blind sometimes. He never noticed, really never paid any attention to his mother's barbs and his wife's reaction until the week before Noreen's birthday. They had invited Leola to a farewell dinner, sending Ken off to hunt deer with his cronies in the great northern woods of Michigan. Ken walked into the kitchen and caught the poisoned dart his mother's lips had launched at his wife.

"Well, what exactly is the problem here that you haven't given me a grandbaby yet?"

Each time, Noreen promised herself that she had endured the last of it, but she hadn't. There were always more painful remarks, purposeful slights, and downright blatant attacks in store.

Ken saw the look, finally, on his wife's wounded face as she scampered to cover her pain and embarrassment. He knew his mother had a sharp tongue, he just hadn't noticed her villainous intention toward Noreen.

Ken was the master of quick and jolly retorts. He had averted many a fistfight in his shady youth by cracking a joke or changing the subject. He reverted to his witty character with a fitting retort to his mother's insensitive comment.

"Well, gosh, Ma, maybe we need to practice more. Come on honey, let's go tend to that."

Noreen slipped her shaking pale hand in his strong, tanned one and walked out of the kitchen, leaving the evening meal to fend for itself. In the privacy of their bedroom, they licked their wounds sufficiently until smiles surfaced and their laughter filled the space.

"How shockingly we behaved," Noreen breathed.

"Yeah, but Mom deserved it. From now on, every time she mentions it, just walk out. She does not deserve to be in your presence when she acts that way, and she certainly doesn't deserve an answer. It is none of her business. She'll figure that out, or she'll be alone. Her choice."

Another blazing example of her iniquitous behavior crept up every single time all three of them rode together in the cab of Kenny's beat-up old Dodge farm truck. Some way or another, Leola always finagled it so that she was sitting in the middle seat, next to her son, which left Noreen feeling ostracized. The conversation was skirted away from Noreen as Leola deftly kept Kenny chatting about one thing and another while Noreen fussed and fumed inwardly, never able to get a word in edgewise. Mostly, Noreen tried not to let it bother her; but one day, it just bubbled out of her as she was talking with Kenny.

"I'm sorry and I know it's petty, but it just puts my nose out of joint every time we go somewhere, and she situates herself right between us. Sometimes she goes out to the truck ten minutes early just to claim the middle seat next to you. It's not that I can't share or even that I have to be next to you every minute, it's just the principle of the thing that's perturbing me. It's like she's trying to break us up or compete for your attention. I keep trying to love her through it, but my approach isn't working."

Ken was startled by Noreen's observation, but the more he thought about it, the more he could see his mother through her eyes.

"Well, we can fix this. The next time we go somewhere, I want you to forget something and go back inside for it."

"Ken Dickson, what exactly do you have up your sleeve?"

"You'll see soon enough," he said as he winked at his perplexed wife.

And so the time came for the three of them to drive to the granary to pick up lime for the fields. Noreen had loaded up a little early, hoping to sidestep the confrontation she knew was brewing. Her presence in the middle did not deter Leola one little bit when she came strolling out to the truck. She climbed into the driver's seat, effectively nudging Noreen over to the passenger door. Leola was none the wiser that her cool maneuvering days were about to be pulled up short when Noreen feigned a forgotten purse and returned to the house.

Moments later, Kenny and Noreen emerged from the house together, walking arm in arm enraptured in their conversation. Kenny briskly walked his bride to the driver's side and helped her up into the cab, leaving his meddling mother no option but to grudgingly move over and allow the new woman in Ken's life to occupy her rightful place by his side in the coveted middle seat.

The hierarchy had been cleanly established without incident. Now that Kenny was alert to the mischievous ministrations underfoot, he placed his allegiance upon the head of his wife and came to her aid whenever the need arose. This was a small thing, a symbol really; but to Noreen, it bespoke love. Even though she was not a wilting flower, it felt affirming to have him step to her defense. She felt cherished. When Noreen needed Kenny, he was there, faithful, true and forever…in almost all things.

But there were exceptions, there are always exceptions. In every marriage, there is an adjustment period, a reorganization of priorities and patterns. One of the things Noreen loved about Kenny was that he was very social, very. He could talk to anybody about anything, anytime. He reminded her of her own father who flitted from table to table in their family restaurant, putting everyone at ease.

The memory of those long-ago days was darkened by the persistent memory of his drinking and how it had tainted their family. Funny how the traits that make a person so appealing in the beginning can turn to frustration and aggravation over time.

It had seemed that history was repeating itself, rearing its ugly persona with a pint of ale in hand. Ken had fallen into a habit, a bad habit as far as Noreen was concerned. He took to stopping into the village's only beer garden now and again at the end of a hard day to chat and commiserate with the other farmers in the area, to just be social. The rain was scarce, and the crops were threatened. He was worried; all the farmers were. If only Ken had realized that a bigger threat was lurking at home.

More and more often, Noreen found herself alone in the evenings. He would lose track of time, forget to call, and stroll in about bedtime, expecting that his supper would be warm and waiting for him.

"Maybe I'm just being overly sensitive because of my Dad's drinking," Noreen wondered for the umpteenth time.

Noreen loved him and placated him...for a while. She had been praying for wisdom and insight. She had asked the Holy Spirit to send the right words, but no matter what she said or did, Kenny continued in his ways.

Noreen was dismayed. On the one hand, she loved Kenny wildly; but on the other, she knew oh too well what havoc was caused from too much drinking. She had lived that life growing up as a witness to her father's overindulgence. She was too proud and too strong to ever tolerate that behavior in her own life. More importantly, she would never want her children to grow up with that example and that burden. Could this be the reason why God had not sent children to them yet? She had to change things, but what to do?

It was clear that they had fallen into a pothole in their married path. Kenny was being careless with his time and his attention. Noreen patiently and lovingly explained to him that she would not stick around to see where the drinking drove them; she already knew, too much really. She had been down that road and regardless of the potholes she would not live to repeat her mother's actions.

One star-speckled night as Noreen rocked alone on the front porch, the old scars that had been held together by optimism and excuse making broke open to reveal the very real and very tender memories from her childhood. She recalled keeping her mother, Anna, company while her dad drank and socialized with the menfolk at their restaurant. Her mother's eyes were too often swollen and haunted, a result of too many tears and too many prayers building up, unanswered, collecting in a heap.

There were days when the weight of being married to a drunkard had nearly crushed Anna's spirit, and it showed in the way she moved, slowly, methodically as if the very joy had been squeezed out of her life. Sometimes she couldn't trust herself to speak; her voice would surely belay the pain lurking in her soul. She fought to keep her own personal pain out of sight of the children, but they knew. They knew.

Like so many women of the times, Anna believed that an unfulfilled marriage was better than no marriage at all. Either way, Anna had wanted better for her daughters, much better. How many times she had uttered her veiled warning to Noreen and Sue Ellen, "Marry in haste, repent in leisure."

Noreen had been certain that she herself had married wisely, but if that were true, how did she then find herself in this untenable situation? Where were the answers to her prayers?

Hmm, maybe she had the answer inside her all along. "I need to do things differently than my mother did. Can too much forgiveness ever be wrong?" She felt the steely cold prickles of her Irish temper tiptoeing up her spine, and she turned to face the problem.

The rocking chair served as a catapult to action. "Enough!" she wailed as she sprang to her feet and ran into the house. "I will not subject myself or my future babies to this drinking. I won't have it. He will have to choose, me or the bottle."

With frenzied movements, Noreen began to pack an escape suitcase. She had made up her mind. She was leaving her beloved Kenny and the humble life they had carved out of nothing but love. It was hard, so hard, but she could see no other way around it. She couldn't force Ken to comply to her desires any more than he could force her to stay and endure it.

He was free. She was free. They made their own choices and the consequences that flowed so naturally, unhurried and unbidden. Her decision was born from logic and necessity, but plenty of anger and fear to go around. Her head would rule the day, come hell or high water.

And would it be hell? Her Catholic roots intimated as much. Could she be forgiven for breaking her marriage vows of good times and bad? How would she ever explain it to everybody back home? Her mother, of course, would welcome her in, would fully understand the gravity of the offense, the hopelessness of the addiction, and the lives that are affected willy-nilly when alcohol rules. Lives that didn't ask to be neglected. Lives struggling to survive and thrive against all odds. Lives adrift without purpose or purposeful love. Forgiveness was something that Noreen needed to wrestle with another day.

Surely Ken couldn't love her and continue with this behavior night after night. Satan had a hold of him and was tightening his grasp. Noreen tried to surround her husband and their life with prayer, to fight off this drinking habit. "He's taken leave of his senses altogether."

She had tried to talk to him, but so far, it had not made one iota of difference as far as she could tell. Where was the man who abandoned his dreams of becoming a dentist to be with her here? Where was he? At the tavern! That vision just did not fit with the man she knew, the man she loved. Perhaps God wanted her to handle this one, and so she would.

With the suitcase packed and stowed under the bed, Noreen stumbled into troubled sleep. She was awakened by Kenny's clumsy efforts in the kitchen as he tried to resurrect dinner, hours too late. Much too late. Much too late for what really mattered. Noreen buried her head under the blankets and offered one final plea to God.

"Bring him back to me, Lord. If it is best for us, good for us, please fix this! Free him from this desire to drink and turn his eyes and his heart toward you, toward me, toward our home and our future. Heal this threat that is tearing our marriage apart."

Noreen said a Rosary late into the bowels of darkness, praying ceaselessly for a miracle, for protection, for a way out of the path she had chosen only as a last resort: to leave her husband, her soulmate, her heart. She was bereft with grief yet resolute in her decision to leave Kenny the next night if he chose the bottle over her again. She would endure the excruciating pain of a broken heart tomorrow. The thought meandered around the room until it landed in the most preposterous heap, smack in the middle of her awareness.

But tonight was not tomorrow, so over and over she prayed. She said a powerful prayer to ask St. Michael to join her prayer barrage. "Please send up prayers, St. Michael, to protect us from Satan and any plan he might be hatching to destroy our marriage, our life.

"St. Michael the archangel, defend us in battle. Be our protection against the wickedness and snares of the devil. May God rebuke him we humbly pray. And do, thou, oh Prince of the heavenly host, by the divine power of God, cast into hell Satan and the other evil spirits who roam about the world, seeking the ruin of souls. Amen."

Sometime before the first rays of sunshine hit the top of the rickety old farmhouse, mere moments before the rooster rose to begin his task of alerting all of nature to begin a new day, a miracle was brewing. Noreen was not privy to this information, for if she had been, she would have leaped with joy from her marriage bed and fell to her knees to praise the God who listens to all prayers.

Instead, Noreen began her day much like any other, but with one exception. She knew the horrible truth—or she thought she did—that this would be her last day with Kenny, her last day in marriage. Her heart was dragging on the floor with each step that took her one moment farther away from her beloved. Each moment of that fateful day, Noreen bombarded heaven in prayer.

She spoke little to her husband, for truly it had all been said before. He spoke little to her, not out of indifference, but because the consequences of his actions the night before had clipped his wings and rendered him less ambitious, less spirited, less spirit-filled. His trapeze had somehow slipped from his grasp, and he was plummeting. His head raged, and his stomach revolted against the choices he had made the previous evening—truthfully, many evenings.

A vague gnawing tiptoed through his misty brain, "Is this really the life I want? Was last night really worth all this? Is this really why I gave up dentistry or being a titan of business or an airline pilot or any other career path? Am I living my passion? Is this the warm and loving life I promised to build with Noreen or has something or someone hijacked my efforts? How in the world has it come to this? Why do I keep doing this? It's not that I crave the drinking—honestly, that's the least important part of it. I'm in a bad habit, for sure. I need to think about this, when things quiet down and I feel up to it. For now, I have work to do, and that's gonna require every ounce of strength I can muster." As quickly as the thought flitted into his consciousness, it dissipated, leaving Kenny to scrutinize his actions and priorities another day, another time.

The day flew by too quickly; they all do. What with the cooking and cleaning and farming, there's no time to stare at the clock or watch a pot boil. But the pot was boiling, under the surface as clearly as the robin hopped across the freshly mowed grass that Ken, nursing a hangover, had attempted to mow that day.

The steam was rushing upward, screeching, sputtering, unnerving everyone in the vicinity. Whether it would boil over and squelch the flames beneath remained to be seen.

"Miracle. I need a miracle." Noreen believed in them, of course. She recalled the miracle that had freed Kenny from the horrible confines of war only to be captured by the bottle. For this, he was saved for this? It made no sense to her, but she promised to abide by the will of the Lord. He had his ways. Was he testing her faith? Kenny's faith? God would have to send a whopping big miracle to stop the actions that she had already put into motion. She hoped and prayed that something—anything—would happen to change her plight. If not, by this time tomorrow, she will have committed a sin of such magnitude that it would be difficult to face God, no matter how loving and forgiving he was. So she wrapped herself in prayer as a buffer for the calamity that awaited her.

She prayed off and on throughout the day, wrapping herself in a cloak of despair, the fibers roughly scraping her skin and irritating her conscience. Could this really be happening? She tried to think about other options, but they all involved Kenny recognizing the problem, which was dubious.

Grogginess and grief became wayward companions, plodding through the day with little hope or enthusiasm. In the middle of snapping green beans for dinner, Noreen slipped sullenly from her chair. When her knees hit the worn linoleum, she began praying anew. Her marriage was disintegrating, but her faith was not.

Kenny rushed in from the fields and jumped in for a quick shower. When he emerged into the living room, he glanced quickly at Noreen, curled up like a kitten in the corner of the davenport with the dappled sun flickering through the picture window. She stared at him for a long minute, recognizing the face, but with a different man inside. Who was this stranger sharing a house with her? Would today be the day she got her husband back, or would it mark the day she lost him forever?

Her last shred of optimism vaporized as despondency claimed her soul at the precise moment when the neighbor's 1937 cherry red Ford pickup truck pulled into the driveway. He tapped the horn, and Kenny emerged from the house by way of the wooden screen door dangling from its hinges, waiting, waiting, waiting for attention, just as Noreen was also waiting, waiting, waiting for attention. The waiting was over. She had her pride. She had her plan. With the banging of the door, she opened her thoughts to the inevitability of love squandered.

Noreen watched as Kenny blithely climbed in and crucified all her hopes, dreams and most importantly love. She took all three, placed them deep within her heart in a special room that she would never open again. She took the key to her heart and placed it in the lock but could not quite bring herself to turn it. There's always a chance, isn't there?

The finality of that motion filled her with anguish, and she just couldn't do it, not here, not now—perhaps when she reached the security of her mother's arms. Perhaps after the papers were signed and sealed, ending their marriage. Perhaps then she would turn the key and begin her life anew. But just now, she wallowed in her pain and felt the full impact of the sin she was about to commit. A sin that would change her life forever.

As Kenny rode the three miles to town, to spend the evening with his buddies instead of his wife, he didn't know, couldn't know, that his world would be irrevocably altered with or without God's intervention. For as he pulled out of the driveway, tears fell from his beloved's eyes and splashed on the window ledge of despair. With leaden feet, she retrieved the suitcase from beneath the bed and placed it in the bed of their truck.

She sat in the truck for several minutes before she reached for the ignition. This decision was final. There was no coming back from this brink; and her life, as far ahead as she could see it, held no joy, no brightness, no love. How could she stand that life? How could she stand this life? She had run out of options. The cornfields stood in silent testimony as she inched her way down the gravel road. She was driving out of her marriage into an unforgiving world.

Noreen turned her thoughts toward her mother who unknowingly awaited her arrival as she turned the truck down the deserted, dusty, country road. She glanced back at the farmhouse, her home, falling down from years of neglect long before they had become the happy new owners. She had made a loving life with Kenny, and now she was driving away from it. How can this be right? How can this be what God has planned for her, for him?

She smelled the cloud of fine powder coming toward her before she actually saw it. Another truck was approaching and was kicking up a bulbous mountain of dust. She held fast to the steering wheel as a red pickup truck passed her and then pulled into their driveway. Noreen's feet, with a mind all their own, slowly applied pressure first to the clutch and then to the brake as she sat in the truck transfixed, waiting for her brain to catch up.

"Wait, isn't that the neighbor man's truck? Should I keep going? I am leaving as a direct result of his actions, not just tonight but for so many nights past. In the past? The past? Past? Is he my past yet? I have to find out!"

She wheeled the car around, skidding dangerously close to the drainage ditch alongside the gravel road. She turned into the driveway just as Ken was exiting the truck, waving good-bye to his friend. He smiled broadly at Noreen as she pulled up beside him.

"Hey, where are you headed?"

"To my mother's," came the truthful reply.

"Well, can you wait 'til tomorrow to go visit? I have a heck of a story to tell you. You just won't believe what happened."

Noreen guardedly parked the truck and followed him into the house where she learned the particulars of the fire that had totally destroyed the beer garden that night. She listened as he talked of the many wasted nights he had spent there lately and how badly he had been feeling for most of the recent days. He talked about missing her and their time together as he held her hand and silently recommitted himself to her.

Ever so silently, Noreen retrieved the key that held fast all her hopes and dreams hidden away and still floundering in her heart. The love that had nearly been sealed forever, changing the path of her life beyond recognition. But God, in his wisdom and love, had spared her this consequence. He had surely saved Kenny from a wasted life of inebriation, but he had likewise saved her from enduring a life without her husband. She was saved from the sin, or her perceived version of it as sin, that, once released, could have decimated her life, her future, maybe even her relationship with God.

Tears of thankfulness and love filled Noreen as she recognized God's answer to her prayer. She never told Kenny about the suitcase in the truck; there was no point to it really. She carried the secret past his death, almost to her own. It was shared with her daughters as a cautionary example that God's time is not our time and that actions carry consequences. She also empowered her daughters to create the life they wanted and that settling for less than real, honest love was never God's plan.

Marriage is difficult, fulfilling, but difficult. She raised her children to withstand the onslaughts of Satan through the power of prayer. Ah, but this wisdom was imparted to the children much, much later, past the fifty-year marker, well into the future.

Today, Noreen lived in the joy of today where their life was waiting to be rebuilt. She tried to avoid thinking about the past, where trust and love, attention and communication had languished, without nurturing for far too long. The issue of excessive drinking did not enter their marriage for even one day after that fateful fire. Kenny would drink a beer here or there, but he refused the temptation of the tavern life even after it had been rebuilt and sprang back into active and false gaiety.

They Worried…about Babies…but Hid It

Relationships were fragile, that's the lesson they had learned just in time. So they paid more attention to each other and added in some frivolity. A weekly Aggravation game with the neighbors replaced one of his previous beer garden nights, another went to volunteering with various church committees. Square dancing and baseball games brought them in contact with other couples and helped satisfy Ken's socialization need. They also went for walks and became more involved in the Church, including an evening Rosary of prayers just before bedtime when darkness swaddled them into a peaceful respite.

Occasionally, they'd take a drive to the roller-skating rink and reminisce about the night they met and how their lives had entwined from that night onward. What they didn't know, what no young couple ever knows, is while the future unwinds, as surely as a ball of twine, the trajectory cannot be predicted. It's better that way, for had they known what lay ahead, it would spoil the surprise.

Their path had led them here, to land that had not been farmed for years. It was theirs, well, the bank had a little ownership too. Each year, they worked side by side to clear and prep more acreage for planting. The barns and outbuildings were rebuilt or burned to the ground in some cases. They parlayed their meager brood of chickens into a thriving side business and purchased a few milk cows. They were thrilled when the fertile ground brought forth a robust harvest after resting dormant for years. The tiny profit allowed the couple to purchase much-needed farm implements, livestock, and additional acreage. They were succeeding, but they just couldn't feel it yet.

And then there was the farmhouse, which was enormously distressing to Noreen. "The thing is worse than a tear-down, it's almost a fall-down!" She made Ken promise, swear on a stack of blessed Bibles, "Once our children arrive, we will fix up the house and focus our attention on making it a comfortable home. I do not want our children running out to the school bus from this unpainted, ramshackle house with gutters hanging, siding missing, boarded-up windows and broken-down everything."

When calmer thoughts prevailed, she'd tone it down saying, "I understand, really I do, and I agree that our resources and our efforts have to go into the farm, the barn, the crops and the animals, but when we have our family, things will have to change."

Ken knew that Noreen had every reason to complain, and he was relieved that she was willing to postpone her own priorities to give the farm a fighting chance to succeed. He would make the most of the time he had before the babies came, and he hoped that would be soon.

They were happy, mostly, but still there was an unspoken gnawing, an inkling that something wasn't quite right. It was always present on the periphery, but it was palpable nonetheless. It couldn't be ignored—babies! Where were their babies? Certainly, they should have come along by now. It's not that they were actively trying, but they weren't not trying either. They were too busy to turn the fleeting thought into full-fledged worry, but it nested in their hearts; and the weight of it began to grow, especially when Noreen neared thirty.

Ken reassured her often that he loved her no matter what, chubby or skinny, young or old, smiling or not, children or childless. To him, the most important thing was that they were sharing a life together, and in truthfulness, that was what mattered most to Noreen too. But couldn't she have both? She wanted so much to be both a wife and a mother, so she kept vigilant in her prayer petitions. To God and God alone she revealed the longing of her soul, though truthfully, Ken knew.

Hannah, Rachel, Sarah, Elizabeth, Rebekah—all women of the Bible, all barren until God heard the pleading prayers of their hearts and blessed them with children. Could she be next? Was there even a particle of hope left? She was sure of it. So she dared to ask for God's compassion, calling on these brave and faithful women as examples of miracles she was not worthy to embrace.

She grew so weary from fielding questions from townsfolk, who cared of course but hurt her nonetheless. Ken's old drinking buddies would ask straight out, "When are you two going to get started on a family?" The wives more subtly adding, "There's nothing like babies to bind a couple together."

Even her own dad, oozing with impish Irish charisma, joined innocently in on the nudging, "Are ya givin' any thought to fillin' the house with gollybeans? I ain't gettin' any younger, ya know, and neither are you, lass."

One day, a friend from church stopped over for an unexpected cup of caffeine. The two women chatted and laughed, exchanged recipes and words of encouragement. Noreen had hesitantly shared her childless dilemma several years prior and had learned to trust the confidential component of their friendship.

"Remember, Noreen, to call on the Lord. Hold him to his promises. Thank him before your prayer is even answered, then watch the miracle unfold. Of course, the babies will come," her friend told her "when God thinks the time is right. You have to trust and that's the hardest part."

"But what's wrong with right now?" she sniffed dejectedly. "What if it never happens?"

"Then you'll figure out exactly what God is calling you to do and you'll follow that path."

Noreen tried with all her might not to dwell on that ever-present possibility, because the tension was like an open wound, the reality too raw. She found herself growing sullen as she immersed herself in prayer, which usually brought her peace, but there was none to be found.

Noreen's Irish temper snipped uncharacteristically at Ken one day. His innocent offense was that he had attempted to jostle her out of yet another baby mood by trotting out his favorite poem, "It Couldn't Be Done." She had always been amused, if not tolerant, of his repetitions, much more tolerant (spoiler alert) than their future children would be! He thought the optimism inherent in the poem really spoke to tenacity, and she might be inspired, but he missed the mark and found that she was closer to the brink than he had realized.

She instantly threw back one of his other oft-used quips, "He who can remain calm when everyone around him is losing their heads simply does not understand the situation." She thought he *was* being too calm in the face of this predicament.

Despite the worries and the workload, they managed to carve out a bit of time for fun. Playing cards had always been an inexpensive way for the Dickson clan to pass the time during the dust bowl evenings, so it came easily for Ken. Not so much for Noreen whose evenings always revolved around the restaurant, but she good-naturedly agreed to give it a try.

One fortuitous day, while picking up supplies at the Waldron feed store, Ken ran into a man who was new to the community, a rare phenomenon as the village was hardly a destination location. Ed, with his wife, Lois, had decided to try their hand at country living for the sheer novelty of it. He liked to talk and laugh and play cards. They were city people really, and childless, so they didn't particularly fit in with the farming locals; most had nestled in the area for generations with a bevy of little ones. Right off the bat, they shared the status of transplant; even though by then, Ken had lived in Waldron for a half dozen years, it was not the same as local born. Ken invited the newcomers over for dinner and a game of cards but neglected to run it by Noreen.

She was less than thrilled. "Dinner is no problem, but this house, Ken!"

His response was simple, "They'll like us for us, or they won't, simple as that."

Noreen fussed about but finally gave into the inevitable; you just can't uninvite them after all. Her fears were unfounded. Ed and Lois were fun and accepting with no city-folk pretenses. They were just tickled to meet friends in the area.

Lois was barely five feet tall and couldn't have weighed even a hundred pounds. She arrived coiffed in a ruffled dress, balancing on the highest heels Noreen had ever seen. Nevertheless, she bounced around gingerly in the kitchen helping with last minute dinner preparations. Her bobbed and bleached hair barely touched her ears where dangling pierced earrings ricocheted off her cheeks and jaw-bone as she chatted. And she chatted a lot. Her shapely lips were painted brilliant red and she even wore eye make-up. Her voice was at the high end of the spectrum, almost a squeak, but her easy smile and ready laugh somehow endeared her to Noreen.

Noreen took a liking to Lois' spunk right away, and Kenny appreciated Ed's knowledge of politics and current events. The evening was fun and easy, filled with joking, conversation and of course, the cards. One night led to another, and before they knew it, they had become fast friends. When they were together, they just never stopped laughing.

However, what wasn't funny was how terrible the two women were at playing cards. To compound the inequity, they always played men against the women. Both men had grown up playing Euchre, a Midwestern card game, and honed their skill in the service, but the women had never really been exposed to it. Even just shuffling the cards was an embarrassing feat. To make matters worse, the men seemed to enjoy a bit of good-natured ribbing at the women's expense.

After several attempts, and several defeats, the women had had enough humble pie to last a lifetime. So they hatched a plan, as any self-respecting woman would. Each morning, they rushed through their household chores and then met for card tutoring. It was sort of like the blind leading the blind, but over time, it began to pay off.

They started winning a few hands here and there and surprising the menfolk.

But that was not the biggest surprise; the clever women held their shining glory as a secret until it was honed to perfection. On the chosen night, the women casually demonstrated their Las Vegas style of shuffling complete with long stringers of cards from one hand to the other, flipping and turning in midair until the men were dazzled speechless. They laughed until they cried, but the message was clear. Do not underestimate these women! Indeed, the women's Euchre playing grew to rival that of any man and often gave them a run for their money.

Actual money only entered into the card playing when the table boasted men. Ken and Ed were monthly participants at a penny/nickel poker game. However, it was the women who reaped the profits and held the best bets. Each time one of their husbands won, which was quite often, the celebration included dinner out for all four of them. The price of poker could get expensive.

As time went by, Noreen and Lois grew closer revealing many of their dreams over coffee. Their lives were busy, but without children, they had some wiggle room in some of their days. Eventually, the conversation turned to children, a sore subject to Noreen for sure.

Lois had a different attitude about it, one that perplexed Noreen. She had known for a very long time that she would not be able to bear children. Instead of pouting and stomping around about it, she had decided to embrace it and follow whatever dream presented itself. On a whim, she went to beauty school to become a hairdresser. She collected poodles, lots of them, and raised them like children. She scoured fashion magazines and dressed fancy. She traveled robustly, with and without her husband. Her life stood in sharp contrast to Noreen's, but they understood each other and bonded.

No woman likes to talk about her age, but when you are trying and trying to have a baby year after year, the ticking of the clock carries an added dubious warning. Birthdays noted the passing of the years as one age slid unnoticed into the next. Twenty-eight became twenty-nine, and then thirty shadowed the horizon.

In the darkness, she dozed with her head nestled on his shoulder like spoons in the silverware drawer. With her arm draped across his midsection, a tear slid down her cheek, unchecked. Her birthday was coming, and there was nothing she could do about that. His rhythmic breathing soothed her back to sleep but could not stay the thoughts that would live to plague her another day.

"Thirty, I can't believe I'm thirty," she bemused. Kenny who was still twenty-nine for six more months, seized the opportunity to tease her, yet again, but with a new twist. "I can hardly believe how old you are too. Why here you are, heading for forty, and I'm still in my twenties." The shock of that statement hit her square between the eyes. The ten-year birthdays were the hardest to handle, and she struggled with the thought of life speeding by. But his teasing made her laugh unexpectedly and pulled her out of her self-absorbed reverie. She thumped him on his fanny for which the reward was a deep and passionate kiss. Suddenly, her birthday didn't seem all that serious. They had other things to occupy their minds and their bodies.

Noreen's actual birthday was always marked by a solitary celebration, for it was the one important event that wasn't shared with Kenny. She wished for it, hoped for it, prayed for it; but so far, his presence had been sorely lacking on her big day each year. Noreen had the unfortunate bad luck to be born on November 13, which is always the beginning of deer-hunting season. For Kenny, that was a sacred cultural more from which nothing short of death could interrupt.

Hunting season was the epitome of male bonding in the rural Hillsdale County area where they lived. Each year, the men in Ken's life would travel up to their hunting cabin in northern Michigan, built to small, but sturdy specifications by his twin, Curtis, now an accomplished union carpenter. There they would begin the deer-hunting ritual. They would briefly escape the burdens of life, the chores, the worries, the women, the responsibilities and go sit in the woods, in the cold, without twitching a muscle.

If they were successful, they were rewarded with venison; if not, the consolation prize was an avid game of euchre or poker in the evening. Either way, it was challenging and fun. Hunting was one of the truly fond memories Ken carried from his youth, where his marksmanship was honed out of necessity. Rarely a year went by without the long-awaited addition of venison to their freezer.

Hunting was as much a part of Kenny's being as Catholicism was to Noreen. In every good relationship, there has to be a give and take, and Ken's absence from her birthday every year was a gift that Noreen graciously gave with love in her heart and understanding on her lips—no guilt, no pressure. She wished it was different, but understood that it couldn't be.

When she first suggested that he go hunting despite her big day, he threw her his best "Aw shucks I'm just a good ol' country boy" grin and seized her offer by encasing her within his strong, steady arms, lifting her off the ground, and swinging her in circles until she squealed with dizziness. She could feel the metal latches on his worn bib overalls, and she put the memory into her soul for safekeeping. This hunting thing was so, so important to him, and she knew it.

She could have made his life miserable, she knew that. She could have pouted or whined, but instead, she made the most of November 13 by getting together with her parents or Lois or just enjoying a quiet evening alone, sewing or reading. The rhythm of her birthdays rolled out slowly, uneventfully, thoughtfully. She used the time each year to examine the events that had transpired. She buried the memories laden with regrets and shined up the happy memories, put them on the shelf, and admired them. There they would remain year after year standing in tribute to a life well lived.

There were many other reasons to celebrate, lots of changes. All their siblings had married and started building lives. Noreen was especially excited when her younger sister, Sue Ellen, ended up marrying Pete Murphy, Kenny's friend from high school. The four newlyweds would reminisce about their double-dating years, the granary prices for corn, and the latest Detroit Tiger baseball score. They attended Our Lady of Mercy Catholic Church together in the nearby town of Fayette, Ohio. They were neighbors, friends, and best of all, family. The old sibling rivalry, jealousy, and bruised feelings had been laid to rest or at least appeared to be sleeping.

The day that Sue Ellen announced her first pregnancy was a surprise and an awakening to Ken and Noreen. They were happy, of course, but the older sister should be pregnant first, shouldn't she? It's just that they had been so certain that they would have been parents by now, but they weren't, and it hurt.

In the dark, quiet of the night, Noreen cried to Kenny. "I'm excited for my baby sister, really I am, but I want it to be me too. Why isn't it me?" Ken held her so fast against his rock-hard chest that she could feel the vibration of his heart beating and smell the musky scent of maleness. His strength fortified her.

Silently, Noreen wondered if she was harboring jealous feelings toward her sister. The hurt was so deep, yet she couldn't admit it to her sister. It felt like babies were all Sue Ellen wanted to talk about, and each word felt like a knife in Noreen's heart.

"Surely she's not doing that to me on purpose, is she?" She was never quite sure with Sue Ellen, and the old pains from the past made their presence known.

Ken, always the easygoing, good-natured one, soothed her with, "Oh, we will just have to try harder. Are you sure we're doing this right?" And she would act indignant then giggle at his antics. She felt herself relax beneath his touch and allowed herself to be distracted again and again.

Amid the hectic pace of establishing their farming business, the years unfolded faster and faster, yet unmarked by a baby of their own. Sue Ellen and Pete now had several, as did all their brothers and sisters. Kenny and Noreen could no longer ignore the burden in their hearts, and together they redoubled their prayer efforts. Sue Ellen's joy tumbled right over the top of Noreen's sensitivity as she rambled on about all the newfangled baby paraphernalia, playpens, perambulators, collapsible high chairs, and car seats to corral the kids.

Noreen raised her chin and pretended that it didn't matter. But it did matter, a lot! She wished she could be more nonchalant about it like her childless friend, Lois, but she just couldn't give up if there was even a chance that they could be parents.

"You're letting this baby thing get in the way of family, and that's just not right, Noreen," Kenny chided one evening. "Do you remember how many times your mom forgave your dad for all that drinking? She modeled that forgiveness for her children. Can't you find it in your heart to forgive the slights and oversights? After all, she's family, and that ought to mean something."

During her prayer and meditation time, she would examine her soul. Did Christianity define her life and her behavior? How did she sin and when were her actions displeasing to God? Actions were easier to identify, but it was more difficult to see the way that she offended God with her thoughts, her envies, her desires. She fleetingly thought of her sister, Sue Ellen, and the acrimony that had assaulted their relationship since their early restaurant days, was compounded now with the unresolved emotions around babies. It was hard to seek forgiveness when Noreen didn't really feel like she was wrong.

The indecipherable plan for sending children and calling them back home to heaven is held by God and only God, but bombarding heaven couldn't hurt. Ken and Noreen called upon St. Gerard, the patron saint of expectant mothers, to pray with them and to lend his voice to theirs. Together they prayed tirelessly, ceaselessly every day, all day long while they plowed the fields, fed the chickens, hoed the garden, baked and cooked and cleaned. Surely, God could not ignore the multitude of prayers pelting the pearly gates.

It was a Tuesday afternoon, Noreen was away from the farm snatching a much-needed reprieve with her mother, Anna, when the floodgates flew open. At first it was difficult to talk about, but soon, the emotions, fears, and tears exploded on her face. Her deepest feelings about children, or lack thereof, flowed unbidden from her lips, quivering with anxiety. Her mother was such a good listener, and Noreen was overwrought with her childless state.

"Oh, Mom, I love him so much, and I really am happy, except we both just want our own baby. We've tried everything we can think of, followed everyone's well-intentioned advice, even taking my temperature, lying with my feet on the headboard, but nothing ever works." While Noreen was sharing her deepest fears and anxieties, she was careful to shield her mother from the acrimony she felt toward Sue Ellen. Somehow, she knew that her mother would never be able to look unbiasedly toward her youngest child, always the baby.

So Noreen stayed on topic, the topic of wanting her own baby, badly. They talked and cried and prayed for hours together, when at long last, her mother stumbled on an idea. A church friend of Anna's had finally become a grandmother after her daughter worked with a fertility specialist in Toledo, Ohio. "I will go see her tomorrow and get his number for you."

Noreen virtually skipped all the way out to her truck and smiled all the way home with the prospect of a baby on the horizon. She was breathless as she shared the news with her husband. It's true that men can sometimes be too practical and at perfectly wrong times. She wanted him to share her excitement with wild abandon. Instead, he had concerns.

Ever the grounded one, Kenny asked all the sensible questions, much to her chagrin. "How can we afford this? How can we travel so far to see this doctor with any regularity and leave the farm unattended? Will we feel worse if this doesn't work? Is it safe? Will it hurt you? Are you sure? Is this really God's will?"

She cried, and she pleaded and finally convinced Ken that this course of action, regardless of the obstacles, would be worth it. And so they doctored, every month, back and forth, saving up and spending, over and over again for five long years.

The treatment included many medications, vials, thermometer, syringes, with a complex schedule of dosing. Noreen carefully cleaned out a dresser drawer in their bedroom where she could organize fertility supplies. She covered them all carefully with a dresser scarf for added privacy. The doctor had explained that the timing of the treatments was critical. Noreen drew up a daily chart to keep track of the innumerable doses that were to be taken or injected every two hours around the clock. She was so afraid of making a mistake in the night and setting back their progress. The pace was exhausting, but there was a chance, a slim one, but a chance.

The plan was tenuous, they knew that. So they chose to tell no one, not the parents, not the siblings, not their friends. They were filled with hope and faith, but not exactly exuberance. The thought of answering questions about something that was so private and unpredictable was off-putting. So they chose to keep it between the two of them.

That worked well for several years until one day, Noreen noticed that the carefully placed scarf had been moved. Even before she checked with Ken to make certain he wasn't the culprit, she knew her offender by name. Her meddling, snooping mother-in-law had been in her house. She knew her secret, their secret. Noreen was at first mortified, but it quickly turned to anger like steam escaping from a boiling kettle. Helpless to stop it, she raced across the field to confront Leola.

As she stormed up the path to Leola's front door, she did not notice the chrysanthemums blooming in the pot by the door or the gentle breeze rustling the wind chime. So single-minded were her thoughts that she barged straight into the house, letting the screen door bang angrily behind her. The startling sound brought Leola out of the kitchen, dishrag in hand.

Noreen's rage burst directly at her, "You had no right. That is my house, my life, my dresser, my business. From now on, you will not step foot in my house unless I invite you. Is that understood?"

Like any garden-variety bully, Leola was taken aback when accosted. It had never occurred to her that sweet, kind, loving Noreen had such a stout backbone. She offered a heartfelt apology followed by a sentence that was lost on Noreen, "So what exactly is going on here?"

"None of your business!" Noreen screamed without really analyzing the question. She turned on her heel and headed for the cornfield where she searched for Ken through eyes that were blurry from fury and tears. When he stopped the tractor and hopped off, she flew headlong into his muscled arms, glistening with sweat from the day's labor. She collapsed into tears of humiliation and heaving sobs.

"She knows, Ken. She knows about the fertility medications. She was snooping in our drawers."

Ken held her tenderly, rocking back and forth in the middle of the cornfield with the sun warming their backs and the corn tassels whooshing in the breeze. Her sobs were punctuated by the rhythmic hum of the insects until her tremors ceased.

The aftereffects were like a desert wasteland, desolate and barren. That's how she felt, as if her lifeless, dusty womb had failed her, failed them.

"Honey, this will never happen again. I'll see to that. I'll talk to Ma, and from now on, we'll lock our doors." While Noreen appreciated Ken rushing to her defense, there was nothing left to protect. The secret was out. Her privacy had been violated.

When emotions run high, it's so easy to jump to the wrong conclusions. Although Leola had certainly and grievously trespassed into their private business, she had absolutely no idea what she had unearthed. Panic surrounded her as she pondered the health of her son and his wife. With that much medication, there must be something terrifyingly wrong. What if she lost either of them? Their presence nearby had been a Godsend to her in her old age, and she couldn't bear another death.

When Ken arrived at his mother's door, hot and bothered by Noreen's revelation, he found Leola on her knees, deep in prayer. "Dear Heavenly Father, I place my life before you in exchange for one prayer granted. Please, God, whatever is going on in my son's house, through the healing power of your Son, the Holy Physician, let those medications be effective."

Ken interrupted, "Mother, what happened today was foul. How could you do this to us, violate our trust? We've done nothing but love you and care for you—hell, we even moved next to you so we could help you, and now you do this to us. You will never enter our home again unless you are invited, and you will not be invited unless you change your attitude about my wife. You will never speak to either of us about this again. You will not ask questions or make any comments whatsoever. The only thing you can do right now to begin to redeem yourself is to pray for us."

"I'm sorry, Kenny, I really am. I'm always praying for both of you and I'll never stop as long as I live. I know I have wronged you, and it will never happen again. I don't deserve your forgiveness. I'm so, so sorry!"

"Of course, we will forgive you, Ma, but that doesn't change the fact that things are going to change going forward. You have to make an effort here."

God has an uncanny gift for perfect timing. For no sooner had Noreen recovered from Leola's invasion than she received news that was much more invasive, albeit joyfully so.

Noreen was pregnant. Even though the blessing was short-lived, it was progress. She lost the baby and another and another and another, so many that she lost count and confidence. Each time, they shared the news with no one. The fact that they were seeing a specialist remained immensely private. She carried the intense loss in her heart and kept the depth of it even from Kenny, for fear he would terminate their relationship with the specialist, which would erase all hope. Noreen lived for hope.

One day, miraculously, Noreen was still pregnant beyond the first trimester, a first. Visions of toy cars racing around their living room or a doll being cradled in pudgy little hands filled her thoughts. Like the yeast rolls Ken loved so much, latent, quiet, but infused with life and love, bubbling up to change her world. In only six more months, the little one would be fully baked and ready to be slathered with sweet love. Noreen set the timer; she was ready.

When she bubbled out of her clothes, she knew she had to tell those who were closest to them. The future grandparents were over the moon and wept tears of joy and thankfulness. Sue Ellen's enthusiasm was boundless as she wrapped her loving arms around her big sister. "Our kids will have so much fun together!"

Lois shrieked with genuine delight. "Oh, we'll share this baby, and I can be the crazy old auntie who marvels at what a good job of mothering you are doing!" Lois' response was so pure and altruistic that it prickled at Noreen's conscience. Her response to Sue Ellen's baby news had not been so loving, so giving, so selfless. She herself had held back a bit of her enthusiasm because her own situation was unresolved, unfulfilled.

"Confession. I need to go to Confession and get this sin off my soul. I need to talk to the priest about how I can best repent. My jealous attitude was a sin, I know that."

The priest listened to Noreen and talked about forgiveness and making amends. "Go talk with your sister, Noreen. Tell her you are sorry and work to repair the damage in your relationship."

In her prayer life, she apologized to God. She purposefully remembered to ask her sister how the children were doing. She changed her attitude going forward. Her motto, "Don't look back, only forward," served her well in her attempt to procrastinate in following the priest's sage advice. She just couldn't admit her feelings or her past transgressions to Sue Ellen.

Plus, there was so much to do to get ready for the baby, and she had to pace herself, resting often. She wanted to do everything right so there could be no self-recriminations if things ended badly. In the evenings, she propped their little transistor radio on her belly so that their baby could hear the music. The smell of happiness consumed her. She was just sure that it made the baby more peaceful, happy, loved, which was just the environment she wanted for their baby.

"I don't want to do anything to get agitated. This time, this baby has to live. I'll talk to Sue Ellen later. Procrastination, as always, was a very effective avoidance technique, and the sin lingered in her heart.

The pregnancy news was shocking in the tiny community of Waldron as nearly everyone, except Kenny and Noreen, had given up hope. After all, a thirty-two-year-old first-time mother was a rarity in 1953. Michael Gerard Dickson was the first child to receive his one-way ticket into the Dickson clan, followed soon after by Pam, Debi, Alan, Dan, and finally, Molly. Even though Noreen was forty-five by the time that her childbearing years ended, she and Kenny thanked God for the joy each of their children brought to their lives.

When children are born, it is always best that the doting parents cannot see far into the future, for if they could, Kenny and Noreen would have surely gnashed their teeth with untethered foreboding and angst on the day that their fifth child, Dan, was born. It was good that they could not anticipate the pain that was to come, for in their ignorance, they simply welcomed their bliss.

While the new parents were aglow with love for their children, they had been counseled by older and wiser parents to keep the love light always burning in their marriage. Noreen's mom, Anna, was fond of saying, "The children will grow up, really they will, and then you'll have only each other. Don't mourn that day. It's the circle of life, the circle of love. It's so easy to get caught up with everything *baby*, but the danger is that you lose each other. This is the only life you get to live, so live it for you too. Carve time out for yourself and for each other, no matter how hard that is to do. Explore hobbies and friendships, together and separately. It's important. Trust me."

It's true that when babies arrive, changes arrive with them. It has to be that way, but Kenny and Noreen heeded the advice of their elders and did not let parenting consume them. They occasionally hired sitters for a quick unromantic meal at the little diner in the next town, where they found themselves mostly talking about the children. It was good advice, and it cemented their love affair and made them better parents in the long run. They were united as an impenetrable parental entity.

And then there's reality. The children brought untold delight, but also forced Kenny to be true to his word. The house was restored and remodeled before the school bus arrived to take Mike to kindergarten. Curtis had recently relocated to Waldron and his carpentry skills were sorely needed and much appreciated by Ken and even more so by Noreen. He handcrafted the kitchen cabinets out of solid oak planking, and they were one of Noreen's fondest memories of her brother-in-law. He taught her how to varnish the wood with smooth, even strokes. He was generous and loving with his talents.

She watched as the brothers, worked side by side. They were so different, fraternal rather than identical, but there was also an uncanny resemblance beneath the skin, a gentleness, a kindness. She watched as Ken knelt next to his brother, heads together, talking over the current obstacle. They had been through so much and now, here they were, both married with children, creating a childhood for them that they wished they had experienced themselves.

With each new Dickson addition, the siblings scooted over at the family dinner table to make room for one more mouth to feed. Noreen and Kenny became experts at tightening their belts. They bought more acreage to farm and rented what they couldn't afford to buy. The Dickson garden grew larger and larger to accommodate the burgeoning family. Ken's hunting skills helped to fill the freezer, hopefully enough to get them through the winter months.

It was August 30, 1960, in the midst of their sunshine, when there descended a cloud of darkness. Anna Irwin, beloved mother of Noreen, Eldin, and Sue Ellen, died unexpectedly at the age of sixty-four. Her passing was mourned by the entire community of Assumption who had enjoyed her company and her restaurant meals for oh so many years.

The loss settled hard on Noreen, and she wrestled with the newfound awareness that she would never again seek counsel from her mother. She's so young to be gone. The years had not been kind to her with so much of the workload dumped on her capable yet weary hands. The pallor of her skin and the premature jowls bespoke the troubles she had shouldered, mostly alone. She left behind a husband who drank too much, worked too little, but had filled her world with laughter and love.

Had the burdens of his drinking played a part in Anna's early and untimely death or had the Lord simply released her from her heavy yoke? It was not the life that Anna had envisioned for herself or her children, but it was the life that had been assigned to her. And now, she was free. With death, it is always the ones who remain who pay the heaviest price. They have to go on.

For Howard, the loss was all-consuming. Normally his gift of gab could rescue him from uncomfortable feelings, but not this time. He sat in the quiet of their parlor, all alone and swirled his scotch, hoping it would dilute his feelings of loss, of loneliness, of regret. For the first time, he claimed no solace at the bottom of the glass.

When the reality of his wife's death landed firmly in his heart, Howard was overcome with helplessness. His eyelids flickered in an ill-advised attempt to halt the flow of tears before they trickled down his sagging, flushed-from-drinking cheeks and right on past his protuberant rose-colored nose coming to rest in the stubble that had taken up permanent residence on his turned-out chin. Gone was the playful Irish grin that had been his calling card for his entire life. No flirty or witty words flew from his lips as the fierce reality of grief bit into his heart. He wanted desperately to join her, but that wish would not come to fruition without pain. Instead, he would subsequently suffer a debilitating stroke, which would render him practically immobile. There he would linger in penance for nearly ten years until the Lord brought solace to his soul by reuniting the pair in heaven, where forgiveness and love reign supreme.

"My children will never know the unselfish love of a truly doting grandmother," Noreen mused. "I will never laugh with her, cry with her, be with her." Death was frighteningly final.

As Noreen wept, Kenny held her and whispered his words of love. "You still have me. I'm not going anywhere. I can't, you know, because I promised you fifty years, and we're not there yet."

Noreen looked up through tear-laden lashes and trembled with the thought she could not put into words. Her eyes locked lovingly on his, and then a quiver swept through her.

Her heart prickled with the suspicion that the fear of loss was the price of love, real love. As she contemplated the reality of it, she realized that worrying about a loved one dying was a small price to pay compared to the joy she received in exchange. Quietly in the recesses of her mind she whispered, "I would gladly pay the price of worrying about losing him for the staggering happiness of sharing my life with him, whether a week, a day, an hour. I need to cherish the time that the Lord provides."

"What is it, honey?" he asked.

With a little more coaxing from Kenny, she tried, "Well, it's just that what if it was you? What if something happens to you? I never really thought about it much, but people can die, and then what? What would happen to you? To me? To our children? I know we promised each other fifty years, but we don't really decide that, do we? I'm afraid. I couldn't bear to be without you."

Kenny squeezed her tightly and uttered a promise that would scan nearly four decades before coming to fruition. "When it's my time, if it's possible, I will wait for you by the pearly gate. I will stay as near to you as I possibly can for the remainder of your life here, and I will help you get through it. You will never be alone. I will reach down from heaven if I possibly can, if God allows it. If we are separated for a time, we will one day reunite in heaven. I promise you."

Noreen, comforted by Kenny's proclamation, spoken in earnest with love in his heart, nuzzled his neck and fell asleep. She dreamed of her mother and only the happy memories from her youth. She pressed down all the dark drinking memories, the disillusionments with her sister, the fire. She awoke with renewed determination to provide a safe, happy childhood for her own children. In the coolness of the morning, she thanked God for releasing her mother from her burdens; and then almost in the same breath, she thanked him for sparing her children from the damage that alcohol can inflict.

Happiness is often an illusion, coming and going, moment by moment, never standing still long enough to fully engulf life. It comes in snippets, in stutters, and whispers away only to return when you least expect it.

But there is another side to happiness, as any parent will attest. It can be consumed by dishes, cleaning, laundry, and cooking. There are lessons to teach and characters to mold. Children don't raise themselves. Besides the necessities, they require guidance, cuddling, and clean pajamas. The Dickson home was finally full—full of children, full of love, and full of prayers. Kenny and Noreen modeled thankfulness to the Lord, and their children were raised in the faith. They heralded the happy moments with exuberant fanfare and quietly endured the gloomy ones.

The children grew up as they always do and became engrossed in their own day-to-day tasks, but the love that connected them to each other, their parents, and their Creator was forged from their earliest reckoning. A love that was eternal, undeniable, unyielding, and forever beautiful. A love that was destined to transcend the boundaries between life and death…for the parents and the children.

Maybe He Couldn't...Survive

In life, there are direct hits and sometimes near misses; and sometimes, both happen at the same time. The ramifications from a catastrophe can be immediate or postponed for some future date or both. So it was in the lives of the Dicksons one chilly fall day.

The year was 1961, and Noreen, age forty-one, was now pregnant with her fifth child, yet unnamed Dan. The harvest had been a bounding success and just in time as funds to support their family had grown dangerously thin and the seed loan at the bank was due. The family depended on the profit from the harvest to clear the boards with a little to spare to get them through the lean winter months already nipping at their heels.

To help offset the frigid non-farming months, they had added twelve milking cows to their barn. Of course, it added extra chores for Kenny, twice a day both feeding and milking them, but it was worth it to have plenty of fresh, unpasteurized milk for their own family and to sell to the big milk companies. With the purchase of stainless steel holding tanks and milking equipment, along with some dedicated effort, a steady profit infused the family budget year-round.

The bitter weather appeared early that fall, with unexpected low temperatures and howling winds. Ken hated winds—too many bad memories. Screeching winds had been a constant backdrop to his

144

South Dakota days as well as an unwelcome stalker during his Navy time at sea. A strong wind could upend even the most savvy Air Force pilot caught unaware. The winds of fate had also fanned the flames when Noreen's family lost their restaurant all those years ago. No siree, nothing good ever came about with wind as a companion.

On that fateful Wednesday morning, Ken was battling the wind head-on as he struggled to load the last of the cornstalks into the auger. The auger was a clever addition to their bevy of farm implements that made his life a whole lot easier. After the corn was picked and sent off to market, the next step was to cut off the cornstalks in the field, feed them by hand into the auger's sharp grinding teeth that were attached to a conveyor belt, which delivered the chopped corn stalks, called ensilage up to the top of the silo. This allotment would provide the much-needed cow feed for the long winter months ahead at little to no cost, aside from the heavy labor component. This particular batch of ensilage, however, would extract a heavy toll, almost the ultimate price.

Ken knew the dangers of the machine, which is why he never allowed any of his children to help with the time-consuming task. Out of necessity, the equipment was built with enormous strength and torque in order to operate the gigantic chains who's links were the size of his thumb in diameter. Many a farmer had lost a hand or an arm to the apparatus, for once it got tangled in the auger teeth, there was no hope for retrieval, and survival itself hung decisively on the farmer's immediate reaction time to forgo his arm in favor of his life.

Careful was Ken's middle name, but even with that mantle, accidents still happen. It was an unexpected gust of wind that morning that inadvertently blew the cuff of his brown denim Carhartt jacket into harm's way. Later, he would vaguely recall hearing the metal buttons flap with a ting-ting-tinging sound before it lodged in the teeth of the auger. Ken looked down in horror as the machine had its sight set on his hand next and then his arm and then…his actions in this second would determine how the damage played out.

Instinctively, Ken threw his leg up on the side of the machine to break the impact that he knew was on the way. He pulled his arm away from the auger blades, but the distance was closing in as the teeth made easy work of the jacket sleeve and was steadily pulling the hand closer. With all the strength he could muster, he pushed off with his left leg, and at the same time he pulled with all his might on his arm. Beneath the adrenaline, he could feel the arm being pulled from it socket as the auger teeth chattered away in anticipation of his flesh entering the machine. He felt his leg snap in several places as he continued to push and pull through the pain fighting for his life and limbs.

In that moment, he felt the horror he would leave behind with a widow, four children, plus one on the way. It couldn't happen, it couldn't. He would not let this machine inflict that kind of pain on the family he so dearly loved and had fought so hard to create. With one last force of will, he catapulted every cell in his body to resist the impact that was a fraction of an inch away; and in that pivotal moment, he heard a sound different from the sounds of his human body breaking apart. He heard the clanking of the auger gears breaking apart.

Metal pieces began crumbling one after the other into the auger, effectively jamming the mechanism so that nothing more could enter it, specifically Ken's hand. The engine slid to a halt as the expression of terror on his face was frozen in place. In the next second, he leapt into action, pulled the jacket off his body, and left it lodged in the auger.

She heard his scream, and fear gripped her heart. The first thing she saw was her beloved hobbling on one leg with his arm hanging down well past his knee, still attached, barely. There was blood oozing out of every pore in his body from the exertion it had just endured. When he collapsed in a heap on the front stoop, unconscious, she sprang into action.

Noreen had no idea of the events that had just taken place, but it was obvious he was in trouble, dire trouble. She checked that he was still breathing then ran inside, grabbed the phone off the wall, interrupted a party line call, yelling, "This is an emergency please hang up. Kenny had a farm accident!" The neighbors yielded the line and immediately started praying, each in their own homes, for whatever fate had fallen upon their good friend Kenny.

Noreen dialed 0 and asked the operator to connect her to the village ambulance, who responded immediately. She hurriedly returned to Kenny and held his limp hand while she awaited the ambulance. As they loaded his unconscious form onto the gurney and then into the vehicle, Noreen insisted on joining him. Her pregnant belly got in the way, and one of the EMT workers paused to give her a boost. He then corralled both Debi and Alan, both too young for school, and popped them up into the cab of the ambulance where the palpable fear was not as heady.

Prayers flowed from her pores as she enlisted the help of her Father in heaven. "Don't take him from me, please don't allow that. We haven't finished our fifty years. We have so much left to do. The children, Father, think of the children. How will I support them? How can I care for them all by myself? Please hear and answer me with a miracle. I call upon Blessed Mother and all the angels and saints to join me in prayer *now*, ceaselessly, until Ken is returned to me. Thank you for sparing his life against that machine and spare him now for me and this family. If ever a man was needed and loved, this is that man. Bring him back to us, my Lord, I beg you."

The men in the ambulance silently joined in with her prayers as did the emergency room staff and the surgeons scrubbing in preparation for an arduous attempt to save his limps and his life.

Sometimes, the grace of God is swift and compassionate, and so it was on this pivotal day. A miracle was bestowed on Kenny and Noreen with the events unfolding as God the Father willed it, in answer to the wailings of His daughter Noreen, desperate yet faithful.

While the surgery was underway, Noreen used the hospital pay phone to alert both families, the church office and the Waldron Caring Committee. Word spread quickly, and more prayers were added to the bombardment already in full swing, pleading with God for help and mercy.

The doctor's face was grim yet comforting as he spoke quietly to Noreen. "It was a formidable surgery. I suspect he will recover, but the usefulness of the arm and leg remains to be seen. It will depend upon how well the nerves and tendons regenerate and how well he follows the directions we give him. We must shield him from infections. We have done all that's humanly possible."

Noreen took the first deep breath that she had in hours. "Nothing is impossible with God," she solemnly whispered to the doctor with a quiver in her voice. Her thoughts whirled anxiously around in her head and landed with a 'klumpf' in her heart. This will require more than prayers, action, so much action. Who's going to tend to his chores, his wounds, his sagging spirit? Noreen cringed at the thought; a farmhouse full of children is hardly sanitary. It's a steep hill ahead, but at least we'll be together. She sent up a prayer of thanksgiving then launched into action.

A message was delivered to the school that the two older children, Mike and Pam, should go home on the bus with their cousins. Ken's twin brother, Curtis, and his wife, Ernie, would be taking care of the children until Noreen could get to them. Fear flew through Pam's veins when she received the message that her dad had been in a farming accident. She instantly worried that perhaps he might die. It is not a thought that had ever entered Pam's mind before this day, for her daddy was big and strong and invincible; but now, worry plagued her.

A kindly neighbor came to the hospital and delivered the two little ones, Debi and Alan, to their aunt and uncle's house as well. All four children huddled together, waiting for their mother to return for them with good news, "Please let it be good news." It was Mike and Pam who led the bedtime prayers, innocent and heartfelt. "Oh, dear Jesus, bring our daddy home, let him be okay."

Their fears were not allayed until the following day, when their weary and forlorn mother returned from the hospital with an update that he was awake from a lengthy and complex surgery. Over the next few weeks, they were allowed to visit him a few minutes each day to see for themselves that their prayers had been answered. After that, a hospital bed was installed in their living room where he would remain in traction, unmoving for months on end.

The burdens of the farm fell squarely on Noreen, although the neighbors pitched in as much as they could, considering they had their own families, farms, and animals occupying their energies as well. Noreen was fiercely independent and didn't want to be the recipient of their charity, to burden them any more than absolutely necessary. For better or worse, Noreen took on the task of feeding and milking the cows twice a day, along with all of the housework necessary to maintain four hungry children with Dan still waiting to make his initial appearance. Fortunately, and unfortunately, it was winter. Fortunately because the outside tasks were fewer; unfortunately because the twice-daily trek to the milking parlor was encumbered by ice and snow.

As soon as Mike and Pam were off on the morning school bus, Noreen donned winter gear and headed to the barn after first tying Debi and Alan to Ken's hospital bed for safekeeping. She'd place toys within reach, but they would be unable to toddle away from Kenny's constant gaze. He invented many ways to keep them entertained. He would sing with them, laugh with them, read to them, toss their toys to be retrieved, and pat them lovingly on their heads as they went about the business of being kids within the small radius of his bed.

The whole process was repeated each evening, but with one variation as the older siblings could help with the younger ones. Different day, same schedule because nothing changed; the cows had to be fed and milked and the children had to be supervised, somehow.

To Noreen's credit, things ran pretty smoothly. Years earlier, when she had told her beloved that she was a nose-to-the-grindstone kinda girl, she never thought she'd have to prove it quite this much. She rose to the challenge. Really, what options did she have? She owed God a debt for sparing Kenny's life. She was eternally thankful.

One night, about halfway through his recovery, an ice storm descended upon all of Southern Michigan. The distance that Noreen needed to cross from the house to the barn was a solid glare of ice. Her pregnancy was advanced to the awkward stage, when the center of balance is disrupted, about six months along. For better or for worse, that day, she chose Kenny's oversized barn boots because they had deeper traction grooves in the soles. The problem was, they were much too big for her and were as tall as her knees.

Inch by inch, she closed the distance to the barn until it became obvious that the tread had precious little effect on the ice. She had gone too far to turn around when she discovered the plight. Before she could ponder a different approach, both feet flew clearly out from beneath her, and she landed squarely on her baby, snuggled all warm and secure inside her.

Panic seized her as she worried about the health of the precious little one she was carrying and wanted so desperately. The muscles in her abdomen contracted painfully, then ceased. Worry gripped her so fiercely that it plummeted to the soles of her feet and she thought she would never be able to stand again. She lay on the ice for what seemed like an eternity, taking stock of her condition. It surprised her that all her parts seemed to be in serviceable condition, so she sat up and sent off a prayer of thanksgiving for surviving the fall, as well as one to get her out of this predicament.

Standing was out of the question as she couldn't even get her legs underneath her without sliding back to the ground. She closed the distance to the barn by sliding on her bottom in sled-like fashion, minus the sled. Once she reached the barn door, she hoisted herself up to a standing position and continued with the chores at hand. The return trip to the house was easier as it was downhill, and the sledding idea paid off. She had retrieved a plastic feed bag from the milk house and used it to cushion her tush on the journey. Truthfully, with the technique, the hardest part was sitting down and getting up at other end. The cows got fed and milked, and the unborn baby remained quietly peaceful, oblivious to the dangers lurking just outside his cuddly womb. Crisis averted, or so she prayed.

She downplayed the fall to Kenny. What purpose would it serve as there was nothing he could do to help her. Adding his worries to hers was pointless. However, in the quiet of her soul, she worried about the possibility that she might, in some way, have damaged the baby she was carrying so lovingly through this exceedingly difficult time. Only time would tell, for now, one foot in front of the other.

Miraculously, Ken made a full, albeit slow recovery, surrounded by constant prayers. He regained the use of both his arm and leg, and the puncture holes from broken bones healed without incident. Surprisingly, he didn't even walk with a limp; and the following winter, he was back, fully engaged with the farm, the cows, and his growing family. He knew that God had granted him a miracle, and he would not squander the gift.

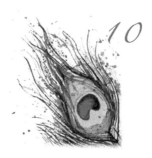

With a Chuckle...They Taught

"Your job is school. No matter what you want to be, no matter what you want to do, a good education will help you." That message was sent and delivered every day, in words, in actions. That family value was embedded in all of the six children from the moment they were conceived.

Noreen would talk to each of her children in utero, a rare practice in the 1950s. She prayed out loud because she knew that the sound of her voice was soothing and because she wanted to be a Godly role model from the second of conception. Her children would learn to pray by her example. She would also sing to them (even though she couldn't carry a tune to save her life). One of her favorite pastimes was to read to her unborn babies because she loved them, of course, and because it made them feel connected and secure. But most importantly, Noreen read to her babies because she knew that early stimulation would encourage brain activity and developmentally increase intelligence, which they valued.

Many mothers of the day saw no reason for their daughters to get a good education, but Noreen vehemently disagreed. She would tell Kenny and then the girls, "You have no way of knowing what your future holds. If you get a college degree or a special skill, you will always be able to take care of yourself and your children, so no matter what, you will be safe."

Ken's accident had been a jolt to Noreen's sense of security. With her thoughts tight, she stood by the bed, folding laundry and whispered quietly into the air, which smelled scrubbed and fresh, "My girls, don't be vulnerable and dependent. Make your own mark, your own accomplishments. Be brave, be strong, find yourselves and your passions, whatever those might be."

Noreen grew pensive as she reflected on her own mother, who was all those things, when it concerned her livelihood. She was a working woman when it was not an acceptable choice. Whether it was out of necessity or passion, she was definitely a role model for self-sufficiency, yet her life was not an easy one. Where would life take her children? An ache rose in her throat, and she huffed back a cry, yearning to discuss so many things with the woman who knew her best. How she missed her mom!

Ken nudged each of the children toward college for a different reason. "You spend a lot of your life at work, so you will be happier if you really like what you do. Plus, of course, money, money, money." The oft-spoken words were accompanied by the all-too-familiar hand gesture, rubbing his thumb against his first two fingers. He liked it best if he could get that gesture right in front of their faces, for impact, for theatrics. Yep, that was commonplace; yep, it always brought a grin from him and occasionally from the children.

When the first day of school arrived for the firstborn, a moment of pride and satisfaction fell down on Kenny and Noreen like a warm, snuggly blanket. They stood radiant, hand in hand, and watched Mike burst through the newly hung screen door, jump off the brand-new concrete porch attached to the freshly painted house, and skip out to the school bus, with confidence. Ken had been true to his word, and together, they embraced the memorable occasion and marveled at how fast time had sped by.

Almost on cue, Kenny trotted out his favorite poem, "It Couldn't Be Done." Noreen smiled demurely as she recognized that the poem was beginning to morph with the passing of the years. He couldn't quite remember all the verses, and some of the word choices became his own rather than the poet's. The rearrangement made him even more adorable, and she quietly smiled her approval.

Affirmation awaited Mike at the school doors because he already understood what would be expected of him there. He knew how to listen, follow directions and politely ask questions. He had been read to so early and so much that he already knew all the letters and sounds. Noreen had even taught him to pick out various words in the stories. He could count, add, and write his full name. He had been preparing for this moment all his short little life, and he reveled in his preparedness. School felt comfortable for him, and he puffed with pride at the accolades of the teachers. The first taste of success not only bred self-confidence, but built the foundation for learning that would launch his school career. He was good at school, hence he liked it.

As children are added to the nest, the challenges increase exponentially. Kenny and Noreen held fast to their values and raised each one to feel cherished as an only child. There were seemingly endless amounts of attention and conversation. Stories were read, words to songs were memorized. There was dancing in the kitchen during evening meal preparation and nonstop knock-knock jokes. Learning takes many forms.

Noreen had long ago forgiven Leola for invading her privacy, the embarrassment of being barren almost forgotten. For the sake of the family, Leola had repented and softened through her later years. Perhaps the erroneous fear of losing her son or his wife to some dreaded disease had helped nudge her priorities into perspective. Or maybe it was the addition of so many grandchildren or the look of contentment that spanned her sweet son's face. Whatever the cause, there was a truce between the two woman who dearly loved one man, Ken.

Pam, Debi, and Alan followed Mike's lead and mastered the Dickson prerequisites before entering kindergarten, but it was never so easy for the fifth child, Dan. Dan's progress was different, not alarming exactly, just unpredictable. Noreen felt ill-equipped.

She couldn't quite figure out what she was doing wrong, but he wasn't responding as the others had. She surprised herself by asking Leola for advice; after all, she was a teacher in her youth. The grandmother was honored to be consulted, and together, they mapped out an education plan that catered to Dan's specific needs. It was difficult and time consuming for sure, but he entered kindergarten every bit the Dickson as the other four children, at least for the time being.

As important as an education was to the Dicksons, learning about their faith was even more so. Attendance at Sunday Mass was nonnegotiable, as was the weekly religious education class where they studied the catechism, the Bible and the history of the Church until it became a part of who they were as people, as Christians.

The lessons emerged slowly, methodically so as not to overwhelm. Like a well-stocked medicine cabinet, the items were lined up to be called upon at just the right time, keeping in mind the proper dosage. Medication, religion and life, in general, were a series of informed and measured choices. Without careful and precise contemplation, nothing made sense.

Children absorb the priorities of the parents, but they also try to clamor for control. They push the boundaries, most of the time, just to see if the adults are serious.

When it came to the Catholic Church, Ken and Noreen were very serious. There would be no boundary pushing. Noreen modeled her prayer life openly for the children. "When I pray for something important, like your spelling test or that the boo-boo on your knee will heal without infection, I can say with full confidence, 'Lord, I am your faithful servant, you know me. You see my devotion to you. In both hard times and good times, I have never abandoned you, please don't abandon me now.'

"Praying doesn't mean I always get what I want, sometimes what I want is not good for me or is not what God wants for me, but prayers matter." The children listened with wide-eyed wonder at the power of their parents' faith.

"Lord, I have faithfully carried the torch that you lit over two thousand years ago and sent down through my ancestors to me,"

Noreen would pray. "I will hold fast to the gift of faith that you have given me. I will faithfully lead my children to you and will guide them in the Church that you started long ago with the help of Peter, the first Pope."

The second most important lesson the children learned, besides religious observance, was obedience. The Dickson children clearly understood the hierarchy and that although they felt like they were the center of their parents' universe, they still knew that they were not in charge. They lived in a world that was firm, fair, consistent, yet filled with plenty of fun and frolicking.

Most family shenanigans were instigated by Ken, who had a penchant for it. One blistery Christmas Eve, the children were gathered in the living room, playing games and reading, when pandemonium exploded on the roof.

Ken leapt from his chair, scuttling the children up the stairs as fast as their little legs could carry them, tumbling, pell-mell over one another. "Hurry, hurry, it's Santa coming early. If he sees you awake, he won't leave presents."

Diving into their beds toes first, the children pulled the covers up to their ears, listening incredulously to the reindeer hoofs and the jingling of sleigh bells. They could just envision Santa leaping from his sleigh as they heard the stamp, stamp, stamp of his boots clamoring toward the chimney. They pressed their eyes closed and scarcely let a breath escape their pursed lips. The two bedrooms, where the six children slept, were so quiet you could have heard a pine needle dropping onto the worn floorboards. Not a muscle twitched as they feigned sleep, hoping against hope that Santa would leave presents.

When the sounds ceased, Mike pronounced, "All clear." They bolted from their beds, raced downstairs, where they were met with heart-wrenching disappointment as the undercarriage of the tree was not adorned with presents for which they had so fervently hoped. Dejectedly, they fought back tears and lamentations, "We should have gone to bed earlier, faster, quieter."

Molly, the youngest, posed the singular question consuming all their thoughts, "Will Santa come back?" Before an answer could be constructed, Ken looked out through the window and shouted, "There's his sleigh, in the sky, quick, run outside and look."

Disappointments were buried as the children rushed to see the spectacle so clearly, articulated by their father. "Look at that front reindeer, it's Rudolph's nose. See the red. Oh, look at the sleigh glimmer in the moonlight. Listen, you can hear him calling to the team. Do you hear the sleigh bells? Well, look at that! Right over there, it's getting smaller. See above that far tree."

The six pajama-clad children stood, shivering in the frigid temperatures, while they peered intently, some seeing the mirage, others trying desperately to see it. However, the real exhibition remained hidden behind them, in the corner of the porch, overlooked in their exuberance to examine the moon lit pageantry of the sky. As they turned to scamper toward the warmth of their home, they finally saw it, a large cardboard box overflowing with presents.

Swirling snow forgotten, their hearts soared while their eyes digested the reality that Santa had, indeed, left them presents. En masse, they dove toward the box, "Oh, this must be yours. Oh, my doll! Mike got his erector set! Whose is this? Did you find your present?" Santa remembered every last one.

When common sense returned, Noreen corralled the children into the house where the Christmas celebration continued well into the night. The last little noggin drifted off to sleep about 9:30 p.m., only to be awakened by the communal alarm clock set to ensure that all six children would be awake and dressed to attend midnight Mass as family tradition dictated. Six little prayerful hands pressed together in thanksgiving for the presents and the fun they had been blessed with that night, and truly, how many children get to see Santa fly away from their rooftop?

The children weren't the only ones that Ken enjoyed teasing. When Noreen turned forty, Ken couldn't resist the all-familiar quip, "Why, you are heading toward fifty and I am just out of my twenties." Of course, he was actually thirty-nine and a half, but it certainly was more fun to play with the years and manipulate the words. What's life, really, if you can't laugh a little?

And then he became uncharacteristically serious and sentimental, "Birthdays come and birthdays go, but my love for you will always be there. I feel guilty that I don't ever spend your birthday with you. Does it upset you, even a little?"

"Oh, Kenny, I know how important hunting is to you, and you hardly find any time to spend with your friends. I love that you have included our sons in this male bonding excursion in the north woods, and I don't spend one second feeling sorry for myself. I choose this. I choose you!" Noreen tried to block a memory that crept up to the periphery of her thoughts, but it slipped in anyway. She allowed herself a second to recall the time when she had not wanted him to fraternize with his friends, a time when he could not be trusted to control his drinking, a time when their marriage hung in the balance. But that time had long passed, and she decisively tucked the thought away and wrapped it carefully in forgiveness.

Ken blinked through his emotions, "I love you more today than I ever dreamed possible. I am a blessed man, and I look forward to fulfilling every last year of my contract." They both smiled at the too-familiar reference to a day far off on the horizon, a date when they would be very old, God willing.

"Hey, did we remember to have God sign that contract?" Ken teased her.

Since there was no suitable reply, she took a deep breath and melted into Ken's broad, muscled chest which boasted the beginnings of a slight paunch from the natural aging process, helped along, perhaps, by a few too many yeast rolls, a place where she felt safe and loved. He held her tightly, kissed the top of her head, and they both fell asleep, exhausted from the responsibilities that filled their days and nights, content in the knowledge that they wouldn't have it any other way.

For all the shortcomings during Ken's childhood years, the one thing, besides a solid education, that he received from his parents was a love of music. Some of the fondest memories he held centered on music being played around the living room after the chores had been completed and during those long, boring days of dust bowl seclusion. Ken's goal was to recreate these memories for his own children, but he wasn't sure how to accomplish this. He had lost lateral arm movement during the farm accident, so he could no longer hold an instrument. How would he ever help his children to enjoy music if he couldn't teach them to play? It was a conundrum.

The thought percolated in the recesses of his mind until he ran into an older couple who lived a ways down the road. Silas and Minnie Robison were childless and retired. She'd been a teacher and he a farmer. Not only did he play a host of instruments like guitar, mandolin, fiddle, and banjo but built them from scratch in his work shed using old barn beams.

Ken ran his fingers across the smooth, glistening surface of the handmade fiddle and felt a catch in his throat as thoughts of his dad filled him with emotion. It had been so long since he'd held an instrument, so long since he'd thought of him, too long.

Ken wanted his own children to experience the toe-tapping, laughter-filled confidence that comes from mastering an instrument. One thing led to another, and soon, all the Dickson children were learning to play guitars, tutored masterfully by Si. They would practice at home daily, sometimes under duress, until the songs came easily, and the family bonding began in earnest.

A jam session occupied each Sunday night where Si helped hone their skills. It was only intended for family fun, until opportunity knocked.

In 1963, the village of Waldron decided to host the first annual Country Music Round-up, organized by a local couple, Arvin and Doris Holland, along with their daughter, Colleen. Not only did they have an overabundance of musical talent themselves, but a gift for promotion and a knack for attracting musicians from well beyond the village boundaries.

When Ken learned that the proceeds would benefit the local fire department, he quickly and easily volunteered his little family band. Some of the children were happy, some not so much; but either way, they rallied their support for the town they loved—well, really, they didn't have a choice.

This was one of the first and most elaborate lessons on community service and helping others that the children had experienced. There was stage fright naturally, but that too was a learning experience; and although it was challenging and time consuming, they persevered—a worthy lesson in and of itself. The shows, which ended in 1979, were a huge success drawing almost unmanageable crowds from miles around.

Some family activities, like church and the family band, were mandated, but many were left up to the individual nature and desires of the children. Some played sports, others joined clubs. They sewed, hunted, swam, and biked. They frolicked in the woods, the fields, and the barn. They'd swing for hours on the tire hung from the big oak tree out front or on the rope swing hanging from the hay mow in the barn. They caught crickets and sold them for a penny a piece to the neighbors who loved to fish. They held jobs and visited the elderly in nursing homes. Their interests were as wide and varied as the individuals they were becoming. Excellent grades and rapt attention to homework were nonnegotiable. They were expected to use their God-given intelligence according to their gifts.

Noreen spent so much time with the children that she knew their unique personalities. She knew that she needed to tailor her nurturing and her teaching to fit the child. She understood that Al had boundless energy and could only be coerced to attend to his studies for short periods. Pam and Debi loved to read so much that they often volunteered and were volunteered to read to Dan or Molly to get out of kitchen duty or garden duty or really any duty.

Mike excelled at math and drawing. Pam and Molly were drawn to science. Debi, nicknamed Debzi D. by Noreen, loved to write and read. Al was a whiz at all of it if he applied himself, and that, of course, was the challenge. Ken and Noreen had laughingly called him Alan Trouble Dickson, though his troubles were small, thanks to their diligent supervision or the grace of God or both—yes, most assuredly both! He made it through the terrible twos and the turbulent teens unscathed, or pretty much unscathed.

Dan had his own unique learning challenges, and secretly Noreen wondered if it was at all related to that dreadful fall on the ice. The day he was born had been both a relief and a miracle, well they were all miracles, but Dan's birth had been shrouded with concern, so the experience was magnified. Her mind wandered briefly to that day in the hospital when she held him tightly to her beating heart, nursed him for the first time and was hypnotized by this tiny, curling toes. She had breathed a prayer of thanksgiving for a perfect boy. Thinking about it wouldn't change a thing, so she tried not to let her mind wander there.

Once all six children were enrolled in Waldron Area Schools, that became the social mecca for the family. Noreen and Ken were busy going to various functions, helping with homework, volunteering in the classroom, practicing sports, and facilitating playdates with friends. So many details, so little time.

One nippy autumn day, Debi was summoned to her parent's bedroom. A surefire signal that something important and private needed to be discussed. She was suspiciously nervous, of course, because it often meant that there was an infraction to discuss away from ever-present sibling ears. What could it be? Her mind quickly reviewed a potential list of topics, maybe a forgotten chore or an incomplete assignment. Maybe there was bad news from the parent/teacher conference.

Her fingers turned pink and then white as Debi gripped her hands tightly in her lap, waiting for what seemed like an eternity. Her discomfort was put to rest by an unexpected compliment.

Noreen began, "Debzie D., your dad and I are so proud of your writing. When we met with your teacher, he told us that you could have a career as a writer if you wanted, so that's something for you to think about when you plan your future."

"No one can choose this for you," Ken concluded with just enough of a serious tone to empower Debi to become the author of her own life.

Surprise and relief were the first emotions that flooded Debi's face as the full impact of the message reached her soul. They had noticed her talents, her efforts, and they were proud of her. Her confidence soared as she accepted the compliment with humility and looked at her parents with newfound appreciation for the effort they put into every aspect of their parenting. They had taken time away from all of the other children, from the household tasks, amidst the nonstop hubbub to spend this private time just with her. Her heart swelled with love, as they all walked out of the bedroom smiling.

Many students from Waldron, including all the Dickson children, went on to higher education. Mike became a nuclear physicist, Pam a hospital CEO, Debi an elementary principal, Alan a youth probation officer, and Molly a physical therapist. If you are paying attention, you will notice that Dan's career is not listed, but that's a longer, sadder, and more complex explanation to be shared later.

Dickson
Picture
Supplement

The Irwin Restaurant, Before the Fire

Irwin's Restaurant

This is where Nowen grew up. We built this restaurant when I was 12. I always worked here, especially in the summer. (identification written on photo back by unknown individual)

The Irwin home/restaurant
Rebuilt After the Fire

Irwin Children—Eldin, Noreen & Sue Ellen

Noreen's Parents: Howard & Anna Irwin

Noreen Irwin

Kenneth Dickson

Twin Brothers: Curtis & Kenny Dickson & Rover

Noreen & Ken with His Parents
Jesse & Leola Dickson

"Put up your Dukes"
Ken Dickson

Ken & Noreen on his Motorcycle

Mr. & Mrs. Kenneth L. Dickson
August 23, 1944
Maid of Honor: Sue Ellen Irwin
Best Man: Curtis Dickson

Ken & Noreen with Mike & Baby Pam

Waldron Mothers' Club
Noreen - 2nd from Right front row
Sue Ellen - 4th from Right back row

Children Seated: Pam, Alan, Dan, Debi
Parents: Ken & Noreen
Standing: Mike

Dickson Farm (after addition)
Waldron, Michigan

Arvin Holland, Ken Dickson, Doris & Colleen
Holland, Pam & Mike Dickson, Si Robison

Dickson Family Band
Al, Mike, Pam, Debi & Ken Dickson

A permanent location at last!
Sue Ellen Murphy & Noreen Dickson helped
to establish the new building in 1990

Ken & Noreen
Fishing at the Cabin

Ken & Dan

Dan Dickson
Waldron High School
Graduation 1980

Seated - Mike, Noreen, Al
Back Row - Debi, Molly, Pam

Final Dickson Christmas
Seated - Al, Melanie, Mike, Noreen, Miranda, Pam, Daneel, Joe
Standing - Pam, Richard, Debi, Win, Barron, Maria, Tiffany,
Justin, Molly, Steve, Joseph, Troy, Jessica

Noreen Dickson
Last Christmas Before Her final
Farewell

Final Gift from Ken to Noreen: Engraved
Box of Memories

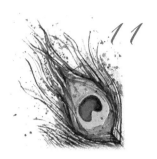

11

They Hid It...from the Children

Schooling offers one kind of learning, but life provides another. In the daily living that takes place in a family, much is taught and much is learned with and without words, intentions, or even awareness.

Ken's gravelly voice was raspy, manly, strong, yet witty and charming too. When the situation warranted it, he would pull out all the stops to get what he wanted, whether a better price for a car, the unchallenged hand of poker or to drive a point home to his children about something or other.

One of his most endearing and irritating traits was his love for and liberal use of sayings, limericks, poems, idioms—his trademark since youth. He could turn a phrase for nearly every situation. When his daughters were getting ready for a date to a nice restaurant or to attend a concert three hours away, he could always be counted on to quip, "Ah, a fool and his money are soon parted." After years of enduring this particular pearl of wisdom, Debi finally hit upon her own witticism, "Yes, but a fool and his money are fun to go out with!" That retort was the only comment that ever stopped him dead in his tracks as peals of good-natured laughter filled the warm cocoon of the tiny living room.

Yes, Kenny was a funny man, and his humor was endearing, most of the time. He used to say, "Laugh and the world laughs with you, cry and you cry alone." For the children, his homespun quips could be quite annoying after about the hundredth time. While they didn't actually dare to visibly do the eye roll, they certainly rolled them on the inside while making every attempt to escape his "words of wisdom" with the arrogance and superiority of nearly every teenager born to this culture. His purpose, of course, was to engage the family in conversation cloaked in laughter as a distraction for the half-hidden agenda of teaching them a tiny life lesson. Parents were sneaky that way.

In the early seventies, when Pam and Debi would come home after a long day at school and a still longer night waiting tables at a nearby restaurant, they would empty their tips out onto the floor to begin the tedious task of counting and rolling the change. Together, they compared the success of that particular evening to other monetary hauls.

Naturally, as can be expected from a teenager, there was also a plethora of complaints about rude customers, domineering bosses, sore feet, and hair that smelled like french fries. He always put the complaints into perspective by chanting, "Money, money, money," with the accompanying thumb rub against the end of his fingers. It was his subtle or not-so-subtle way of saying that choices have consequences—some good, some not so good. It was his attempt to train his offspring to focus their attention on the rewards and remain steadfast toward the goal. This was usually followed by the phrase, "You wanna eat, you gotta work." To the highly sensitive ears of teenagers, it sounded more like a lecture, which of course was never appreciated.

It goes without saying that this particular statement was ludicrous. It's not like the children were expected to chip in one penny for the pleasure of putting their shoes under the family dinner table. It was a systematic preparartion for a time in the not-too-distant future when they would be out in the cold, cruel world, fending for themselves. It definitely set the standard for a stellar work ethic, along with, "Sometimes you have to do without the things you want in life in order to afford the things you need—priorities."

When complaints arose about jobs or bosses and the conversation turned to finding another one, Ken could be counted on to promote the path of safety and security. He knew that jobs were scarce in the rural community. Having lived through the Depression and all that it entailed, he would generally contribute either, "A bird in the hand is worth two in the bush" or "The grass always looks greener on the other side of the fence." Sometimes for good measure, he'd throw in either, "Don't bite the hand that feeds you" or "You'll never miss the water 'til the well runs dry."

Ken Dickson was a sensible man. He used to say that when you are striving for something, you want to be careful not to destroy the good things you already have. Life is a balancing act, and it's hard to be happy in all areas at the same time. Easy does it.

Paradoxically, he had an interesting way of encouraging all his children to reach out beyond their comfort level. When unfamiliar situations arose that nudged forth feelings of insecurity, whether at work or socially, he entreated them to "put on your gloves slowly." In other words, "watch what's going on around you." How are others functioning, what's working, and what's not working? Through the years, those words have jumped to the forefront, unbidden at just the right moment to ease them through the uncomfortable newness stage. "Fake it 'til you make it" was another well-worn phrase that usually followed the first. He was nothing if not predictable, dependable, really.

Ken Dickson abhorred all things related to illicit drugs. His viewpoint was magnified by his prison guard career in his later years at Jackson State Penitentiary, but alas, that is revealing too much too soon. All in good time. Suffice to say that on a daily basis, he saw the dangers and the pitfalls of the drug-laced lifestyle in the world around him, especially lurking behind the prison walls, a fierce testament to lost lives.

Sometimes, Ken sermonized and warned and spouted, but children have only so much tolerance for listening to that sort of thing; so he resorted instead to cleverly phrased warnings and lectures masquerading as poetry or storytelling to work his way around that topic...ad nauseam.

The most powerful anti-drug poem he ever shared was written by a Jackson State Prison resident before he committed suicide through a drug overdose. He is said to have left this poem that was posthumously printed in the prison newspaper with the author listed as anonymous. The poem is reprinted here with permission from Jackson State Prison:

Miss Heroin

So now, little man, you've grown tired of grass,
LSD, acid, cocaine and hash
and someone pretending to be a true friend said,
"I'll introduce you to Miss Heroin."

Well, Honey before you start fooling with me,
just let me inform you of how it will be.
For I will seduce you and make you my slave.
I've sent many stronger than you to their grave.

You think you could never become a disgrace
and end up addicted to poppy seed waste.
So you start inhaling me one afternoon
and take me into your arms very soon.

And when I have entered deep down in your veins,
the craving will nearly drive you insane.
You'll need lots of money as you have been told.
For Honey, I'm much more expensive than gold.

You'll swindle your mother and just for a buck,
You'll turn into something vile and corrupt.
You'll lie and you'll steal for my narcotic charm
and only feel contentment when I'm in your arms.

The day that you realize the monster you've grown,
You'll solemnly promise to leave me alone.
If you think that you've got the mystical knack,
then Sweetie, just try getting me off your back.

The vomit, the cramps, your guts tied in a knot.
The jangling nerves screaming "just one more shot!"
The hot chills, the cold sweats, the withdrawal pains
can only be saved by my little white grains.

There's no other way and there's no need to look
For deep down inside you will know you are hooked.
You'll desperately run to the pusher and then
you'll welcome me back in your arms once again.

And when I return, just as I foretold.
I know that you'll give me your body and soul.
You'll give up your conscience, your morals, your heart
and you will be *mine* until *death* do us part.

Ken felt so strongly that after retirement, he volunteered to speak to schoolchildren about prison life and drug addiction in particular. He hoped that his words might have an impact and save some unsuspecting youngster from a path of incarceration, despair, and even death.

While Ken loathed drugs, there were other less vile habits that irritated him as well. Even though he totally detested gum chewing, no amount of shaming or chastisement could curtail it in his children. Possibly and probably because they had a powerful ally. For a daily treat and without express agreement from him, Noreen allowed the children one stick of Beemans gum, so it had to be carefully protected in order to persevere throughout the day. Her logic was simple: she really liked gum, the children really loved it, and she really loved them. Although he pretended not to notice, it was not without his own dollop of disapproval in the form of a poem he hoped would dissuade, but never did.

"The gum-chewing girl and the cud-chewing cow are somewhat alike yet different somehow. And what is the difference I can see it all now, it's the intelligent look…on the face of that cow."

"Ha-ha," and on they would chew!

Yep, the Dickson parents were thoughtful about how they wanted their children raised. They left nothing to chance; they parented, counseled, modeled, and prayed, mostly united.

Ken's coup de grâce was the same poem he often repeated to Noreen to lighten the mood when times were tough. Through the years, he had dropped all but the first verse, which held a slightly better chance of holding the attention of six wiggly children.

It Couldn't Be Done

Edgar Albert Guest

Somebody said that it couldn't be done
But he (sometimes *she*, depending on the audience)
with a chuckle replied that
"maybe it couldn't," but he would be one
Who wouldn't say so till he'd tried.
So he buckled right in with the trace of a grin
On his face. If he worried he hid it.
He started to sing as he tackled the thing
that couldn't be done, and he did it!

To the captive audience, he lovingly shared the poem to inspire his children to achieve, against all odds, no matter what. The secondary message was almost as clear: follow your dreams and stand strong in the wake of peer pressure. This stanza of the poem was heard so often that it was fully committed to memory by all six children.

While Ken was famous for being gregarious, Noreen had her own more subtle sayings that she sailed out at appropriate times for the educational benefit of her children. Besides the oft-touted, "Love

each other," as a reprimand for sibling disagreements and 'stop worrying' or 'no regrets' came cloaked as, "Look forward, never back."

Sometimes her words had an uncanny way of humbling even
the most self-absorbed child, "People don't think about you nearly
as often as you think they do. They're really too busy thinking about
themselves." While Noreen's children were the center of her universe,
she knew that the whole world did not feel the same, and it was an
injustice to their upbringing to believe otherwise.

Balance is difficult to achieve with a house full of children and
unending tasks. Long gone were the days of lolling in bed with her
husband and marveling at the sound of rain on the roof and listening
to the water wash the world away.

These days, Noreen was always the first to rise; and the first
task at hand was coffee, blessed coffee. She loved watching the sun
summon up the energy to burst up over the horizon, and she'd hold
her breath as the new day dawned, hoping that some of that energy
would rub off on her. That was her cue to get going on breakfast so
it would be hot and waiting for the masses. The rhythm of her mothering was comforting, albeit exhausting.

When the eldest daughter, Pam, started thinking about making
her way in the world, Noreen took her to the attic to go through some
of Grandma's belongings. As she mounted the steep narrow stairs and
crouched beneath the low-hanging rafters, she heard herself groaning
and creaking, which made her feel like a much older woman. Perhaps
it was the memories of her own "coming into womanhood" talks
years ago with her own mother. It's funny how time turns around and
you find yourself on the backside of the same circle, the circle of love.

"Here's a tablecloth we can set aside for you and some dishes
that Grandma loved. We can start your own collection of things to
get you started. It's time you had a hope chest."

Looking back, of course, hope chests are such an outdated concept, but to the thirteen-year-old Pam, it felt like a rite of passage.
Pam's hope chest was as big and empty as the life she still had ahead
of her. "How will I ever fill it?"

Noreen looked lovingly at her. "You have to make your own choices, and I don't expect them to be the same as mine. You will find your own way, your own path, and I will love you no matter what you choose."

So all summer long, mother and daughter embroidered napkins, crocheted pillowcases, knitted afghans and cross-stitched dresser scarves that unbeknownst to them would be deemed hopelessly old-fashioned to the new generation in which Pam would be a card-carrying professional woman. Her mother would stand in the shadows of that future, surrounding her with prayers and love as she would, in turn, for each of her children far, far into the future. But for now, life lessons were taught amidst the stitches.

Each year when summer arrived, at long last, the formal school lessons for all children slid ever so slightly aside to make room for the casual, informal lessons that claim the mind of the ever-observant child as they go about the business of growing up. Of course, there are chores to complete, meals to prepare, gardens to hoe, baseballs to throw, but some events frame childhood by the sheer power of the emotion.

Each summer, the family would skedaddle to their tiny, rustic hunting cabin, located near the Mackinac Bridge in Michigan, about a five hour car drive with six wiggly children. While it was not situated directly on the lake, it still offered many amenities: fishing, swimming, and building sand castles at the ol' swimming hole.

July was the perfect time to get away. The corn was too mature to cultivate, and with the harvest still months away, there was little to do but pray for equal measures of rain and sunshine, which were held solely in the good Lord's hands. So the cares and concerns of farm living were exchanged for the whisper of the wind blowing through the north woods, the smell of pine needles, and the splash of gentle waves on the docks, shorelines and swimming children. Their indoor toilet at home was exchanged for a two-seater outhouse and the faucets for an outdoor hand pump, complete with a bucket and lots of little hands to carry the water into the cabin. The novelty of that wore off pretty quickly. Cabin life was refreshing and difficult, what with no TV, no radio, no indoor plumbing, and no real privacy, about six hundred square feet for two adults and six children. Most of the time they were outdoors anyway and the children reveled in this change of pace. Actually, they all did!

Most evenings, right at dusk, the children could be found with their noses pressed to the inside of the car windows, eyes on alert, as their dad drove them around the country mile, looking for deer. The counts usually lingered around one hundred; when they topped that, it was cause for great celebration, which meant ice cream for sure. Noreen kept the official nightly record so they could compare their successes.

They watched for other critters too—turkeys, a glimpse of a bear, a porcupine, an eagle perched on a pine tree—but the all-time highlight was a magnificent peacock standing tall and proud right in the center of the country road, plumes on display.

Ken slowed the car and let it roll silently forward. In the hush of the cool evening with just enough breeze to ruffle the feathers, an aura of holiness enveloped the occupants as they watched in wonderment. Dan was the first to whisper, "It's like his feathers are covered with eyes." Ken spoke reverently, "It sure does, the eyes are called ocelli and are a reminder from God that he's watching out for you not just right now, but always. If you stay alert, you can find lots of messages from God in the world. Of course, there's the rainbow, remember that story? And God helps our corn grow tall and you too," he grinned as he tousled Molly's hair. Then he continued. "God filled the whole world with so many things to make us happy. God nodded his approval when each of you were born—sights, sounds and tastes, like ice cream," which brought a united whoop of delight from the populace and signaled a tasty end to the evening's excitement.

Then in predicable fashion, their father broke into song, "He's got the whole world in his hands… He's got chocolate ice cream in his hands… He's got the whole world in his hands."

He couldn't hold back his glee as he pointed out to the children, "See, even God likes chocolate ice cream best." The older children groaned, the younger ones giggled, but everyone welcomed the idea of ice cream, whatever the flavor.

One memorable date, July 23, 1968, at the end of their vacation, the Dickson family was traveling home to reclaim farm life and move toward harvest. The much-anticipated profit would finance the family expenses for the upcoming year, God willing. This money was also used to purchase the seeds and fertilizers for the following spring, when the entire farming process would begin anew.

For most of the early part of the trip, the children napped; but there were many stories read aloud and singing abounded. There were sibling spats, of course, but were always matched with the same motherly words, "Love God, love each other."

Once in a while, in those moments, Noreen would have a flashback to her own childhood, when her pent-up frustration with Sue Ellen would threaten to bubble over into unkind words. Before they were spoken in haste, Noreen would tamp them down deeper and deeper so as not to unduly embarrass her mother in front of the customers. Is that the best way to handle childhood feelings? Maybe not, but it was all that she knew and all that she had experienced. Don't speak it, don't acknowledge it, and it would just disappear, right? I'm sure Sue Ellen will get her comeuppance someday. Abruptly, she reminded herself to live in the present and look forward, never back.

As the family traveled farther south and familiar towns faded into the rearview mirror, an uneasiness filled the front seat of the car, and unspoken words passed between the adults with a series of ominous looks. In a fraction of a thought, it seemed like the general scenery had taken on an eerie transfiguration since they had traveled this way at the beginning of the month. The feeling was surreal, as if they were hallucinating.

It was apparent only to the parental eyes that severe storms had catapulted the area into dishevelment and destruction; entire houses were gone. Barns lay in a shamble, windmills flattened. They thought of the lives that had been ruined or worse.

His hand reached for hers as they silently prayed for those affected and that the horror they were witnessing would ease before they reached their little corner of the county. As they drew closer to home, their prayers seemed to be having little effect; for instead of lighter storm damage, it was becoming clear that their home and their crops had been directly in the path of the recent tornado.

Limbs and debris littered the gravel road as they turned the corner that led to their home, making their passage nearly impossible. Their tear-brimmed eyes rested with gratitude on the house still standing. The next glance told them that the crops had not been so lucky. The fields that should have boasted six-foot tall cornstalks laden with sun-ripened ears were, instead, flattened to the ground. Not a stalk was left standing. There was nothing to harvest, nothing.

The contrast between the adults in the front seat and the children in the rear was stark. Hardly a breath escaped from Kenny and Noreen as they realized the utter devastation of their livelihood and the inexorable calamity that had befallen them. The hullabaloo in the backseat was deafening as laughter, clapping and cheering filled the car with excitement at the prospect of re-uniting with their pet turtle, Emory. Their little eyes did not register the misfortune that had befallen their family. They saw only their home, where they were happy, safe, and loved. As it should be, for serious worry belonged to the adults.

But the lives of children are not always stress free. There are struggles and sadness that might seem trivial from an adult perspective but hold substantial worry in the hearts and minds of the young. It was not the flattened fields that caused distress to the young ones but the overturned turtle tub that allowed for their pet's release back into freedom. As the children ran to the area, they began to call out for their beloved turtle, "Emory! Emory!" They were hoping against hope that he would hear them (turtles can hear, right?) and return, maybe. Ken and Noreen joined the children, wrapped them in their arms as they all cried together, tears of loss, tears of sorrow, tears of mourning.

When at last the house was quiet, in the still of the evening, after all children had been consoled, fed, bathed, and tucked tightly into bed, Ken and Noreen held each other in silence, allowing the grief to nearly consume them. He wrapped her tightly in his arms, inhaled a deep shaky breath, and led a prayer of thanksgiving for lives protected and a home to house them.

The tender moment, so laden with worry, was lightened by Ken's raspy voice, whispering towards heaven, "Somebody said that it couldn't be done…" A smile escaped her tearstained lips in spite of her grief. She'd heard it a million times before, but he fairly glowed with self-satisfaction; and truly, what else could he say.

Tomorrow, they would clean up the rubble and begin anew. Tomorrow, they would make a plan. But tonight, tonight, they would just hold each other and take solace in the fact that they had each other. They had six beautiful children alive and safe. Things could be replaced, repaired, but lives were precious, and they understood that to the core of their being. As they lay there trying to count their blessings, they had no idea that one day in the not-too-distant future, one of their blessings would be taken from the security of their arms. Fortunately or unfortunately, the future holds the future; this night was claimed by the current disaster and the love they held for each other.

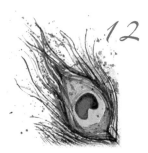

Somebody Said...Opportunity Knocks

He had wanted to be a farmer, but the tornado had effectively blocked that path, at least for now. He had to focus on the pragmatics. There were children to feed, bills to pay, and no harvest in the foreseeable future. They had lived off the profits from last year's harvest with the expectation that there would be another cache this fall. With the death of that dream, Ken needed to figure out a way to make money now.

There were pitifully few jobs available around their tiny hometown of Waldron, Michigan. Farmhands were usually neighbors or friends who volunteered. Thankfully, Ken got hired at a nearby factory in Pioneer, Ohio, where he endured the mundane pandemonium for the entire winter. The wages were low, but they could survive, just barely. When spring came, a decision had to be made. If they were to plant crops again, they would have to borrow seed money to do it. If the crops failed again, they could lose the farm because they would never be able to repay the loan.

A sharp prickling ran up Ken's back as he remembered his parents' plight. The dust bowl had extracted a huge price from them. Not just the farm and equipment, but self-esteem, pride, happiness really. "And that's the danger of debt," Ken told Noreen. "Do we dare risk everything?"

Fear crept in like ants to a picnic, unexpected, uninvited, unwelcome. Whoever said you could live on love alone never had to feed six children. The time for a decision was now.

They had both lived through the depression and knew that the dangers were real. Noreen remembered a neighbor whose farm and house were mortgage free, but he had taken out a small loan to build a chicken coup. Times turned hard; he couldn't repay the loan and lost the entire farm and house. That story had marked her as a child, and the retelling of it to her own children had leveled the same result. It was a heart-wrenching advisory to remain debt free and play it safe.

The wounds of Ken's childhood came rushing back with full force. He would not let his love of farming take his own children to the depths that he had endured for so many of his young years. There had to be another way to put food in their bellies, clothes on their backs, and heat in their home.

It broke his heart that pancakes and bean soup became the main fare more often than not. The venison-laden freezer had been depleted months ago, and deer-hunting season was months away. The children, innocently, grumbled as children often do without knowledge of how their words bit their daddy to his core. "Aw, not again!" they murmured.

"Why can't we buy school lunch? It's pizza day!"

"Can I go roller-skating with my friends?"

Something had to change. The factory job was just marking time. It didn't pay well enough to support six children, and it didn't allow him enough time to plant crops, even if they did decide to gamble and borrow the money. A short frustration later, they needed a new plan. So they prayed.

The answer came innocently lolling off the lips of Pete Murphy, Sue Ellen's husband, over a bottle of Orange Crush at the Waldron gas station where the men had met after the baseball game to quench their thirst. Pete had traded farming for a career as a prison guard at Jackson State Penitentiary and had heard a rumor that they might be hiring. It would be quite a drive to Jackson, about an hour, but the pay was stellar and the benefits unmatchable. If he could stand the work—and that was a mighty big *IF*.

For the next few days, the thought ricocheted around in his head. It was not how he envisioned his life, but he was way too far down life's path to go back to school and chase his dentistry dream. He had responsibilities, six minor ones and one major. He knew Noreen would support him with whatever he chose, but he just couldn't see a way to make college a reality at this stage of his life.

The prison! Could he hate it any more than being cooped up in the factory doing mindless tasks day after day for a pittance paycheck? Somehow his train had been jolted off the track and he was going nowhere fast.

The driving distance to the prison was a real consideration. They could relocate, of course, but he just couldn't raise his children in the big city of Jackson, Michigan, population 50,000 when they so loved living in Waldron, with a population of 532 including the cows! It boiled down to safety; a country lifestyle and peace of mind meant a lot.

He couldn't make this choice alone; he'd tried that once, and it had not gone well as he recalled with mirth. She definitely will have an opinion, and it affects her nearly as much. He had to talk with Noreen. Together, they looked at the opportunity from every angle and finally decided to apply for the job. They would stay on the farm and rent out some of the land and try to farm the rest when he wasn't working at the prison. That would keep the children in this safe, protected community where everyone knew everyone and watched out for each other, sometimes too much, but that was the trade-off.

They hired Kenny straight away. Here was a big, strapping, hardworking, clean-cut veteran with good values and a family to feed. It was a good bet that he would show up for work and follow protocol.

The benefits of working as a prison guard were many. The work was interesting and ever-changing. You had to always be alert, on your game. He knew that his words could make a difference in the lives of an inmate here or there. Otherwise, he resorted to his alter ego tough guy, groomed in his youth out of self-preservation as he was always the poorest and the newest kid at school. The difficulty of those days, long past, solidified his resolve to keep his children in the same school for all their years, forging fond friendships and building memories. He commuted to work at the prison to preserve their childhood. He would make every sacrifice for them and for Noreen, whatever was necessary, whatever was best for them.

For the first time, the Dickson children had health insurance. For the first time, Noreen had the security of knowing that their golden years, glinting on the horizon, would be financed with a regular pension check. She smiled thinking ahead to quieter times when child-rearing would end, leaving just the two of them.

Hearing her mother's words with her "yester-ear" flooded her heart with love, for her mother and her husband, "Marry a man who makes you laugh, and your life will never be boring." Well, her life certainly wasn't boring. She was filled with unexpected melancholy, wishing that her mother were alive to share her life, give advice, and marvel at the unexpected twists and turns that engulfed her days.

The years working at the prison were a financial boon to the family. They were able to pay off the farmland completely and build an addition on their tiny home: a recreation room where the children could spread out a bit, invite friends over to play pool or ping-pong, or have a slumber party. Ken built a baseball diamond on part of the acreage, which acted as a backup when the school field was occupied. Secretly, Ken had hoped that his children would love the sport as much as he did, but their interests led them elsewhere, and he acquiesced gracefully. He respected their individuality so long as they were well-behaved, drug free, and productive. Like most parents, he just wanted his children to be happy.

For the first time ever, Noreen and Ken could relax a bit. They weren't rich, by any means, but they had enough. The checks were dependable, the hours steady, the routine predictable. The month-long vacation to the cabin was reduced to two weeks, but the quickly growing children were easily fed, clothed, and shoed. They could even buy a cafeteria lunch once in a while and go roller-skating or to the movies with friends sometimes. Life was easier, and the family flourished.

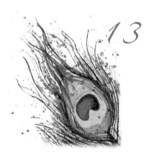

But She Would Be One...to Listen

There's a lot of commotion raising six children. Sometimes, it's hard to hear, really hard to hear. There are lunches to pack, homework to complete, bedrooms to clean, baths to be given, gardens to grow; and then there's the cooking and the laundry and the cleaning, not to mention refereeing sibling spats. Noreen wouldn't change her life for anything, but every day, just for a few moments, she would indulge herself by taking a coffee break with her sister, her closest confidant yet sometimes distant rival.

Most of the time, that coffee break was confined to a phone chat, but they lived close enough that occasionally, they ran over to each other's houses. Now that Noreen had children, she and Sue Ellen had lots more in common. Now that both husbands worked at the prison, they had more sister time; and mostly, that was good.

The two families, the Dicksons and the Murphys, not only shared some DNA; they shared the community, the school, and their church. Their faith was as strong as the ice that clung to their rooftops as the Michigan winter engulfed them. Attending Church every week was as much a part of their weekly routine as watching *Lawrence Welk* or *Hee Haw*. Neither would be missed without a serious reason.

They would share the latest news about the children and support each other through the daily routines, the worries. Together they joined the Waldron Mother's Club, the PTA, the Friends of the Library, and the Athletic Boosters. They helped raise money for the local fire department and the school. They were busier, happier than they ever imagined. Together, they could discuss anything—well, almost anything.

A volcano between Noreen and Sue Ellen was brewing, bubbling deep within, threatening to erupt. The smoke sometimes made them irritable, clouding the space and the peace between them. Neither spoke of the impending danger. Both Noreen and her sister hoped that the dreaded conversation would never reach the surface, but as they were soon to find out, some lava cannot be contained and is bound to see the light of day, one way or another.

Attempting to extinguish a volcano is exhausting, the sisters were discovering. So it felt as each morning dawned, Noreen found it increasingly more difficult to leap into the day enthusiastically. She was groggy, sluggish and muddlingly inefficient, even with a dose of full octane coffee. She thought she was coping, but—well, maybe not. Why just yesterday, Kenny had questioned her, "What's going on with you? You seem so distracted, like you're not really here with us."

In all the years that they had been married, she'd only kept one secret from him, the suitcase in the truck the night she almost left him because of his drinking. But this one—oh, this one was too elusive, too hard to pin down. She didn't know what to think about it, and she wanted time to just make it go away. She certainly did not want to talk about it to anyone—not Kenny, not Sue Ellen. No one! This situation felt like an uncomfortable sliver you get in the bottom of your foot from walking barefoot under a pine tree. It didn't seem important in the beginning, but over time, it could not be ignored. It needled you until eventually, you just had to act.

So Noreen languished in the denial stage for far too long to be good for her health. She tossed and turned every night, and when she finally fell into a fitful sleep, the dream would come. It was not scary exactly, just unreal. As nights turned to months, Noreen began to pay more attention. Could God be sending her a message?

The dream was always the same. She heard a voice, a man's voice, deep and resonant, calling her by name, calling her to action. At the end of the dream, she would jolt awake, shaking her head, and refusing to even consider the content so clearly illuminated in her dream. She was too busy, far too busy raising a family and supporting Kenny on the farm to take on another task. He would never approve; they were barely keeping up as it was. The outside activities that they participated in were all related directly to building a better environment for their children, their school, town, church.

But this dream threatened all that. It was not better for her family. In fact, it would force her to spend precious hours away from them. It would be physically and mentally challenging. How would she ever know where to even start with a task so overwhelming? This couldn't be what God wanted, could it?

In another home, not far away, God delivered the same dream to Sue Ellen, night after night, disturbing her sleep, wreaking havoc on her frazzled nervous system. Because she wasn't sleeping well at night, she would doze off in the middle of a sentence or when packing the children's lunches. Once, she even fell asleep behind the wheel of the tractor and drove it off into the freshly planted rows. Peter was not happy.

Sue Ellen found a quiet corner of the barn and just screamed her frustration to God, "Something has to give. I need to sleep. I'm falling behind in my chores, and Pete is getting irritated with me. I can't do this thing, I just can't. I don't have time. I have no experience. I'm really, really sure that this is just my imagination."

Both sisters were shouldering the burden of this dream in silence. They both were feeling like they were entirely alone and, truthfully, that they'd gone a bit batty. In the light of day with full reason intact, the dream seemed far away and forgettable, except for the vague needling at the back of the neck, a gentle reminder...of what? The dream of a crazy person? Imagination gone awry? "This is not enough to make me believe it, so I won't. I can't."

The dreams became stronger and more forceful until one gloomy, overcast Tuesday, Noreen invited herself over to Sue Ellen's kitchen for coffee. "I need to talk, to tell you something. I can't talk to anyone else. I need your help to put something to rest, finally and forever."

As Noreen poured out the gist of her reoccurring dream, it felt like the full force of the volcano was erupting right in the middle of the sunny Murphy kitchen. Sue Ellen sat in awed silence, her heart beating out of her chest, her hands clammy with perspiration.

When Noreen finally paused to take a breath, she crumpled into tears of relief and embarrassment. "I know you must think that I'm crazy."

"I do," said Sue Ellen. "And I'm crazy too, because I have been having the exact same dream. I'm exhausted, overwhelmed and confused from it. How is this even possible, and what in the world does it mean?"

Noreen was too stunned to speak as she listened to Sue Ellen tell her tale, an experience all too familiar because she too had lived it in her dreams. The magnitude of being plunked smack-dab in the middle of a miracle pushed all the words out of Noreen's mouth. She sat in silence, crying tears of joy or fear or maybe reverence. She slowly reached out her hand and clasped her sister's quivering one as tears slid from their eyes. No matter the differences they had experienced in their relationship in the past, this they shared as co-conspirators.

Minutes seemed like hours before Noreen finally broke the silence. "It seems that God has nudged the most unlikely candidates to do this staggering thing. We have no experience and nothing to offer. We don't even have an idea of where to begin."

"Why us?" Sue Ellen mused.

Noreen took a sip of her neglected coffee too cool to be enjoyed and winced. "Maybe, He chose us because he knew we would say, 'yes.' He knows our hearts, and He knows that we are faithful. Maybe we should just trust Him."

The two sisters hugged, cried, and looked at each other with a newfound insight. This concurrent dream to help the poor could not be ignored. It was much too much of a coincidence to be their imaginations run amok. They didn't know what they were going to do, but they did know that action would follow. How? When? Where? They couldn't say; the only clear answer was who and what.

They held each other and prayed. They vowed to do the work placed before them by the Lord. That night, both women slept peacefully in their beds. The dream came, but they were not awakened. They rose in the morning fully rested with a sense that action steps were being outlined. They knew, with all certainty that the decision to comply was the hardest part.

They had agreed to help clothe the poor, but how does that happen? They knew that there was a local headquarters for St. Vincent de Paul in Toledo, an hour away, but there was nothing in the Waldron area; it was too sparsely populated and so very impoverished, from the world's perspective. Hmmm, perhaps God knew what he was doing. The thought brought a smile to Noreen's lips. She remembered her mom's insightful words, "There are no accidents."

The sisters knew that the overarching goal of St. Vincent de Paul to relieve poverty, suffering, and loneliness matched the tenor of their dreams, so they began their research with a phone call. They learned that the St. Vincent de Paul Society was founded in 1833 in France, but wasn't established in the United States until a decade later. The conversation was encouraging as over 4,300 such facilities had already been established, so they would have knowledgeable assistance. The priest on the other end of the phone line explained that the current facilities assisted an estimated twelve million Americans who were struggling to feed and clothe their families every year.

"If you pursue this mission, we will be here to help you every step of the way. You will not be alone. We have procedures in place, and we can help you with the necessary paperwork. We can even get you started with food, clothing, and household items until the local community donations take over."

As outlandish as it was to accept the challenge, the next hurdle before them would be far more difficult, sharing the news with their husbands. Neither Kenny nor Pete were going to be in favor of the endeavor, but Irwin women, inspired by God, were basically unstoppable. They couldn't tell God no, so there really was no other option but to put their foot down and insist.

Noreen was not used to being at odds with Kenny, and it was going to be disconcerting. They usually agreed on most everything, so this was uncharted territory. She prayed for a week for the Holy Spirit to prepare Ken's heart. Then she prayed another week for just the right moment to present itself. It began to feel that maybe she was procrastinating, because—well, she was! Finally, she prayed for courage and for the Holy Spirit to speak through her and help her words find fertile soil in the garden of Ken's heart. It was hard to find the perfect time for such a volatile discussion. First, she needed a time when there were no children around; and secondly, she needed a time when he was home from the prison but not working on the farm. A rainy day would be perfect.

Her mind flitted back to the glorious farming days of their early wedded days when the rain served as an excuse to loll around in bed together and accomplish nothing of importance. Her nostalgia for the lazy days spent playing cards and laughing together, without all the hubbub of child-rearing, seemed so long ago. Her mother's words sprang live in her head, "Always be careful what you pray for, it may just happen." How they had prayed for these children!

Noreen tried not to worry, but practically speaking, she knew that the children's lives were bound to change when she took on this mission. There would be less time for baking, less time for talking, less time at home together. She was sure she could make it work, with a little adjustment here, a corner cut there. Really, she had no choice. God had spoken, really spoken to her. "How is that even possible?" she pondered over and over in her heart.

In the end, she simply trusted in the Lord and initiated the discussion to a much-startled and less-than-enamored husband. As with most things, beginning is the most difficult step. Ken listened patiently, but the expression on his face was not favorable. With tears streaming down her face, Noreen's earnestness could not be denied, and who was he anyway to stand in the way of God's work?

"You and I have always valued education," Noreen continued. "We teach our children to step forward in the face of fear and uncertainty. This is my learning opportunity. I am being called to help the poor, underprivileged members of our community. I don't know exactly how to do that. This is all new and a bit scary too. I never expected it, never even wanted it, but I'm being called to do this. Do you really think we should just tell God, 'No thanks'?"

Ken was dumbfounded. The dual dream, of course, was compelling. He wondered out loud, "Do you really believe that it's possible for a message to come directly from heaven?" Noreen hugged him and whispered simply, "I believe."

Their discussion continued, and Noreen emphasized the many blessings God had sent their way. "We prayed, and you were spared from a probable death in the Navy overseas. We prayed and were somehow able to find and afford this farm. We prayed for parenthood, and we now have six little miracles living with us, perfect treasures from God. He granted us a miracle when you survived the farm accident. God helped us to get back on our feet after the tornado, which could have been our undoing. He has always helped us find a way through the challenges that come our way. How can we deny Him this when He so graciously heard our most earnest pleas? He has stood by us always, and now, He is asking us for faithful service."

Sue Ellen was experiencing a similar response when she approached Pete about the dream and the resulting plan. Both sisters emphasized that the eldest of their children had graduated and left the nest, leaving the mothers with a bit more time. The husbands silently frowned, they had other plans for that 'bit more time' and it did not include their wives working away from home for free. But, in the end, the men were helpless to resist, and the quest to follow God's will began in earnest.

So the sisters followed what little guidance they had received nearly two months prior when the dreams had abruptly ended and reality took a firm hold. First, they petitioned the Toledo Diocese to allow them to open a St. Vincent de Paul satellite in Fayette, Ohio, where their parish church was located. They would give away free clothes, shoes, and household items to the poor living in the community and nearby areas. *Free*, that was the edict.

The priests tried to convince Noreen and Sue Ellen to sell the donated charity items for a small fee like most of the other St. Vincent de Paul stores. Both sisters gasped in unison, "Oh my goodness gracious, NO!" Later, when they laughed about the priest's shocked expression, they realized just how clear and authentic their dreams had been. They had both been shown in their dream that no fees would be charged in this new facility. Period. God had spoken!

Once the paperwork was completed and the diocese gave approval, the difficult task of finding a location ensued. With very little funding and no way to generate resources from the sale of the donated items, which they hoped would roll in, they started brainstorming ideas. They spread the word around town that they were searching and then trusted the Lord to lead them to an affordable location.

They filled their hearts with prayers and waited. The answer that came was far from what they expected. "Sometimes, God tests and strengthens our faith through hardship," chirped Noreen. But little did they know just how hard it would be as every rose is likewise accompanied by thorns.

The rosy news was they had a place to distribute the clothing; the thorny part was that the location was outdoors in the wooden stanchion behind the lumberyard. The owner told them they could set up every Saturday, because they were closed, but would have to take everything away at the end of the day. The sisters were not rebuffed and sent up prayers of thanks that their mission would begin.

In anticipation of opening day, 1977, the Diocese of Toledo delivered a small truckload of clothing to the Murphy farm, much like a mission-starter kit. Pete helped his wife load the bags into their pickup truck the night before.

At five o'clock in the morning, two alarm clocks heralded the dawn of a new day in both the Murphy and the Dickson homes. The sisters jumped from their warm and cozy beds to greet opening day, only to discover that Mother Nature had dropped an unexpected gift: snow…everywhere…and adding to the hardship was the near-zero temperature.

Michigan weather is always unpredictable, but who could have imagined that this oh so important day would be oh so frigid. It would be so much more difficult. Was Satan behind this? Was he trying to dishearten them? Stand aside, oh, evil one.

Without any outward complaint, the women bundled up in double coats, scarves, hats, and mittens and set out into the darkness to prepare for the onslaught of patrons. They knew that the job was daunting, but they had underestimated the physical exertion required to heft the truckload of bags up onto the wooden pallets, already covered in snow. The wind fought their every movement as they folded the garments, juxtaposing them on sheets spread across the lumber. The wind nipped at their cheeks turning them a brilliant crimson, but still they toiled on.

Word had spread slowly through the community, so the stream of patrons was scant, but they dribbled in bit by steady bit. By the end of the day, the women were frozen to the core and bone weary with twenty or so bags of clothes left to pack up before they could return home.

As they headed for home, it felt like an eternity before the heater kicked in and started to warm the cab of the cherry-red truck. They spoke little for their chattering teeth made the effort nearly impossible. The roar of the truck engine down the snow-covered country roads meant that relief would soon be theirs. The shivering subsided first and, finally, blessedly, their numb feet began to tingle with warmth. By the time they reached home, Noreen and Sue Ellen were chatting comfortably with the hardships of the day far behind them.

The first few weeks were slow going, but word spread mouth to mouth; and by the end of the month, they had distributed everything they had in their possession. "Well, if we have nothing left to pass out, I guess we don't have to open next week," spoke Sue Ellen with a wry smile. Noreen just shook her head. "Well, we have to at least show up to turn away the patrons."

God's message rang clear the following week, when the sisters arrived to a mound of donations, jackets, sweaters, hats, boots, and kitchen supplies. Donations from around the community had trickled in all week as the various churches had announced the St. Vincent de Paul initiative from the pulpits.

Kindhearted, loving people dropped off bags and boxes at the lumberyard where management turned a blind eye to the growing pile out back and graciously accepted them.

There was even a baby bed and a high chair. One very pregnant customer had come checking for just those items for three weeks in a row. "Oh, I hope she comes today," mused Sue Ellen.

Noreen didn't answer; her heart was caught in her throat, and she could barely breathe. In a wrinkled, stained, and badly worn flowered pillowcase, she had just uncovered a treasure that rendered her speechless. High above her head with both hands, she held up an antique painting of Christ, surrounded by an intricately carved frame. When her sister turned, she caught sight of the painting and likewise stopped breathing, mesmerized by the artist's ability to capture in the oil paint, love, compassion, and holiness. The eyes of Christ smiled across their humble accommodations, which was much like the meager manger several thousand years before.

When their wits finally returned, they avidly discussed the fate of the treasure. "We could sell it and purchase a few newer items like socks, underwear, maybe food," offered the ever-practical Noreen. "This painting cannot be relegated to only one home. What if we hang it each week to mark this location for His name?" suggested Sue Ellen.

Noreen pondered her sister's words until she felt the peace that comes from genuine agreement claim her. "Yes! Perhaps everyone who sees this masterpiece will be moved by the Spirit to do whatever it is they are being called to do. Every day, our work will be blessed."

Sue Ellen couldn't have said it better and the two sisters found a moment of perfect harmony. From that day forward, the Christ painting was hung on the stanchion post before anything else was unloaded.

That first winter was the hardest, and they would have loved to throw in the towel. But it really felt like God was testing them to see just how deep their faith ran, and they did not want to be caught wanting in that department. They were stout, and they would endure whatever the Lord sent their way.

By the time Christmas rolled around, Noreen was beyond overwhelmed. In a good year, she didn't have much appreciation for the fanfare of secular Christmas traditions, because she felt they detracted from the importance and holiness of the Savior's birth and because she already had enough on her overfilled plate.

Kenny, however, had always been crazy about everything Christmas. One Saturday, he showed up accompanied by all the children plus boxes of decorations. He jumped out, so proud of himself, and they proceeded to decorate the lumberyard, draping garland, lights and tinsel.

The sisters looked on as the Spirit of Christmas frolicked all around. Noreen wanted to explain to Ken the impracticality of it all, that it added another nice but unnecessary task to her long list. On a normal day, even with no complications, she barely had time to get the donations set up before the customers started arriving. Truly, what sense did decorations make in an outdoor lumberyard? Plus, at the end of a long, cold day, the last thing she felt like doing was taking down decorations only to be put up again the following week.

"I just wanted you to be surrounded by the joy of the season while you worked," he explained with love oozing out of his doting heart. It was hard to fault the poor man's motives.

For a second, she wondered if it was bleeding; she was biting her tongue with such consternation. She recognized the thoughtfulness of his actions but cringed at the frivolity of it. "Four weeks," she thought to herself. "I can do this for the four Saturdays in December, really only three since technically, he put them up today. More work, ugh!" How would she keep up? Didn't he know this was the busiest month with so many folks looking for warm clothing, Christmas gift-giving items, not to mention a huge run on toys and stuffed animals. For him, she could keep quiet. It brought him joy, and that brought her joy.

By spring, thankfully, God must have taken pity on them because He sent a prominent and well-respected businessman, who wished to remain anonymous, to their rescue. He owned a fixer-upper house conveniently located almost directly across the street from Our Lady of Mercy Catholic Church. There were woodchucks in the basement and raccoons in the attic, but St. V's nestled comfortably on the main level. Even though there was no water or heat, there was electricity, and at least they were in out of the elements; and more importantly, they could leave the clothing set up from one week to the next. What a blessing!

Word spread far and wide, and the St. Vincent de Paul satellite became a haven for people who were down on their luck. Several of the local churches donated funds, and the sisters bought food stuffs to distribute—eggs, cheese, milk, bread in addition to distributing government surplus items such as butter and cheese. As the weather warmed, many of the townspeople began to drop off excess vegetables from their gardens. Throughout the summer, patrons could pick up apples and onions, peaches and peppers to help stretch their supper rations and fill their children's bellies with healthy, bone-building food.

From time to time, a wayward soul would stop in with a sad story about running out of heating oil or having the electricity turned off. Sue Ellen and Noreen would help as much as they could, but the real gift was the Christian love that spread beyond the walls of the ramshackle house that served as a launching pad for their ministry.

And launch they did! The Toledo Diocese had been astounded by the number of patrons and the amount of donations. During the early years, much of the stock was brought down from the Toledo overflow, but there came a point when the tiny Fayette satellite became self-sufficient. From time to time, the sisters even sent their overflow on to Toledo. The generosity of the community was evident by the number of consistent volunteers from Our Lady of Mercy

Catholic Church and other churches in the area. They worked tirelessly side by side, smiling, talking, and often praying together.

Life at home was crazy at first, with so much of Noreen and Sue Ellen's time going into the setup and launch; but slowly, they settled into a routine. The children helped when they could, and even Kenny and Pete started showing up more regularly to heft the bags onto the sorting tables, which was an enormous relief to the ladies. They did much of the handyman work around the dilapidated house and helped organize the donations by building racks and shelves whenever they could catch some time between working at the prison and on their respective farms.

It seems that we never appreciate the smooth-flowing, calmer times until calamity hits and sets our world into a tailspin. Kenny and Noreen were fast asleep in their beds when the phone jangled them awake. Ken was the first to reach the only phone in the house, hanging on the kitchen wall. Noreen was right behind him, wringing her hands so tightly her knuckles were turning white. "Good news never comes in the middle of the night," she whispered almost to herself.

Noreen watched anxiously and listened to every word her husband said, hoping for clues to the midnight alert. Kenny shook his head uttering, "I see. Uh-huh. Oh, that is terrible. Can I do anything to help? Have you called Pete and Sue Ellen? Should we come there? I see."

Noreen almost collapsed from holding her breath. As she exhaled, she planted her feet firmly and put a hand on Kenny's arm. She mouthed the words, "What is it?" But Kenny was too engrossed in the conversation, and Noreen was left to worry for what seemed like hours but was truly just a few minutes. Her mind raced; has something happened to one of her sister's children? They were older, so it would not be unheard of for them to be out this late.

And it had been a dreadful evening. The crack of thunder and the glare of lightning from the colossal rainstorm had brought her own children to their bedroom doorway several times. The temperatures had plummeted as the cloud cover took hold and the storms locked the world in an icy grip. Sleep seemed impossible, so for a bit, the family stood on the front porch wrapped like mummies in blankets, hooting and hollering, laughing and yodeling into the storm.

As a Navy man and a farmer, Ken knew storms. He had grown to love their power and untamed majesty. It took him back to his youth in South Dakota when the dust bowl rains were cause for a frolicking celebration. Ken and Noreen did not want their children to cower in the face of storms, from nature and otherwise, so they taught them to enjoy the spectacle with a brave heart and just rejoice in the knowledge that God was present.

"Did you know that our Lord made this beautiful rainstorm for us to enjoy?" Ken paused for effect as six little heads bobbed up and down. "And did you know that he did the whole thing using only his left hand?" That brought out the questions:

"What?"

"Are you kidding?"

"How do you know that?"

Ken looked 'em straight in the eye and supplied all the answer they would need: "Because the Bible says that Jesus sits on His right hand…" The older children roared with laughter, and the little ones didn't understand the humor exactly but laughed because everyone else was laughing, because it was fun, and because it helped make the storm seem less scary. They shared more jokes and stories that they'd heard at school or church, and everyone enjoyed the clean, fresh smell that follows a sound rainstorm in Michigan.

And enjoy they did until Noreen scooted them off to bed. She paced the floor for a while longer, waiting for the pitter-patter to be replaced by the sleepy sounds of children resting contentedly in their beds. She had barely fallen asleep herself when the phone rang.

No matter how hard she tried, she could not glean any real clues from Ken's side of the conversation. "Yes. Okay. I'll tell her. Oh, it was a banger of a storm. We'll talk more later."

Finally, blessedly, the phone call ended. The receiver was still in midair when Noreen exploded with questions. The look on Ken's face silenced her as he held both of her hands in his.

His first words brought relief, "Everyone we know is fine. No one has been hurt." Noreen exhaled; what else mattered, really? People, that was the important part of life. Everything else was expendable, replaceable, props for the lives being lived all around.

His next words brought sadness, "The roof at the St. Vincent's house fell in, and everything is ruined. Tomorrow, we'll see if any of the tables or shelves can be salvaged, but there's nothing that can be done tonight. Oh, I'd better call the owner just to see if he needs any help securing what's left of his property. What a senseless loss!"

So there it was, all of her hard work, and it comes to this. Well, what was the point? *This* was God's plan? It just doesn't make sense. And then the tears fell, not from the loss, but for all the people who would suffer and go without necessities, because this storm, this beautiful and terrible storm, had ruined everything.

How is it that one minute, they were filled with awe and wonder at the very thing that caused such destruction and pain in the next minute? Life really is complicated. God really is complicated. Arm in arm, they returned to the bedroom where solace was waiting and love abounded. "Tomorrow, I'll think about this tomorrow."

The cleanup had already begun in earnest by the time the children were off to school, and Ken and Noreen met Pete and Sue Ellen at the site. The two men had called the prison to explain that they wouldn't be working that day. It was an unusual request, but their women needed them.

The owner of the house met them in the driveway with the saddest expression on his face. Here, he had tried to do the right thing, but had just made a mess of things. Thank goodness the storm had not hit when St. Vincent's was open. But as it was, things were such a mess—water dripping, plaster hanging, everything soaked. The carpet squished around their boots as they trudged through the house, leaving indented footprints as testament to the path they took.

Noreen had hoped maybe, just maybe, the operation could be saved, but the storm had taken its toll. Walking in a daze, she rounded the corner and ran into Sue Ellen standing over the tables that the men had just built, but now ruined. The weight of the rub-

ble had bowed the legs, smashed the tabletop. The water had slith-
ered everywhere. The sisters fell into each other's arms and sobbed for
a dream unfulfilled, for the help that the poor would not receive, for
the fruitlessness of their efforts.

"Why bother if this is what comes of it? We would have been
better off helping our husbands and tending to our children. Why
did God call us to this task only to have it obliterated?"

They worked the rest of the week throwing everything into the
dumpster. What else could they do? Noreen made the obligatory
calls to the diocese, canceling the truck that was scheduled to pick
up excess clothing, cancelled the monthly statistic report meeting,
and she put a notice in the local paper that donations were not being
accepted. The St. Vincent de Paul Store was closed.

In her productive haste, skittering here and there, Noreen did
not consider the Bible verse, "You were running the race so well. Who
has held you back from following the truth?" (Galatians 5:7). Had
she considered the possibility that Satan was helping her stumble,
she might have made different choices. Fortunately, God recognized
it and intervened on her behalf. He was strong when she was weak.

The documents, receipts, and records were thoroughly soaked.
Sue Ellen just couldn't deal with the soggy boxes of papers. She felt
overwhelmed and was barely able to function coherently. "You're
always the stronger one, sis, you do this."

Noreen smoldered as she silently gathered up the papers, remembering the childhood pattern of shouldering her sister's chores. She
felt the pointedness of Sue Ellen's comment clawing at the back of
her neck. "Why do I always have to take on the tough tasks? I don't
want to be Martha."

As Sue Ellen tugged at a pile of rubble in the main room, squeals
of awe and astonishment escaped her lips. For buried beneath the
heap was the antique painting of Christ, which had hung so prominently on the wall. It had survived! Even the ornate frame was in fine
condition. A miracle? Probably. A sign? Possibility.

"Noreen, come out here right now." Noreen bristled at yet
another order from her baby sister. "I'm working in here," she replied

with more attitude than she meant to reveal. The sarcasm slipped over Sue Ellen like a salamander on moss-covered rock.

Wordlessly, Sue Ellen led her bedraggled big sister out of the room filled with pessimism and peevishness and into the bright, hopeful rays of God's love shining down from a nail on the wall that held the hope for tomorrow. A hope that had been lost but now was found.

Noreen, however, had slipped into a crevice of darkness, feeling as if her efforts to follow God's will had been in vain. St. Vincent's had failed. She smiled at the picture; she tried, but she could not find the optimism that was so characteristic of her. In this moment, Noreen felt the stirrings of future rifts that would rise up between the sisters.

As the days passed, Ken tried to pull her out of her despondency. He took her out to eat at their favorite diner in the next town over. She smiled and ate, but her heart just wasn't in it. She had little to say and appeared not to be listening to much that Kenny had to say. She didn't even laugh at his jokes, which was unusual.

To add to her burdens, all of Noreen's old childhood jealousies and recriminations toward her baby sister starting sprouting up in her. "Why do I have to do the paperwork? How come this falls on me? Mom always gave me the toughest jobs just because I was older." On and on swirled the thoughts, the recriminations, the guilt, and the discontent with her sister's lot in life, with her own. She wallowed in her own private dark night of the soul. It's not that she didn't pray to be released from her thoughts, her feelings, she did, all the time. It's that she received no answers, no signs, no help. Where was God? Had she offended him so grievously? Would he ever forgive her? Could she ever forgive herself? Could she forgive her sister, really forgive her? Together, they had failed God, and that knowledge ate at her heart.

Sometimes when things seem to be most hopeless, a ray of sunshine splits the darkness, bringing with it a glimmer of what life could be, should be, may be again. Noreen's salvation came in the form of a phone call from the Toledo diocesan priest.

The family was gathered at the dinner table, when the ringing disturbed them. Noreen was just lifting a forkful of mashed potatoes to her lips when her son, Alan, handed her the bungee-corded wall phone. "It's for you, Mom."

"Hello? Mrs. Dickson, is that you? Is everyone all right?"

At first, she thought the priest was calling for the data report, and she was gathering the courage to admit that she hadn't even begun to assemble the details. When the papers had dried sufficiently, she had crammed them into a box and stuffed it into the back of the closet. She just didn't have the stamina to move forward, unravel the numbers. The memories were sharp and nipped at her with the knowledge that St. Vincent's was closed, and her efforts were fruitless.

Her attention snapped back to the receiver in her hand as she replied,

"Yes, no one was injured, but everything is ruined, and I feel terrible about it all. I just don't know why this happened. It was going so well. We were helping so many people."

There was a long pause at the other end of the line. Noreen was sure his next words would be about the report that was overdue, so she was startled when he began, "Mrs. Dickson, I have good news for you."

"The diocese has been so pleased with how smoothly things have been running there. The number of customers has been steadily increasing, and there seems to be a solid core of consistent volunteers. We are particularly pleased that you have reached out to the other churches in the area. It's so Christlike and builds understanding and goodwill. I know that you, personally, have been a good ambassador, speaking during their church services, and spreading the word that we are all called to serve together. The number of clothing donations has surpassed what is collected in our main Toledo location, and we have come to depend on your surplus to help the poor here. It is a testament to faith that this satellite has thrived and helped so many of God's children in need.

He continued, "For quite some time now, we at the diocese have pondered the suitability of your current site. The house was a Godsend, and we join with you in thanking God for opening up the owner's heart to help this fledgling ministry. Never once did you complain about the lack of heat or the poor lighting. The tiny rooms create a hardship, we know, for the tables and the traffic flow. But yet you rejoiced in the space and made it work." Noreen was not sure where this was heading, but she listened intently.

"The storm has rushed our timeline, but it is time nonetheless to look beyond your current location. The diocese is willing to fund a pole barn building project if you are able to find a feasible location. I know that you have all been through a lot emotionally and physically getting through this setback. God has not abandoned you, and neither will the Diocese."

Noreen was speechless and caught only snippets of the conversation that followed. The call had come out of the blue, and she did not have time to process his words. "Bless you, let me think about it and talk to Sue Ellen and our husbands. It's been a trying time," she stammered, trying to cover her shock.

"I understand. Take all the time you need to consider expanding the work that has been set before you. There is no pressure. Just want you to know that there are options. Please pray about it and get back to me when you are certain how you want to proceed."

After she hung up, Noreen thought about the priest's last sentence. "Certain? Nothing is certain? Maybe God, by way of the storm, was telling me that my mission is over. Maybe it's someone else's time to step forward, send them the dream. How does anyone ever figure it all out? I'm just so tired, I can hardly think."

The rest of the meal was spent discussing the news. Ken was less than enthralled as he had already begun to imagine a life with his wife at home, like the olden days. "I have to tell Sue Ellen and Pete so they can think on it, pray on it." Though the call to Sue Ellen was brief, it was met with mixed feelings, especially from Pete. Selfishly, the husbands wanted their wives at home. Spiritually, they wanted to follow God's will. In the end, after much soul-searching and mountains of prayers, faith won out, and the sisters stepped forward into another new adventure.

The following year was challenging in ways they could not have imagined. The red tape involved was tedious and confusing. Sue Ellen and Noreen had different ideas on how to proceed. They searched for answers and found themselves bickering over minor slights or sharp retorts. The sisters' relationship stumbled. They were bruised, burdened, and seriously overcommitted. They struggled to move forward but caught flack not only from the men at home but from the other sister. Hard feelings siphoned away their joy and left a sticky mess.

The sisters attempted to wash away their discontent with each other, but it was only superficial at best. They thought they had forgiven each other and moved on to the matters at hand, but what is forgiveness? And how do you really know if your heart has healed from the ugliness that was allowed to enter it? These questions would come to light again in the future, long after the mind had forgotten what the heart remembers.

Years later, the urgent message that Kenneth brings to Noreen, from beyond this life, is centered in forgiveness. It would have nothing to do with accomplishments or savings accounts or even the children. He brought no advice for beating the stock market or when to buy property and where. The real reason that Ken broke the silence of death was to cleanse the heart of the woman he loved with proclamations and directions so simple, yet so very hard to complete.

The enemy is pride. It gets in the way of spiritual growth. We hate to admit our faults, our shortcomings, our mistakes. We hate to humble ourselves before those who have quarreled with us. The negative feelings fester and grow and harden the heart against the love always present but shaded by the altercation.

Sue Ellen and Noreen both tried to get past the misunderstandings and essentially, they succeeded, on the outside anyway. They had hugged and forgiven, and Noreen tried to tell herself that it was the last time they would need to forgive each other—only it wasn't.

Together they attacked the task God had placed before them, to clothe and care for those in need. They put notices in the paper seeking land donations for a St. Vincent de Paul building. They were invited to be guest speakers at some of the local churches, various service clubs, schools, town meetings, and local libraries.

One Sunday, Noreen was invited to say a few words to their fellow parishioners of Our Lady of Mercy Catholic Church. She felt funny speaking there, sort of like "preaching to the choir." Certainly everyone in that small, close-knit community must already know all the details of how the project worked. Many of the parishioners were already volunteering and donating both funds and gently used items.

So Noreen spoke about the people in the community and how they had benefited from the free donations. She spoke not so much about the project but the way it affected people, the workers, the customers, the neighboring churches. "We really never know how our actions affect others, sometimes positively and sometimes not so positively." Noreen looked up and saw her sister in the pew and unintentionally reflected on their tumultuous relationship. How easy it is to talk about love and forgiveness, but how much more difficult is it to put it into practice.

Noreen shook herself out of her reverie and finished with a plea to the congregation. "If this work is important, it cannot be continued with a handful of people. It must be accomplished with all of us, pulling together for the good of those in need. We are all on a mission of God. Please help find a place to build this facility for the sake of those who cannot speak for themselves."

After Mass the president of the Parish Council, the local church governing board, approached Noreen and offered to call a special meeting to brainstorm solutions. In the end, after much discussion, they agreed to allow a pole barn to be erected on Church property with the understanding that if the St. Vincent store ever closed, the building would revert to the Church. The diocese hesitated briefly before agreeing.

At last, a home. A real home for the St. Vincent de Paul store. A place where those in need could come, without money, to secure the things they needed. Whether it was warm coats, boots, sweaters, shoes, dishes, books, toys—whatever the need—there would be hands to help. Noreen and Sue Ellen hugged each other gleefully.

The worst part was over, or so they thought. Neither of them had any knowledge of construction. Instead of worrying, at this point, they just trusted that God would provide. And He did.

The building grew up from the earth like a sapling reaching for the sky, strong and steady and just as miraculous. The perfect building surrounded by imperfect people, still harboring grudges and resisting forgiveness.

By the grace of God, something wonderful has risen from tragedy, again. Faith. It all boiled down to faith, and there was plenty of that to go around.

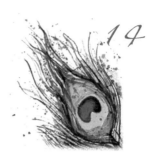

He Started to Sing…but Died Young

Parents die first. It's just the natural order of things. God designed it that way because the loss of a child can feel too devastating to endure. And yet sometimes, for whatever reason that we can never fully comprehend, it happens. It happened to Mary as she knelt at the foot of her son's cross, and it happened to Leola as she held her dying son during his last breath of life in this world. Both mothers knew that their sons were in God's hands, but both struggled under the burden of loss and grief. Sadly, Noreen's initiation to the unenviable league of mothers who have lost sons, would soon commence.

So let's not beat around the bush anymore. As dreadful as it is to put into words, Dan died. It was not some terrible car accident or disease or an addiction problem that killed him; he literally died from stress. Oh, there's a fancy name for it, all right, electrolyte imbalance triggered by stress overload.

Dan was relatively short for a man, about five feet eight inches or so, with compact well-defined muscles, honed from hoisting bales of hay on the farm plus daily weight lifting with his football buddies. He had flashing blue eyes, thick blonde hair, and a strong straight nose, reminiscent of a Roman soldier. He walked with a spring in his gait, arms swinging and head held high, resplendent in the fact that he was loved immensely by all—family, classmates, teachers, neighbors, and pretty much everyone he met, especially the females. Of course, the list of adorers was somewhat stifled due to the suppressed population of his rural hometown, big fish/little pond scenario for sure.

One day in 1978, with a brand-new driver's license in his wallet, Dan successfully pleaded for the freedom to drive to Saturday night Mass independently. Deviousness percolated as he was giddy with the excitement of unleashed freedom. The idea of being able to sleep late the next morning, while the rest of the family went to church, was a major appeal. His younger sister, Molly, begged to ride along for the adventure. He agreed under one condition. She could ride with him only if she did one small errand and kept one small secret. She agreed without asking for details.

Young Molly was nervous as she snuck into the back of the church and quickly captured the weekly bulletin, visible proof of attendance. She escaped unnoticed out the back door. Danny and Molly cruised around, hoping no one they knew would spot them and tattle to the parents. For years, the secret lay between the siblings, bonding them even closer.

Outwardly Dan was Catholic, though not overly so, much to his mother's chagrin. He drank a little, probably smoked a bit too, behind the school, the barn, or the big willow tree. He was loyal to a fault and that's what endeared him to everyone. He was real, not perfect, but warm, funny, kind, and loving.

Except, of course, when he donned his football gear. Then and pretty much only then, he was fierce. What he lacked in stature, he made up for with gumption.

Unfortunately his prowess on the field was not matched by classroom success. Dan struggled at all things school. Though his parents battled against a label, everyone knew it, and nobody cared a hoot.

College presents a difficult transition for many students, but it is particularly challenging for those with a learning disability. Students who are good at school have a better chance for success because they have internalized what it takes to "do school." They have skills and experience, and they are more resilient. Past school successes have filled them with confidence in their abilities, in their intelligence, in their organizational strategies, in their study skills. They may not be brighter or better than poor students, but they believe they are.

Dan was none of those things. Kind and sweet, yes; popular, ambitious, athletic, absolutely; but academically confident, no. Schoolwork was a struggle for him, and he knew it. Everyone knew it, but it was never talked about. Report cards in the Dickson home were a private affair. The siblings suspected, of course, but it was not discussed. Report cards were serious and confidential and were only shared with parents behind closed doors, each child taking turns entering the parents' bedroom, which was the only room in the house which afforded privacy. In that way, there was no opportunity for comparison or for teasing. Punishments and praise were meted out confidentially.

By the time Dan graduated, the pattern had been clearly established by the four older children that college was the next step. Dan avoided it, for a while, with miscellaneous jobs around the area— gas station attendant, farmhand, paint crew, construction grunt. He lived with several siblings in different locations and worked hard to establish a career, any career. But real careers are hard to launch without training, and Dan eventually decided to try college, whether out of real desire, a competitive spirit or lack of appealing options, it was hard to ascertain. For better or for worse, and the latter turned out to be more accurate, Dan chose Northern Michigan University.

If you've never experienced the north woods of Michigan, you are missing quite an experience. Regardless of the season, the view is spectacular. The air smells fresh and clean like someone just scrubbed it with Pine-Sol. The hardy buds pop miraculously through the late snows and swell the branches of the trees so they can get a leap on the short growing season. The water runs in rivulets to the rivers, the ponds and the surrounding Great Lakes. It's crystal clear and cold— oh, so cold.

Way too soon, spring erupts into summer; and the animals, fish, and insects gorge on the plentiful food bursting forth as if a splendid buffet had just materialized. A scant few months and the fall chill starts claiming the nights. Fall is in the air, and all manner of life begins the arduous task of preparing for the sparsity of food and intense cold that marks the end of the growing season.

That fateful fall, Kenny and Noreen drove Dan to his selected college, every bit of six hours one way. The farther they drove north, the more spectacular was the color show. The leaves were brilliant shades of red, orange, yellow with green and brown sprinkled in for contrast. There were times when the pavement was hard to see because the falling leaves had obliterated the road. Still they drove on, with trepidation in their hearts but a resolve to help Dan follow his dream wherever that might take him. His life, his choice.

Dan had decided to become a forest ranger. "Best job ever," he touted. "You get to be outside almost all of the time. You help find lost hunters and create a plan to protect, not just the woods, but the animals and the lakes too. I'll get to help with scheduled burns and treat pests and diseases that creep in. Because of me, future generations will get to enjoy Michigan's natural resources," he boasted.

Dan made friends at college easily and seemed to find plenty in common. They were a hardy lot. Dan loved the ruggedness surrounding the Northern Michigan campus, quite near the family cabin. He snow-camped with his buddies with nothing more than a sleeping bag and a backpack. He excelled at all his survival classes, but those were the only classes where he met success.

The Dickson family missed Dan at the holidays as the drive was too long to be practical, and besides, he had plenty of homework to complete. Occasional phone calls were filled with animated accounts of sleeping in a snowbank just to prove it could be done. He was learning to track wildlife and watch for signs of illness or distress. Unfortunately, he did not transfer that knowledge to recognize and observe the signs of his own distress, building day by day, course by course, assignment by assignment.

By the time spring break rolled around, the phone calls had dwindled away to nearly nonexistent. Noreen grew more uneasy as silent weeks rolled into months with no word from her son. Finally, she phoned Dan's roommate, because her son was just not answering the phone. Noreen was surprised when the roommate handed the phone to Dan, lolling around in the dorm room. She asked a thousand probing questions of him. "Why didn't you answer the phone? How's school? Are you eating enough? Are you warm enough? Are you keeping up with your classes? Do you need a tutor?" The usual concerned-mother questions rolled off her lips in an attempt to engage her son in conversation so she could gauge the situation. Dan gave her little to work with, incredibly stingy with his words. "I'm okay," he fibbed.

When Kenny got on the phone, the questions were reduced to one, "What's going on?" He heard Dan sharply inhale before responding, and when he did finally speak, his voice cracked, belaying the emotion present just beneath the surface. "Dad, I really just want to come home for spring break. Can you come get me?"

Ken wanted to say, "Are you kidding me? That's a really long and expensive drive for only one week. Besides, you'll be out for the summer soon." But there was something in Dan's voice that halted his common-sense assertion. Instead, he said, "Sure, we'd love to come get you. We're lonesome for you too."

A six-hour trip up north followed by a six-hour trip back downstate all in one day with questionable roads that time of year was ludicrous. To make the same trip all over again ten days later was even more insane. But they loved Dan, like all their children, and something in his voice was unsettling. Whatever the reason, whatever the inconvenience, whatever the cost, Dan needed to come home, and come home he would.

An uneasiness hung in the car on the journey north to claim their son. Neither parent could quite put their finger on it, but it was there nonetheless, strong as steel and every bit as cold. They spoke very little, each in their own thoughts, in their own prayers. They said a Rosary together and prayed for each of their children's needs, but Dan's needs were at the forefront. There was no room for peace with the restlessness that plagued them.

When they pulled up to the dorm, Dan was sitting on a snow pile with his luggage. It was odd. Why wasn't he waiting inside? Didn't he have schoolwork to do? Wasn't he cold? Where were his friends? Dan bounded to the car, all smiles; and all their previous uneasiness faded into the contentedness of being reunited with their fifth-born child. They hugged, kissed, cried with joy, then began the long journey home.

Dan chattered away about his college experiences. Everything seemed fine, at first. In that moment, he was a healthy, content college freshman so happy to be reunited with his family.

They had hoped to drive out of the snowy areas before nightfall, but the slushy asphalt turned to ice. The ditches along the road bore witness to that fact as they held deeply entrenched cars that had passed that way and been snared by the icy, cruel claw of Mother Nature at her worst.

At this rate, the six-hour drive back to the farm would easily take ten; but if he needed this, it was worth it. Whatever it took to help him find himself, find his dream, find his destiny, they would do it.

The Dickson men were gentlemen and never walked away from an opportunity to help someone in need. A young girl driving a lightweight Pinto hatchback just ahead of them in the road, slipped off the road and landed with a *klumpf* in the ditch. Ken and Dan stopped, pushed her out of the ditch, only to have her slide back in the moment she accelerated. The car was too light and not meant for the challenges of winter driving. Since cell phones had not been invented, they decided to deliver her to a pay phone at the next rest area about thirty miles ahead. Anyone who has traveled through northern Michigan understands that civilized exits are few and far between.

Noreen listened with interest to the conversation that ensued between the two youngsters in the backseat. She was traveling home from college too and was hoping to see her boyfriend that night, but plans are often prone to change when winter weather intervenes.

The two talked about the demands of college and compared workloads. Through eavesdropping, Noreen was able to glimpse a side of her son that had not surfaced before. He was struggling with school. How could she not have known that? Why had he not told her? Certainly, she had asked him how it was going, time and time again, yet he had always brushed her inquiries off with one-word responses such as, "Fine" or "Good."

A different story surfaced as he chatted with this girl. Term papers, the worst. Oh, and midterms to study for, interviews to conduct, a text analysis, and a research project to complete. Ten days was a short period to accomplish so much. "Well, I've been working at it pretty steady," she confided, "but there're just so many assignments. I'm only about half done. The research part takes the longest. Now I just have to write it up. It's hard to squeeze in any fun."

After the girl was dropped off, Dan grew somber, deep in his own thoughts. Noreen tried to chat amicably. "What do you want to do when you get home? Do you know if any of your high school buddies will be home too?" Nothing worked, until…until she started asking him about schoolwork.

"So how's your psychology class?" He shrugged and told her that he had a paper due the day he got back to college. "How much of it have you completed? What do you mean none? And is that the only class with homework that has to be completed over the break?" Noreen's chest grew tighter and tighter as she listened to all the assignments that were due right after break.

She was alarmed when she learned that he had not started any of it—the term papers, the essays, the book reports, the interviews. Nothing—he had tackled none of the prep work to allow for successful completion of even one of the assignments.

The cause was simple, or so she thought. Dan must be overwhelmed, over his head. Yet he seemed to be eerily calm. Except for his shaking hand, which belayed the terror within, he looked to any casual observer to be handling the pressure, shouldering the stress. But was he? Noreen wondered first to herself, later to Kenny.

Once they finally arrived home, Noreen threw herself into cooking and baking. She wanted Dan to have a good break, a healthy break. He had lost weight at school, and that was odd; most college freshman gained fifteen or so pounds. The cafeteria food is so plentiful, and Dan always had a big appetite. It just seemed strange.

And stranger still, no matter what she cooked, he only pushed it around his plate, picked at it. She fixed all his favorite dishes, but nothing excited his appetite, captured his interest.

Ken offered to drive Dan to the closest big library in Adrian, Michigan, about an hour away. When Dan hesitated, he reminded him about his assignments, which were due in ten days. Some of the siblings living nearby offered to help gather the books and collect the research documents, but Dan procrastinated. "Oh, tomorrow. Today I just want to be home."

It became apparent that Dan was overwhelmed and worried about school, which found its legs in procrastination. When he started feeling listless and distanced himself from family and friends, his folks noticed.

When he began to talk nonsense and could no longer focus, they were fiercely alarmed. So much so that one night, they took him to the hospital in Jackson, Michigan. They felt foolish for what was so seriously wrong to warrant such an action? It was uneasiness, an inner voice. So they listened and acted.

The hospital admitted him and kept him for a month for observation and therapy. They experimented with pharmaceuticals, but nothing seemed to help. They ran test after test but could find nothing seriously wrong. They blamed it on stress from school, and everyone understood the truth in that.

Maybe he had traveled a path too steep for his abilities, but it's the choice he made. He was headstrong and opinionated, like all of the Dicksons. Noreen so wished he would have listened to her plea to go to a community college nearby, but he loved the outdoors and the wilderness of the north woods was enticing.

When Dan returned home from the hospital, he seemed a bit better. By that time, it was obvious he was not returning to school. Noreen and Ken were sure that once that pressure was removed, he would bounce back to their talkative, outgoing son, but their optimism proved short-lived.

Dan was in a downward spiral, and nothing seemed to pull him out. He wasn't interested in anything. His parents tried to get him to walk down their gravel road to the corner every day. That was their goal, a mere quarter mile. If they could just get him off the sofa into the chilly country sunshine, surely, their real son would resurface.

Dan continued to talk about school and the work he still had to complete, acting as if he were still actively participating. He kept thinking and worrying, around and around, until his hands would shake. He lost more of his appetite every day and became pathetically lethargic. He was not thirsty and could only be nudged to take a small sip of water. Nothing captured his interest, and he grew frighteningly quiet as days turned into weeks and dark commas punctuated the tender skin beneath his troubled, blue eyes.

The doctor was calming and had helpful advice. "Keep his life calm so his nervous system has a chance to rebalance itself. He's been through a trauma. The pressure from college may have dissipated, but it is still very real to Dan, and he needs time to recover. If he isn't noticeably improved by next week, call me again."

The week would pass with Noreen and Kenny walking on eggshells trying to keep day-to-day stresses and annoyances from reaching Dan. They would talk soothingly to him, pray with him, try to laugh with him. His eating habits had not improved, and he was still drinking precious little. Dark circles formed beneath the baby-blue eyes that used to dance with mischief.

The parental faces became tense and drawn, haggard with worry. Ken noticed, for the first time, the wrinkles that surrounded his wife's eyes and the jowls that announced middle age. Where had the years gone?

His gaze returned to this full-grown man before them who only yesterday was born, their precious son, whose very existence was a miracle. They called the doctor and tried to get an appointment, but the schedule was booked up well into the following week.

"We're worried about him. Something just isn't right," they pleaded with the receptionist. "I'll have the doctor call you." The doctor did call them back, several times, and explained, "Your son has experienced severe stress overload. We've run every test possible, and there is nothing physically wrong with him. It will just take time. Call back in a week if the situation has not resolved itself." Noreen sat frozen, holding the phone and not knowing what she could do to help her baby.

And so it continued, until the point that Dan's stress level pressed the strength to live out of his body, and he sought peace in the next realm as his mother held him, weeping tears of distress that ran rivulets down her trembling face and onto the sallow cheeks of her twenty-three-year-old baby. Dan met his maker on July 14, 1984.

When the EMTs arrived, she wouldn't let go of his hand. As tears fell freely, she cradled herself against the warmth already waning from his body; together they created their own Pieta. She leaned her head into the scent of him, to inhale him in a failed attempt to capture the essence of his life. While they waited at the hospital, her fingers entwined his with a ferocity that couldn't be shaken. The hospital staff entered the room with warm voices, gently nudging the bespectacled woman to let him go. They explained that they needed to take his body, but she held on ever more tightly. If she refused to let them have him, perhaps this nightmare would vaporize, like all bad dreams that evanesce in the light of morning. Insight finally dawned on her, it was a flawed plan.

As Ken eased her toward the door, she turned and took a step back into the room and stood there for a second, as if for the first time that night, she absorbed the enormity of what had happened. She pulled free of Ken's embrace and rushed back to the bed that held her son captive. Fresh tears cascaded down her blotchy face, so tired, so worn, so hopeless. Couldn't God grant them a Lazarus moment and raise him from the dead? (John 11:1–45). This miracle was not to be granted; others would come, but not this one, not now.

Death is such a strange thing. The doctors called it electrolyte imbalance, which means that his electrical system stopped sending signals to his organs to continue living. A simple IV could have saved his life had anyone known, even suspected, the problem. The autopsy showed he was severely dehydrated. All she knew is that her son was gone, forever.

Ken and Noreen held each other and wept with a sorrow that was deeper and more profound than anything they had ever experienced. It was more painful than their separation during the war years, even more heartbreaking than their barren years and the scores of miscarriages they had endured. The thought that he was beyond their reach, beyond their help, was unbearable. Was he also beyond the reach of their love?

It seemed like their tears would never stop. For Kenny, there was an element of déjà vu. He remembered his own mother's grief over the loss of his brother Clifford. He had stood witness to her pain and learned firsthand that mourning could be catastrophic. His mother, Leola, had never truly recovered, and he worried that the same fate might befall his wife. His mother's tears had stopped spilling outward but took up residence inside, causing a far greater calamity in her soul.

Noreen's sobs were so wracked that she couldn't draw a breath and coughed convulsively. His arms cocooned her lovingly until she slumped in his arms. Her warmth gave him strength as he fought to keep her spirit alive. He couldn't let her turn into his mother. He willed her to survive, to be strong, to rise above this piercing loss.

Ken had witnessed the slow, steady demise of his own parents' relationship after Clifford had died. The sorrow should have brought them closer together, bonded them in their misery; but sorrow is capricious, and their lives imploded instead. Perhaps if they had shared their feelings, they would have survived the grief and helped the remaining children to do the same. Instead, well, they didn't.

He had to do it differently this time. He made his presence known to her hovering lovingly. He brought her steamy mugs of coffee, which burned her throat, so raw and swollen, but it forced her to feel something, anything.

With his heart overflowing with emotions and grief, he reached out toward Noreen and the children, not away from them. He chose to share his tears and his sadness only if they were paired with faith and love. When he felt overwhelmed, he hugged someone—Noreen, the other children, neighbors, fellow parishioners. More and more, he saw them responding in kind. They filled the air with prayer and looked beyond their personal tragedy to the world all around. Love always finds a way.

It's not that parents believe that their children come with guarantees to live long and fruitful lives, but they just always expected; it was a common assumption, that children should outlive their parents, not the other way around—never the other way around. Everyone understood that, embraced that, held fast to that. It was the natural order of things, an unwritten contract, wasn't it? So how is it that the two most important women in Ken's life had each been forced to endure the unendurable?

The Bible teaches the importance of releasing a deceased loved one into the loving arms of the Father. After the crucifixion, Jesus said to Mary Magdalene, "Woman, why are you weeping? Whom are you looking for? Stop holding on to me, for I have not yet ascended to the Father. But go to my brothers and tell them, 'I am going to my Father and your Father, to my God and your God'" (John 20:1–2, 11–18).

At odd times throughout the day, the reality would jump into focus, and they would yearn for their son's physical presence. As the days passed, Noreen's laughter vaporized; and she became lost in her longing, her prayers, too grief-stricken to concentrate on much else. She wanted to withdraw from life, because she was so weary of putting on a brave front. It took every effort she possessed to barely maintain a speck of a smile and force back the tears welling up in her eyes. It would be so easy to isolate herself behind her grief and to shut out the world, but Kenny nudged her forward, outward.

So many thoughts consumed her. Repeatedly she asked herself what she might have done differently to keep her son alive. There were no answers, no recriminations, only the facts, her son was dead.

Unanswered questions tumbling around in her head and in her heart. Where was her son now? Would she ever see him again? What happened after death? Her strong Catholic faith heralded heaven, but was there more? Her long-ago, city-slicker friend Lois used to talk about reincarnation as if it were real. Noreen had argued the Catholic stance, because it's all she knew and it was what she believed. But now, maybe there's more that even the Catholic Church did not, could not, openly embrace.

In the quiet of her soul, the unanswerable questions assaulted her without mercy. Is this really the end for Dan, or is it a beginning? Is it possible to get another chance at life? Was Dan beyond their love, beyond their prayers? Was he at peace? Was he with her parents in heaven? Could he hear them, see them? The thought brought her up short. "What kind of a role model am I then? Would he be proud to call me his mother now?" There was no way to know for sure, but if there was the slightest chance, even a glimmer of hope that he was spiritually nearby, then she would be the mother that he deserved, that they all deserved.

She stepped into their black-and-green tiled bathroom and closed the door. A flick of the light switch brought instant brightness and made her squint in the mirror. She looked at her grief-wracked face, somehow holding itself together. She was startled that she still appeared almost whole on the outside, even though her heart was broken to smithereens on the inside. How is that possible? Her pale hand quivered as she tucked a wayward strand of hair behind her ear, revealing a blotchy complexion and overly red eyes brought on from wiping too many tears, for far too many days. She had to pull it together, not only for herself, but for Kenny and the children, all grown now, yet floundering as well.

She prayed and she asked her son, her dearly departed son, to pray with her. Then she asked Ken. Together, they swallowed their sorrow, gulped down the sadness that threatened to engulf them, and salved it with prayer. That was the only thing that they could do for their son, for themselves, and for the remaining children very much alive.

When all Dan's brothers and sisters gathered at home, Noreen and Ken summoned their strength and presence of mind to offer another life lesson: death. For all their grief, they were still parents— albeit parents of adult children, but parents nonetheless. As horrendous as this was, there was still an opportunity to strengthen their children's faith, to teach a lesson about love, peace, and living with ambiguity and the unknown.

Noreen, her green eyes bloodshot and red rimmed, began by sharing a quote from Eleonor Roosevelt, her heroine, "You gain strength, courage, and confidence by every experience in which you really stop to look fear in the face. You are able to say to yourself, 'I have lived through this horror. I can take the next thing that comes along.' You must do the thing you think you cannot do."

She inhaled sharply, reached for a tissue and continued, "Losing a child is the worst thing that could happen to me, the thing I've always feared most. If I can get through this, I can live through anything and so can you. No matter what life throws at you, if you persevere, you will come out on the other end stronger, more resilient and more confident in your ability to handle the next hardship. Life is not always easy. Be brave."

"We all feel the loss of Dan, there's a hole in our hearts and that hole will remind us forever that life is short. It will remind us to live well, love always, and stay connected with our Father. I know we wish we had been more appreciative of his presence, more careful, more attentive, more aware of what a gift he was to our family. No matter what you are thinking or feeling right now, remember that Dan knew that we all loved him and he loved us. Hold on to that thought and store it deep in your heart."

Noreen's words caught in her throat as she sobbed softly. Seamlessly, as if they had rehearsed it, Ken picked up the conversation and continued the lesson, "We will see him one day, but until then, we have to go on. We all have lives to live. If we curl up and die, the tragedy is magnified. There is plenty of love here in this room to sustain us. We have each other and, God willing, many more years to devote to our family, our friends, and our Church. We will never forget. We will carry our love for Dan and the pain of his loss together in our hearts until we are one day reunited in the presence of God."

"God's ways are not our ways. We have no way of knowing why God called Dan home, no one knows. Maybe to save him from a future calamity or painful disease. Maybe He has a new calling for him. Maybe to test our faith. One thing is for certain: how we conduct ourselves in the difficult moments of life defines who we are as people, as Dicksons. This is a time to prove what we are made of, in our hearts, in our minds, in our souls. We must not fail this test. We must remain faithful to the end of our days."

As the sibling closest in age to Dan, Molly stepped forward to wrap her arms around her parents; the other siblings followed her example until they were all standing in a heap in the center of the room.

Noreen broke the tender moment. "I could not stand it. I would never be happy in heaven without every one of you there with me. Your dad and I never expected that one of you would get there first. Now Dan is waiting for us to join him. Pray every day, hold on to your faith. Share it with my grandchildren and my great-grandchildren someday. Love God, love each another."

Tears were streaming down every face now, and sobbing filled the small living room of their simple farmhouse. Though the room had long since been remodeled, it couldn't deny the telltale signs of family. There were nicks in the baseboard where the little boys had crashed their Matchbox cars. The wall mirror had a chip out of the corner where a curling iron had once been dropped (I won't name any names). The family portraits filled one entire wall and bore witness to the lives that began their journey here, in the bosom of this family. Now the well-worn room absorbed a new essence, the presence of death, which could have collided with the family had it not been buffered by love and faith.

Love was ever present here in this house. It was palpable. It lived in the walls and the carpet and the hearts of the people who shared the same name and the same faith. There was no denying its presence and the presence of God. This house had stood sentry to legions of prayers through the years and was not a stranger to heartache and happiness, both shared lovingly with each other and with God. It was a way of life, a cherished path.

And now, Dan walked that path without them. He wasn't alone, they firmly believed that. God would receive him and love him as a loyal son, of that they were convinced. But beyond that, what else did they really know or understand about heaven? Precious little.

As the months passed, the family healed outwardly. They went back to jobs and chores and responsibilities. They reconnected into their lives, all the while knowing that Dan would never go back to his. How tragic was that?!

One night, Ken and Noreen were swinging on the porch swing shivering under a gold, hand-crocheted afghan to ward off the spring chill. "Kenny, if you die first, after the fifty years you promised me of course, wait for me at the pearly gates. Promise?" Kenny wasn't smiling. Fifty years did not seem so far away anymore. "I'm not going anywhere without you. God will just have to understand that!"

"Seriously, wait for me. I want to see your face right away when I get there. Better yet, let's just die together of old age."

They had laughingly needled each other with those words for many decades, but now, they just didn't seem as funny. Would anything ever be funny again? Death had touched their family, and the burden it left was far too heavy to carry alone. Even with God, they sometimes buckled from the weight of it.

They both grew somber, and the tears started again as they missed Dan together. Where was he exactly and what was he doing exactly? Would he be waiting for them? Why couldn't he be granted fifty years to enjoy his life instead of a scant twenty-three years? He was taken far too soon, had hardly begun his adult life. There were so many experiences he would never have. It was just unfair.

Their tears made chilly paths down their cheeks and fell into their laps, moistening their pants. Tiny, mist-sized droplets splattered onto his tanned, manly hands, worn and weathered with the years. His knuckles were chapped, split and calloused, strong hands which gave testament to the fact that he had worked hard to give his family a better life. He protected them from all manner of discomfort and catastrophes, but he could not protect them from this. As the sun was captured by the horizon, they watched the dancing shadows overtake the eerie night.

"Come on. One foot in front of the other, honey. Don't look backwards, only forward." And up they stood and went into the house to find a distraction for their pain and an expression of the love that still burned strongly so many years later. A love that had left traces, incontestable proof, that they had weathered many of life's challenges.

As Noreen nuzzled close to her husband and looked up into his sleepy eyes, she had no way of knowing that her troubles had only begun. Dan would not be her only loss, for all of life ends in loss one way or another. But those were worries for another day as she wrapped herself in love and peace, if only momentarily.

Six children, six beautiful, holy, vibrant, kind, loving children. They had fought and struggled to get each one of those babies, and they were profoundly precious to them. They had taught them, prayed for them, praised them, listened to them, loved them. They were responsible for them. And then there were five...a tragedy beyond endurance.

A Trace of a Grin…Here They Come

Life has a way of moving along, even if you're not ready, even if you don't want to go. And so it was with the Dickson family; weeks turned into years and flew by. Ken and Noreen were lovingly distracted by six beautiful and faith-filled grandchildren, Jace, Jessica, Troy, Justin, Barron, and Daneel (who, yes, bears the name of the son they lost). He wasn't lost really, just absent. They knew exactly where he was.

Kenny and Noreen were doting grandparents, just as they had been doting parents, but without the responsibilities. They fished with them and baked cookies, even taught them how to garden, hunt, and sew. The children loved to play in the barn just as their parents before them did. They collected bugs and leaves and sometimes a baby bird or two. Noreen read them stories, and they helped her cook. Kenny was famous for tumbling on the floor with the grandchildren, not quite as spry as he used to be but spry enough to please them. Visits to the farm were always intriguing.

When you have your children late in life and then have six, the retirement years tend to overlap the child-rearing ones. So it was that Molly, the youngest, was still at home when her dad retired.

Golf was a hobby Ken had taken up in his retirement and had shared with Molly. It provided a wonderful platform for interacting with her, especially in the summer. They would disappear for an afternoon, away from duties and chores, and just "be." They'd enjoy the fresh air and sunshine along with the challenge of the game.

As Molly grew into her busy teen years, the grandchildren lined up to take her place next to Grandpa on the course. The best part about golfing, according to the grandchildren, was the golf cart. He often let the little ones chauffeur him around. It was a sleepy, rural course in the village of Morenci, Michigan, just fifteen minutes from Waldron, so there was plenty of leeway to break a rule or two.

With golf, it feels like you are in another reality. You escape your daily routines and fly freely over the gentle slopes, pausing occasionally to send a ball sailing along with you. In that relaxed setting, Ken really got to know his grandchildren, what they thought, who they were, what they liked and didn't like. He listened to their dreams of the future as their innocent words expressed the boundless possibilities, unedited, untethered.

The tepid days of summer brought out the lightning bugs to chase as far as the eye could see. Noreen provided the jars and sat on the porch, watching the grandchildren crisscross the yard, capturing handfuls of bugs all aglow. It reminded her of the not-so-distant days of parenting. A little spoiling was a good thing.

Ice cream—there was always plenty of ice cream to celebrate the sultry summer season. Ken was very vocal that the only acceptable ice cream had to be chocolate. Ridiculing Noreen about vanilla continued to be an amusing pastime, at least for Ken. It grew a little weary for Noreen as she thought to herself, *ENOUGH already.*

She smiled. She understood him. Men! Funny how it never occurred to him, not even once, that their own freezer was perpetually stocked with chocolate ice cream, never vanilla, as a silent testament to her love for him. Chocolate ice cream made him happy, and that was reason enough.

The grandkids were another thing altogether! They loved Superman ice cream and bubblegum and blue lagoon and rainbow sherbet. Sherbet? Is that even ice cream? Really? Ken laughed at their preferences, shook his head, and continued unsuccessfully in his quest to convert them to the only true ice cream, chocolate.

Ken, being the jokester the he was, couldn't help himself. Once when Mike brought his new wife, Winalee, home to visit, Ken couldn't resist a bit of good-natured fun. Win was a city gal, so it made the prank even more fun; she never saw it coming.

Win was a horticulture aficionado and enjoyed picking Kenny's brain about plant growth and natural fertilizer, another more polite name for cow manure. He explained how he used the tractor to scoop out the paddock and load the manure into a spreader to be dispersed across his acreage, which kept the soil strong and resilient.

Her brain started percolating, and that should have been her clue to slow down and proceed slowly, but it wasn't. She flew head-long into Kenny's plan for a bit of fun, at her expense perhaps. Win suggested that she could collect a bit of manure to take back to the city for her plants, to which Ken readily acquiesced. He had her just where he wanted her.

The adventure started with the right equipment—knee high rubber boots, much too large for her petite, feminine feet; and a gigantic scoop shovel, also way too large for her tiny frame. Add to that a huge metal bucket, and you get the idea. With the stage set for mischief, Win waded into the two-foot-deep cow manure with excitement and optimism, full of visions of flourishing foliage.

The entire family stood or sat on the high wooden fence that corralled the milk cows into the outdoor feed pen. Had they thought ahead, they would have brought cameras; but as it turned out, the event was to be captured and preserved in collective family memories only.

As any experienced farmer could predict, Win was going down. The cows, of course, were curious and waded toward her to get a closer look. Win, as predicted, was not prepared for their massive size or the fact that her boots had now been suctioned down into the manure, and she could not move. When she tried to escape, her feet slipped cleanly out of the boots and into the manure where they were rendered clean no more. Amidst uproars of good-natured laughter, the city girl was initiated. She was a good sport, she had to be, and in the end, she got more than she had expected—she became part of Mike's crazy family for better or worse and lots of places in between.

Summers held a more leisurely pace for educators and Debi, living just an hour away, visited her parents often, especially now during their communal grieving. The grandchildren loved the amenities of the farm, and their grandma's good cooking. The ample opportunity for ice cream was just a bonus.

On one such visit, Debi noticed that her parents were just acting strange. They kept looking at each other with meaningful glances. It wasn't long before her father got right to the point.

"Justin and Barron, why don't you go play outside on the tire swing while we talk with your mother." The boys were happy to oblige.

Ken did not suggest a bedroom chat, but just jumped right into it. "Your brother's death has been difficult in so many ways, but it reminded us that God can call any of us home at any time. We want to be ready, so your mother and I decided to get our affairs in order. We prepared a will and made our funeral arrangements. While we were deciding about the funeral hymns and the scripture readings, we had an idea of something else we would like, and you are the only one who can help with this."

Ken paused to catch his breath, and Noreen stepped in, "We are so proud of your writing, and we were wondering if you would be willing to write a poem about our life that could be read during the funeral mass."

The thought of her parents death hit Debi right between the eyes. She knew it could happen, actually that it would happen someday, but that day was not this day, and she didn't want to think about it. It was too sad, too painful.

"Oh, sure, I'd be happy to write something," she hedged with a somber heart.

Ken pushed her for a commitment, "We just thought that summer might be the perfect season since your workload is so much lighter. Do you think you could work on this before you start back to teaching in the fall?"

A quick intake of breath, then she exhaled slowly, gathering courage and calming her bereaved heart from the mere thought of losing her parents.

"Yes, I'll get you a rough draft later this month," she answered, struggling to keep the emotion out of her voice. Then she shared her thoughts, "It's pretty hard to think about right now with the pain from Dan's death so fresh. Just promise me that we won't have to use the poem for a really long time." Debi whispered the words solemnly in an attempt to keep the hysteria from rising. She just couldn't lose them too.

Ken's jovial response lightened the tone, without really answering the question, "Well, your mother *is* getting pretty old." To which, Noreen, so accustomed to his banter, simply smiled and ignored him. She reached for her daughter, so alive in the here and now, and hugged her tightly. No further words were necessary.

There were moments when Debi was able to keep the grief at bay, times when her thoughts would turn to other things, her children, her teaching, her life. But grief is a tricky adversary; it does not play fair. It would besiege her from behind and startle her with its ferocity, feral and vicious, biting and twisting, inflicting emotional lacerations and bruises so deftly they felt physical. It would grab her by the throat until only a whimper could escape.

"How long will this last?" she wondered, out loud, not for the first time. Her father's wisdom soothed her, "It will last as long as it lasts, but it changes shape and sneaks up on you. That's why you can't anticipate the ambush and that's why it hurts so much."

"Sometimes, Dad, I forget Dan's gone and then when I remember it's like I feel his death as if it just happened."

"I know sweetheart, with time the sorrow will ease into nostalgia and thinking about your brother will bring warm thoughts, bittersweet, but the fierce pain will give way to acceptance. The memories will bring you comfort. Trust me on this, I lived through my own brother's death and I was much younger than you." Silence rose up between them, each absorbed in their own thoughts, sharing the moment and the pain. Noreen smiled weakly, they would all get through this together.

A large family brings with it a lot of activity and a lot of distractions. Ken and Noreen relished their time with family, especially during the summer months. Jessica and Troy, the grandchildren who lived in Kansas, would fly out for several weeks to enjoy a bit of the slow-paced rural lifestyle, which always included a trip to the cabin and, naturally, lots of ice cream. They even learned how to make ice cream the old-fashioned way, cranking and cranking and cranking; the taste of a bygone era.

It's funny that even as generations grow up, the things that tickled children also tickled grandchildren like Grandpa's black bear tale around the cabin campfire, which always ended with, "Don't feed the bears—yourself." He'd seen it on a sign somewhere and had added it to his collection of witticisms.

So nerves were on edge when later, Jessica and Troy walked their friends home to the cabin next door. Through the dark eerie woods, they dallied, thinking about that story and feeling nervous about the night sounds, the crickets, the leaves rustling, the crack of twigs beneath their feet.

Suddenly, they heard a huge commotion in the undergrowth heading their way. When the growling commenced, they knew they were in trouble, so they did the very thing you should never do when faced with a charging black bear—run and scream. At the exact moment just before utter mayhem, Grandpa jumped out of the bushes and laughed his rolling belly laugh! He had a sense of humor for sure, twisted sometimes, but very funny.

From that moment on, every time they heard Grandpa's recitation of "Fuzzy Bear," author unknown, they remembered this moment and smiled.

> Fuzzy Wuzzy was a bear.
> Fuzzy Wuzzy had no hair.
> Fuzzy Wuzzy wasn't fuzzy
> was he?

All the grandchildren loved summers, but for Justin and Barron, who lived nearby, the very best time of the year—better than Christmas or Easter or even Fourth of July—was Halloween. Ken had a gift for making it exciting and tickling their fancies.

The kid in him was just plain fanatical about the holiday and he would plant his pumpkin patch right next to the road for the sheer pleasure of chasing high school students, bent on thievery, out into the darkness, often with his rifle in tow. Shots fired into the night sky brought squeals of terror from the teens who hightailed it outta there only to revisit the patch another night.

From the villagers' perspective, "punkin'" snatching was a quaint, rural ritual. The farmers planted them, and the youth tried to collect them. Steal is much too harsh a word. That, of course, meant many late-night punkin' patch raids. There was really only one rule, jack-o'-lanterns were off-limits.

Most everyone respected that jack-o'-lanterns were essentially family pets. Children lovingly named them, primped them, and fawned over them. They were carved, painted, lit, and loved. Jack-o'-lanterns took on a life of their own and magically glowed in the dusky night air. They were a member of the family, albeit a short-lived member, but loved nonetheless. That kind of Halloween magic was not to be messed with. It was just not cool to snatch them. No one was *that* desperate for a punkin'.

There was one time, however, when the dreadful crime was committed, even though it was frowned on by adults and teenagers alike. One young man in the rural farm community, who shall remain nameless, did snatch a jack-o'-lantern and smashed it right in front of the house. The community was indignant, aghast, the parents were horrified, the children cried.

In the end, it was the teenagers who turned him in, and the owners of the jack-o'-lantern pressed charges. In his defense, since he really didn't have one, the would-be offender cited all the punkin' snatching that took place in the Waldron community, which was, of course, true. The prosecutor brilliantly illustrated the profound difference between a beloved jack-o'-lantern and a plain, ol', run-of-the-mill punkin'. It was a slight, but important distinction that made all the difference.

The wheels of justice reigned supreme, and a sentence was issued that thoroughly satisfied the victims and the community while setting a precedent for any future wayward jack-o'-lantern snatching. It is refreshing in this age of litigation to find a sentence that is entirely without a monetary penalty. The judge ruled that the following Halloween, the delinquent jack-o-lantern thief was to spend the entire night on the porch protecting the offended family's jack-o'-lantern. It was quite a painful penance as it obliterated any hope for the offender to participate in the Halloween pumpkin antics that year.

The rituals varied little from year to year. When the big night arrived and trick or treating had ended, all the little ghouls and goblins, fairies and cowboys would fall exhausted into restless sleep, hampered by the massive quantities of sugar they had consumed. For the older children of the community, the night was just getting started.

As darkness fell on the sleepy village of Waldron, the teenagers could be found loading up all of the punkins' they had been snatching and hiding for a month in their barns or basements or in the gully behind the old oak tree or by the creek in the woods—any place secluded enough not to be discovered. They were not worried about the adults finding their stash, for they were purposely not looking. The kids were hiding their pumpkin collection from other marauding groups of friends. The kids would hijack the pumpkins from one another, back and forth until the big night arrived. Alan, the fourth-oldest sibling, so loved this tradition! He swore that he once had the same pumpkin stolen a dozen times before Halloween night. Someone would take it; he'd capture it back, only to start the whole process all over again. But in the end, it didn't matter; thanks to the farmers, there were plenty to go around.

Teenagers piled into pickups and traveled to the four corners of Waldron to participate in the age-old custom of smashing punkin's in the street. Before the night was over, the only stoplight in town was rendered useless because no cars could travel through the intersection but for the ten-foot mountain of punkin's blocking the junction.

As morning dawned, the local farmers would participate in their own time-worn tradition, using their front-end loaders, tractors, and dump trucks to clear away the oozing orange seed-ridden debris. No harm, no foul, no arrests. Virtually, no other vandalism took place—no tagging, no broken windows, no theft. Just kids having fun and adults looking the other way…and smiling, ever so slightly at the memories of their own punkin' smashin' youth.

There were old traditions and not-so-old traditions associated with Halloween. Kenny had invented a new way to delight the grandchildren. Each October, when the crops were harvested for the winter and the workload was lightened, Kenny would design and build ever-more-creative surprises for the trick-or-treating grandkids.

The parents played along and parked waaay down the road, behind the barn, so their car could not be seen from the house. They would sneak ever so quietly up past the barn, making every effort to silently move in the shadows. If they succeeded, they could climb up on the concrete porch, that had mattered so much to Noreen back in the day, and scratch on the window or giggle through the screen door or make scary noises. Sometimes they had their own surprise tactics, like shining flashlights into the room or shaving cream on the window.

Ken would jump out of his chair and come running outside, but the grandkids, always faster had sprinted around the house. While Grandpa wasn't quicker, he was definitely smarter. Before they could make the lap around the house, he would run out the back door to snatch them up when they rounded the corner.

Sometimes the scenario was upset by Kenny's maneuverings. He would be mischievously absent from his chair when they arrived on the porch. They would peak through every window to surprise him, but the surprise was on them. He might be found hiding behind a tree, lying in the ditch, or hiding in the garden. Once, he even drove out of the barn on a tractor. Sometimes, he wore spooky masks or a funny painted face. No one could predict what shenanigans awaited them at the Dickson farm.

One year, Kenny built a haunted tent over the swing set by draping a tarp, adding spooky lights. He even wired it with scary sounds and hung pieces of cloth to blow in the wind. That year, he was not sitting on his chair by the window or hiding outside. They were sure they would find him in the haunted tent, but they were afraid to look. Instead, they quietly looked in all the usual places, but to no avail.

Just when they were about to give up, they heard a *click, click, clicking* sound, almost like words filling the air around them; and then they heard their grandpa's voice calling to them, mocking them, attempting to scare them. At first, they thought it was coming from the spooky tent, so they gathered their courage to look inside. Silence abated as the screams pealed out of them with delight and turned to laughter. A tape recorder had been set up in the tent with their grandpa's voice speaking to them. When they heard their names being called from a different direction, they spun in circles, searching and searching until they collapsed on the ground.

"Your grandpa loves you. He loves you this…MUCH!" In that moment, the children saw him, and their mouths fell open in amazement. The full moon illuminated the sky and cast a gray shadow on everything below. It was one of those magical nights when time seemed to stand still but for the ticking of the clock and the silly sounds of Grandpa jumping up and down on the roof over the front porch!

Laughter filled the night air and quickly turned to begging as they tried to convince their parents to let them climb up on the roof too. Common sense was the better part of valor, and their pleadings were denied. Kenny laughed as he remembered another time, when his own children would crawl out on the roof with him to catch a whisper of the breeze and share a moment of family bonding. But that seemed like a lifetime ago, and children today were raised much differently—safer, probably—but he yearned for the carefree days when all the dangers of living were kept in their place.

After all, he had kept his children safe when they were young anyway, even with a pretty regular dose of high-spirited mischief, that he mostly instigated. Of course, calamity was predominantly kept at bay because Noreen, the more cautious one, nearly always stepped in just before things went awry.

Kenny's thoughts momentarily whisked him away as he bemused the fact that nothing could guarantee the safety of the children, or the grandchildren for that matter. Just a few short years ago, he would have stood tall and proud that he had ushered all his six children safely and securely into adulthood.

Ah, but the raw memories of Dan and all that had transpired momentarily caught in his throat. Unexpected tears threatened to bely his sentiments, and he wanted nothing to spoil this moment for these precious grandchildren. Instead he reached for all of them and embraced them in a quivering hug, reminiscent of the hugs given to his own children just yesterday, or so it felt.

"What's the matter, Grandpa?" they wanted to know for grandchildren, like children, had an uncanny way of sensing the emotions of the adults they loved.

"Oh, Grandpa was just thinking that someday I wouldn't be here to hug you like this and I wanted to make it a big one so you remember me!"

"But where are you going?" Barron wondered aloud. "We want you to be here, all the time, when we come. It won't be fun if you're gone away."

The carefree giddiness that ruled the day only minutes before evaporated into a serious conversation, a very serious one, and Ken really wasn't prepared for it. But children follow their own timeline and ask the questions at the time that makes the most sense to them and he would not deny them the answers that they so innocently sought.

"I'm not going anywhere for a really long time, I think. But someday, when I get to heaven, you better believe that I will keep praying for you."

Justin, the older brother, thought about it for a minute before adding, "But, Grandpa, if you're there and we're here, we won't be able to play together. Will you be able to talk to us and read us stories from heaven? Will you even be able to hear what we're saying? Will you be watching us on Hall'ween?"

"I'm not sure, but if I can, I will! If God allows it, I will stay very near to you. You can always talk to me, and I will try very hard to answer back."

The words skittered over little Barron's head as he just wanted to get back to playing, "Okay, Grandpa. Cross your heart and hope to die, poke a needle in your eye?"

"Ouch, that doesn't sound so good. How about we just shake on it?"

They all did the funny handshake, the one that was guaranteed to bring out the giggles in any kid. It was a tried and true strategy purposefully implemented with the sole intent of changing the subject. Like Barron, Kenny really wanted to talk about something else, anything else. Heaven was a subject too complex to address all in one sitting. Enough questions and enough answers for one night.

This single, innocent moment was destined to resurface again, first as a memory and then as a motivator to communicate from heaven. The innocence of the conversation, laced with unseen potential, found a niche in Kenny, where the memories nestled unnoticed for years. A conversation that would prove to have an unpredicted and profound effect on the entire Dickson family.

It Couldn't Be Done...yet a Contract Was Fulfilled

"**F**ifty years! We've almost reached the fifty-year marker... that's five zero, with the same woman. I not only raised six children with you, Noreen, but I got to see you grow really, really old!"

"Kenny!" Noreen, caught unaware, yelped. "I can't believe you said that!"

"Well, it's true, Noreen." She missed the teasing light in his eyes as he reeled her in. "You are soooo much older than I am."

After nearly fifty years, he'd never grown tired of taunting her. She was just so easy to tease. With retirement at hand, he would have much more time to devote to that particular pastime.

Retirement had been good to them. Finally, they could spend every waking moment together if they wanted, and most of the time, they did. They bought a little trailer in a retirement community in Florida to escape the challenging Michigan winters. It was nice to explore new areas and experience a different lifestyle than the cabin or the farm.

However, they could never have foreseen that their Florida refuge, which brought them such joy, would also be the site of such fear.

For it was in that tiny mobile home, far away from their children, that Kenny had his first heart attack.

Noreen screamed when he fell to the floor, "Kenny, are you okay? What's happening? Are you hurt? This isn't funny, stop it!" When she didn't see the telltale crinkles forming beside his baby-blue eyes or the merriment dance across his weathered face, she knew it was for real. She sprang into action and called 911, but her disturbed words were barely discernible, "Hur, hlp, com quik, not laughing, prblm, no breathn, srus." The conversation ended after she was finally able to grab hold of her fear, if just for a moment, to provide the address, and just seconds before she broke into inconsolable sobbing. Every muscle was shaking as she gasped for air that eluded her.

It was just not fair; they hadn't been married fifty years yet. She remembered that they had laughed about renegotiating their contract with God at their fiftieth anniversary. It was funny then; it wasn't so funny now. She knew that they had been blessed, but still it was too early. She couldn't face it, she wouldn't. Instead, she prayed with all her might for a different resolution. If there was a chance to save him, she was begging for it. Surely, God would understand her fear and misery, wouldn't He?

"Oh, God, if you could let this cup pass me by..." (Matthew 26:39 and Luke 22:42). Her thoughts turned to the originator of those words, Jesus in the Garden of Gethsemane, the night before he was to be crucified. She felt guilty for asking God to save her husband when he seemingly turned a deaf ear to his only son's pleading for the same mercy. God had his reasons that we cannot fully understand. Even knowing this, she fell to her knees, begging God for more time.

The ambulance arrived quickly and whisked Ken away. She wanted to ride along, but they discouraged her. Driving was not something that she felt comfortable with in the best of times, but now, she just couldn't face it alone. The lady next door was the designated emergency driver, and Noreen gratefully accepted. It seemed that the people in their retirement community were all too familiar with the scenario. They had seen it far too often, so preselected roles made sense, albeit a tad fatalistic, yet, in the moment, comforting.

Things flowed quickly and smoothly. There was someone to drive, someone who volunteered to call family members, someone to lock up their trailer while they hurried to the hospital. Others brought food, picked up their mail, and notified the neighbors of what had transpired. Many bowed their heads together and prayed for Ken's recovery, knowing that others with similar episodes had never returned.

When positive news arrived, a collective sigh of relief spread through the community and landed with the loved ones in Michigan and elsewhere across the country. Ken was one of the lucky ones; his heart attack, thankfully, was small, help had arrived quickly, and the time was not right for his final farewell. That would come, of course, but not this day and not here, so far away from family. The doctors said he would make a full recovery. They left the hospital less than a week later with a list of mandatory reforms: more exercise, fewer baked goods, no stress, a small aspirin. The list went on interminably, but they thankfully welcomed the reprieve from catastrophe. Noreen told herself soothingly that this would be the last time, but she was kidding herself.

Good intentions rarely alter actions if left in the theoretical phase. Ken made a small attempt to behave himself in the beginning, when the memory was fresh and the fear was very real. He complained that all he was allowed to eat was sawdust, which offended Noreen, who was trying to redesign her recipes to be more health conscious. Ken laughed that it was too little, too late, and why bother.

"Really Noreen, when it's my time, I'd rather check out eating one of your legendary yeast rolls with buttercream frosting." Her good intentions to reform his lifestyle were not well received.

Time, as always, is the enemy and has an uncanny way of blurring memories and weakening the resolve to reform toward a healthier vein. "If I can't eat, really what's the point?" he complained often, with boyish zest.

"Well, honestly, Ken, I thought I was the point," she sighed. "I thought our family was the point. I thought that your help with the poor at St. Vincent's was the point. Don't you want to stay with me and enjoy these grandbabies? Isn't that more important than anything else?" To which Ken had no retort. She was right, of course, but oh, how he hated to admit that, mainly because it would require a change to a life that he dearly loved just the way it was.

She was hard to argue with, she always was. Maybe because she made so much sense or maybe because he just didn't have the heart to tell her that if he couldn't have a real life, he didn't want one at all. God heard him even if Noreen refused to do so.

And time marched on as it always does. It seemed like they turned around three times and the day was upon them.

"We made it," Noreen exclaimed. "I can't believe we really made it! After all these years, we're finally celebrating our fiftieth wedding anniversary."

Kenny had surprised her with dinner out, and they had spent the better part of the evening gazing into each other's eyes across the table. To him, she was just as beautiful, just as beguiling, and just as spirited as she had been that first night. It was a somber celebration with both of them cognizant of the frailties of life.

Always the kidder, Ken had whispered, "Well, I haven't decided if I want to renew the marriage contract or not. Fifty years seems like a good run. Maybe I'll consult with some experts"

Noreen shot back, "Over my dead body." To which Kenny replied, "Now who's trying to get out of the contract? Well, let's just take it a day at a time and thank God for every minute he gives us."

They sat holding hands and remembered back through the years, the good times and the not-so-good times. They lived to see their children grown and even had time to spend with grandchildren. It's funny that they didn't feel so old. If they avoided mirrors, they could even believe they were newlyweds, laughing about how old they would be in fifty years. The years had slipped by one by one, until now, when they piled up to fifty.

The heart attack that killed him came a few months later in Michigan surrounded by those who loved him most dearly: his wife and his children. Well, maybe the grandchildren should have been there. If they had they would have seen a man serene and at peace with the destiny of his life. He had lived a good life, a happy life. Was there anything else that mattered in that moment more than the fact that he knew the Lord and loved fully and completely those who were entrusted to his care?

He loved others too—the patrons of St. Vincent's, his neighbors, the fellow parishioners at Our Lady of Mercy Catholic Church, even the panhandlers they passed sometimes in Florida when they drove for groceries. He could see the goodness and the holiness that God had designed into each and every person. Noreen was jolted into the here and now by the incessant beeping of the ventilator attached to Ken.

She hoped that he could feel her love as he lay so still and silent now on the bed that would not release him. She had been avoiding it, but the time had come; there was no point in delaying the inevitable. She knew what she had to do.

She clung confidently to a Bible verse that kept returning to her thoughts, "Verily, verily I say unto you, He that heareth my word, and believeth on him that sent me, hath everlasting life, and shall not come into condemnation; but is passed from death unto life" (John 5:24).

Noreen called the five children to his hospital room at the University of Michigan Cardiac unit when she knew for absolute certain that his condition was terminal. The second heart attack had blown out nearly half of his cardiac wall, and he was being kept alive by the *thump, thump, thumping* of the life support unit.

Debi was the first to arrive because she lived the closest. "He hasn't even left, and I miss him already. Nothing will ever be the same."

"No, it won't be the same, Debzi D., but it will be okay. And it's going to be okay because we have each other, and that's the blessing of family love. We'll always have his love and our love."

The fourth oldest child, Al, and his wife took a bit longer to arrive, because they had a new baby to bundle up. When they walked into the hospital, Noreen swallowed her sorrow to exclaim over the miracle of life beginning anew in the same room with her husband, whose life was slipping from him, from her.

The rest of the children began to arrive, harried, breathless, tear-streaked faces with heavy, hurting hearts. Noreen greeted each one with a brave, love-laden smile. She wiped away their tears, kissed their cheeks, and hugged them with all of her strength.

Together, for the last time, they entered Ken's room as a family and circled the bed. The room was silent and awkward. No one knew how to proceed or what to do. Emotions were high as they squeezed each other's hands and tried to stay back the sobbing. Even though she was surrounded by her children, Noreen had never felt more bereft as the life support system chugged on toward the certain destination on the horizon, like a dependable train that always arrived on time, and the time had come.

The silence was finally, blessedly, broken by Noreen as she led the children in prayer. They sang Kenny's favorite gospel songs from his Baptist days and recited Bible verses. Sentiments and memories were offered and shared as one after the other spoke of the things that matter most—faith, love, perseverance, kindness, hard work, honesty, forgiveness.

After everyone had their say and shared their love, Noreen reached out and took her husband's hand. She smiled at his face, limp and unresponsive, the sun speckled skin hanging in layers across his stubbled chin, consuming his neck once pulsing with life and vitality. With a prayer on her quivering lips, moist from perspiration and tears, she unclasped her Confirmation cross from around her neck and laid it on his laboring chest.

One by one, each of her five children reached beneath the neckline of their shirts and likewise removed the cross necklace that had been hanging there since their own Confirmation day when they stepped forward and accepted Jesus as their personal savior for the first time as adults, or almost adults. Each one placed their cross on their father's chest, rising and falling in shallow rhythmic breaths as dictated by the monotonous breathing apparatus controlling his life, preserving his presence, avoiding the unavoidable.

As Noreen gazed in amazement, she finally understood the depth of the mission that drove their marriage: five children stood where once there were six. Yet all five stood as faithful servants of the Lord. They had walked this earth wearing the symbol that epitomized their faith, rich and varied. The Confirmation crosses had been a physical symbol as well as a constant reminder to the siblings and to the world that they had dedicated their lives to follow the Lord. They had not wandered from that decision and stood firmly planted in their faith, all of them.

Pam remembered something their dad had once told her, "You are never really dead as long as someone remembers you. I will always be alive in you. Just remember me. The good things you do in life live on in other people who pass it on to other people in other places and they send it on through the generations. That's what I've done with you. Now it's your turn. Be good to each other."

Silence fell deafeningly in the small, cramped hospital room. They held each other and prayed the Lord's Prayer through teary, blurred vision with a passion that rattled their hearts,

And in the next moment, with a brief nod from Noreen and a soft, sad smile, the respirator was inactivated in accordance with Kenny's wishes and God's will. For a moment, a brief moment, collectively, they hoped that a miracle would befall them. Maybe, just maybe, he would open his eyes, and all would be well. But God had other plans, as Kenny breathed his last breath and slowly faded out of this life and into the next, without protest, without incident, filled with faith and obedience and love, always love.

Ken was on a challenging adventure without her. His now infamous words, matured and morphed with the passing of time, flitted across her grief-wracked brain, surprising her and comforting her. She repeated them over in her head using Ken's words rather than the poet's (sorry, Edgar Albert Guest). Ken had done it, and she wished he hadn't.

It Couldn't Be Done

Somebody said that it couldn't be done, but he
with a chuckle replied, that maybe it couldn't,
but he would be one who wouldn't say so 'til he
tried. So, he buckled right in with a bit of a grin
on his chin and if he worried, he hid it and he
tackled the thing everyone said couldn't be done
and he did it!

The doctor interrupted the somber family time to unceremoniously record the time of death and the date, November 13. The
significance had not escaped Noreen. It was her birthday, and the
only one in fifty years that he had shared with her. The irony weighed
heavy on her heart. She had never begrudged him his yearly hunting
excursion with the men, and the coincidence of having him here with
her on this, of all dates, was painfully poignant. She remembered the
last fifty birthdays spent without him, content in the knowledge that
he loved her.

It was much, much harder to accept the fact that not only would
he never spend another birthday with her, but he would not spend
another day with her. With a heart burgeoning with pain and loss,
Noreen wept and fell into a restless sleep about 4:00 a.m. on the first
of many nights without her soulmate. The darkness engulfed her in
soothing blue shadow, a place where finally thinking, missing, and
aching were not in the forefront; a place of nothingness where her
spirit could restore itself in anticipation of tomorrow's burden.

The funeral Mass was a holy event with just the right amount
of optimism, mingled with tears for the loss felt by the mourners.
The family's faith told them that Kenny was in God's hands now, but
their hearts recognized how empty their own hands felt.

After Holy Communion, with an imperceptible nod from the
priest, Debi climbed the two steps of the altar leading to the ambo.
She stood before the microphone, trying to compose herself.

Crying will ruin this moment. I have to do this for dad, she thought to herself.

She looked out at the grief-ridden faces in a nearly packed church. Family, friends, neighbors, co-workers, and everyone who had been impacted by their father's legacy, a testament to a life well lived.

Her voice cracked with emotion, but the tears were kept at bay as she began the task assigned to her just a few years before, when both of her parents were still alive. She solemnly read the poem they had nudged her to write after Dan's death. They had kept it tucked away in Noreen's cedar chest, with all the important papers relating to their death.

Circle of Love
by Debi Dickson

The great-grandmas and grandpas of years gone past
Sent a heritage down that they meant to last.
The dream was that love would envelop our lives
And not die a memory in some dusty archive.
Because life is a circle—a circle of love.

Dad and Mom began their life as one.
It wasn't all easy and full of fun.
There were hard times and lean times
And downright mean times.
But their life was a circle—a circle of love.

God blessed their marriage with children galore,
And he helped them support us, no easy chore.
Through diapers and dating their wisdom sustained us.
Though we seldom admitted it, the mere thought pained us.
Life is a circle—a circle of love.

As their family grew, their love did the same.
Wherever they were needed, they always came.
The house was quite busy with three girls and three boys,
But they cherished us always, embracing the joys.
Life is a circle—a circle of love.

Our music was a unifying source.
It was hard to find time to practice, of course.
As our own lives expanded, we grew away from the band.
But not the lessons we had learned firsthand.
Our circle was changing—our circle of love.

We learned how to work and to strive and have fun.
We learned that our love was held tight by each one.
Kindness and sharing intermingled with spats,
Along with giggles and wrestling and a few tears, perhaps.
Our lives were a circle—a circle of love.

We learned about sports, hunting, fishing, and sewing.
And many other things that were well worth knowing.
These skills they taught us with unbelievable patience.
Plus they took us up north for numerous vacations.
Life is a circle—a circle of love.

As life mates were chosen, our family grew.
The folks welcomed each one because they knew
The stages of life come full circle with time.
It was viewed as a blessing, a passage sublime.
Our circle was growing—our circle of love.

The love we were raised with we shared with our spouse,
And allowed that inheritance to permeate the house.
It wasn't too long before grandchildren came,
And we passed love along to them just the same.
Our circle was changing—our circle of love.

When Dan went to heaven, the circle did not shatter.
Love binds us together, location doesn't matter.
Though some live far and some live near,
The circle's intact, we hold it dear.
Our family's a circle—a circle of love.

Mom and Dad displayed pure, unbridled delight
At successes and dreams often shared late at night.
They would listen with kindness and wisdom and pride.
Always letting us know they stood by our side.
They nurtured this circle—our circle of love.

Each Sunday we would celebrate Mass
Because they knew God's love would last.
Our circles begin and our circles end
As we're cradled in God's eternal hand.
God starts this circle—this circle of love.

Dad's life has come full circle now.
It happened so quickly, I don't know how.
But God, in his wisdom, has beckoned him home.
We are each living testaments, wherever we roam.
That his life was a circle—a circle of love.

The challenge to us as we head down life's path
Is to pass on their legacy, so it will last.
We need to love one another and all those around
So when our circle ends, God's trumpets will sound.
Let's make our life a circle—a circle of love.

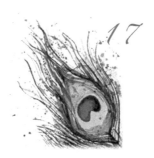

She Would Be One...Instead of Two

She was roused from her slumber by the first spark of sunshine. Rising up between them, all the fifty years that came before loomed in those first rays of light, and Noreen bravely faced a future without him. This day would forever place a marker in her life, the *before* and the *after*. As she went about her morning tasks—making only her half of the bed, brewing coffee into only one mug, pouring out only one daily vitamin—she felt like she was swimming in a bubble, and she couldn't swim.

The weight of her burden was exhausting, and she wandered without purpose. As she walked by the hook that held his faded denim bib overalls, she pressed her tearstained cheek to the cool, hard metal clasps, remembering how he used to hug her so closely to him. She inhaled the scent of him still clinging to this world, but for how much longer? "I'm not ready to let you go, but I don't have a choice," she winced. The season was ending.

She sat down with her coffee and reached for a yeast roll, his favorite. How could she sit here eating breakfast as if the world were still a normal place, as if she had not just had her heart torn from her chest the day before? How could she move on from that, and what would be the point? Her reason for living had been driven from her life, and she felt like a wooden spool devoid of the cotton thread that was wound so securely. At the peak of the spool's usefulness, there was purpose; but empty, it was merely discarded without a thought.

The pounding in her head would not relent; her throat ached, along with her heart…that had also abandoned her. Her eyes were sore and swollen from shedding oceans of grief-ridden tears, the lids so heavy and bloated she could hardly lift them. She fought to keep them open because when she closed them, his face appeared, and the longing to touch him was unbearable.

The harsh reality of the morning after fell heavy upon her; Kenny had fulfilled his fifty-year contract; there would be no renewals. The decision was final.

After Kenny's death, the soft, gentle voice of God within her was muffled. Noreen wondered if she could continue to do God's work. What could God have been thinking? How could she serve the Lord now that she was alone and had lost her helpmate, her rock, her love? Ever since the weather nearly destroyed the St. Vincent project, Kenny had been by her side, working and helping. He had been there to lift the heavy bags of donated clothing onto the sorting table with uncanny timing just when she was ready for them. He built shelves and racks, fashioned an automatic door closure, hung curtains, carried out trash, and talked to the customers. He was truly a jack of all trades and reveled at the opportunity to make someone smile.

He talked her down when petty disagreements surfaced with Sue Ellen over this policy or that practice at St. Vincent's. Most importantly, Ken smoothed the social awkwardness with his carefree chitter-chatter and his eagerness to engage absolutely everyone in comfortable conversation. He made the patrons feel welcome because, well, they were.

But all that was over. She felt hollow and eviscerated. Her lungs bellowed from the agony of unexpressed loss. She gripped her pain with such veracity that she thought her hands might actually bleed. Her self-shattering tenacity was debilitating. Life would never be the same, and she wanted to wallow in her own self-pity, to sit down and grieve for every miserable remaining day she had left of her own life until God ended her purgatory on earth.

She wanted to, but she didn't. As through every difficult situation, her faith prevailed. She remembered her own advice, passed on glibly to anyone listening, "Look forward, never back." Now what? Could she follow her own advice?

The grief over Kenny's death brought her back to the very brink where she hovered after Dan's death. Like a deer caught in the headlights, every moment startled her. However, this time, she recognized the signs of despair, and she knew how to cope.

This time she was saying good-bye to a seventy-two-year-old man, not a twenty-three-year-old boy. At this age, death was expected—not easy, but expected. She found comfort knowing that her precious son Dan, dead now for over three decades, was welcoming his dad into the kingdom of God. She could almost imagine Kenny catching him up on the happenings here on earth, how the Detroit Tigers had fared this season and the past thirty seasons. They had a lot of ground to cover. The comings and goings of the siblings and his old Waldron friends, surely, were high on the priority list. Dan must be feeling happy, excited, and loved. He would enjoy giving Dad the grand tour.

She wondered, not for the first time, what heaven was like. Were father and son engaged in any of the familiar activities that they loved like hunting, fishing, joking, talking, and playing poker? That thought brought a smile to her grief-ridden soul when nothing else could.

"On my bed at night I sought him whom my heart loves—I sought him but I did not find him. I will rise then and go about the city; in the streets and crossings I will seek Him whom my heart loves. I sought him but I did not find him. The watchmen came upon me, as they made their rounds of the city: Have you seen him whom my heart loves?" (SGS 3:1–4b). She reached for his pillow and cradled it to her chest for a heartbeat before releasing it. "I'm alone, but not lonely thanks to my children and my work at St. V's, but I miss you! I miss us," she admitted softly to herself and maybe to Ken if he was listening.

Noreen sought him in her sleep, in every waking moment, until exhaustion and desperation gave way to peace and acceptance. One night, she was awakened from a sound sleep by a pressure next to her on the bed. The edge of the mattress compressed as if someone were sitting down. She knew it was him; she could sense it and feel it. She breathed in his presence and was soothed by his love, ever present, ever alive. It's true, she thought, "Love never dies!"

Noreen remembered with solemnity, the rainy evening when she had fallen off Ken's motorcycle. In his youth he had always liked excitement, which was precisely why he chose to train as a fighter pilot. That characteristic had lain dormant for so many of their married years, when safety and security were mandatory for survival, yet here he was, off on a wild and edifying ride without her. The thought made her smile, and she wished that she could jump up and join him, pressing her young, trusting body against his strong, muscular back, with full confidence that he would drive her safely to their destination.

Instead Noreen sought comfort in church. The Catholic Church had housed generations of worshippers, where prayers were shared and answered, hearts broken and healed, love offered and received. In the sanctity of the Mass, she relinquished her grief to God as her ancestors before her had done. It was in the celebration of the Mass that her husband often made his presence known. For over fifty years, they had sat together in the same pew, he on the end spot where he could rest his arm, damaged and aching from the farm accident so, so long ago. She was always by his side, week after week, year after year, until now, when she was the solitary occupant sitting alone in the well-worn, family pew, fourth from the front, to the right of the altar.

One day, shortly after Ken's death, Noreen was praying in their pew before the Service began when she felt someone nudge her over. She looked up only to discover there was no one there, physically. If she closed her eyes and quieted her mind, she could sense him standing beside her. She smiled up foolishly and scooched over in the pew, leaving his spot empty to be filled by his soul taking a brief reprieve from heaven. She hoped it were true; she felt it was, but nothing was certain anymore. But just in case and because it felt so good, from that day forward, she always left his end spot in the pew empty. "I am with you always, even unto the end of the world" (Matthew 28:20).

Eventually, the gnawing ache of missing Kenny began to subside. It's not that it just vanished, but the painful grip loosened just enough to begin her life anew without his physical presence, loosened enough for her to breathe. She started viewing her memories differently. Instead of focusing on the pain and loss, when her thoughts turned to him, she forced herself to remember the happiness there. She started smiling at the funny things he used to say, instead of crying because he would never say them again. She reveled in the memory of how he sashayed when he walked, rather than torment herself with the knowledge that he would never move again. She made yeast rolls for herself and allowed his appreciation to infuse her with love. In short, she helped him live joyfully in her memories.

A single mug of coffee in the morning began to feel familiar. Little by little, Noreen established new routines, her routines. She started a morning meditation with her coffee instead of rushing into the news as had been their practice throughout their marriage. She bought vanilla ice cream, instead of his favorite chocolate, because she really did prefer the simplicity of it. She still missed him every moment of every day, but she stepped forward bravely and resolutely, repeating her own words to herself, "Look forward, never back." The gaping wound was healing, but the scars would never disappear. When the time is right, life has a subtle way of nudging itself in front of grief, relegating itself to the forefront.

"My life is not over, and Kenny would not want me to wallow in my grief. We've talked about this." God had graciously and lovingly answered their prayer for fifty years together, spoken with jest in the bloom of their youth. "Why, oh why, hadn't we prayed for sixty or seventy or more?" As Kenny and Noreen and all of us learn, there is never enough time. The challenge is to make the most of the time we are given.

Noreen was weak and vulnerable when the unexpected knife wound came from the most unlikely source, her sister. Sue Ellen's voice jangled the phone line as she revealed the truth about the unresolved mystery from their youth. She giggled with glee at the chaos and drama she had ushered into the family all those years ago by hiding their dad's belongings so Noreen would get blamed. She was proud of her ability to one-up her big sister and become the savior of the day at Noreen's expense.

As grapes in a wine press, Noreen felt the squeeze of her sister's words. She felt betrayed, hoodwinked, sabotaged. How could she not have sensed something else at work? She had missed the clues, never suspected her sister's involvement. The keen edge of jealousy hung between them. Noreen's pain and disillusionment swelled to engulf her.

If truth be told, however, the sharing of this long-ago secret was not an intentional malicious act, for the real wrongdoing had unraveled years before when Sue Ellen portrayed herself as the good daughter and cast Noreen as the nitwit. Sue Ellen did not intend to hurt her already-wounded sister; today, she had succeeded at that in their youth. In actuality, she thought her sister already knew that she had been behind the missing items, a careless prank by her estimation.

Silence screamed between them through the telephone wire followed by a swift and chilly good-bye. Noreen reeled from betrayal and held her sister responsible for the mean-spirited thoughts and recriminations that seeped into her already grieving heart. Perhaps if she had been stronger, she could have resisted. If Kenny had been there to act as a life preserver and float her gently to the surface, she might have made a better choice. But he wasn't there, and she couldn't swim. In her fragile state, she fell into the swirling abyss of blame. She felt the waters raging, threatening to carry her away in the deluge. The chasm was too wide for crossing, and Noreen swallowed her sister's betrayal without a word of protest.

She tried to throw herself into her work at St. Vincent de Paul, but Sue Ellen's mocking voice reverberated in the recesses of her mind, never far from the surface, infecting everything she did. She knew she was being curt, quiet, and cantankerous with her sister.

Sue Ellen stood innocently by, not recognizing what had spurred this obnoxious side of her usually complacent and amiable sister.

It only took a few minor spats before Noreen succumbed to retaliation. "You take it over then. All of it. You can be in charge of St. Vincent's. Go ahead, be the president. I relinquish it all. I don't need this grief, I have enough of my own. I quit. I'm retiring. Enough of this!" In an ill-advised attempt to escape the confrontation, Noreen swirled around too quickly flinging her body headlong into the door frame. She grappled for the air as her arm landed on a stack of donated books which toppled nosily to the floor preventing a swift and graceful exit. She winced with pain as she regained her footing and kept moving out the door, hugging her arm to her chest already exploding in agony.

Once she reached the safety of her automobile, she pressed her angry foot to the gas pedal leaving a plume of dust in her wake. Moments later, she recognized that she was unfit to drive, so she pulled into the A & P parking lot to catch her breath. There she sat rocking forward and back in the padded cloth seat attempting to calm her nerves. Her arm ached from the impact, yet she hardly noticed. As one hour turned into two, she felt her pounding heartbeat slide into a regular rhythm and the ebb and flow of normal breathing return. She slipped the gearshift into drive and eased the vehicle slowly into the street, heading away from the St. Vincent d'Paul Store for the last time and toward Ken's gravesite. Her words clawed past the lump in her throat, reverberating first in her head and then off the hard surfaces of the car's interior, "What have I done?"

As if it had a mind of its own, the car navigated the path to the nearby cemetery. The peonies were in bloom, Ken's favorite. She leaned on the tombstone to try to catch her breath and her sanity. It was a safe spot, a holy spot. During their marriage, the task of caring for the graves had been a regular outing that they had shared together. All of the family graves received fresh flowers and perennials were planted as a tribute to the family love they had inherited. She hoped she had instilled this value in her children as she would hate to see the ancestors final resting places neglected, not to mention her own. She didn't know if it were true, but she hoped that the deceased could hear her prayers, her thoughts, her conversations as she tended their plots. She wanted them to know they were loved and remembered.

She knew that God created each of us lovingly from dust and to dust we would return. You are born, you live, you die, and the cycle continues ceaselessly. With sadness, she allowed her eyes to wander to the older, untended graves. Would that be her one day? Would the next generation diligently honor their ancestors or forget they even lived, loved. Would this precious spot that held her beloved son and her soulmate one day give way to the moss, to the weeds, to the forgotten. She shuddered and focused on the only things that truly last, faith, hope and love. She prayed for these gifts for her family members alive and deceased. She prayed for the generations, yet unborn. She pointedly included her sister and felt the bitter pang of remorse for allowing her pain and hurt to guide her actions.

Sue Ellen was bewildered by her sister's harsh words and hasty retreat. They'd had disagreements before but had always rose above them with sisterly love. Where was that love now? The words that had escaped her own lips only weeks before never entered her mind. An inconsequential utterance, spoken blithely in lightheartedness, had created a mysterious canyon too wide to cross. The raging waters of anger rushed too loud for talking. A bridge could not be built.

Maybe It Couldn't...but He Did It

The first words Dad spoke were lost on us. We were stunned by disbelief. At the sound of his voice, a voice we had not heard for fourteen years, Molly, my sister, and I stopped dead in our tracks. We stood motionless in the middle of the cafeteria of the retreat center, each experiencing a private epiphany with Dad. It seemed like long minutes passed before I could function sufficiently to look out of my own reverie to notice my sister by my side, though it was probably only seconds. One look and I knew, without a shadow of a doubt, she was experiencing the same thing.

A fellow conference attendee, Kimberly Egberts, who unbeknownst to us was a spiritual healer, stood quietly in front of us, speaking words that barely registered. "Your father is here, and he wants to talk to you. I can help you hear his words more clearly if you wish." Molly and I both reached out and touched her forearm and, with a trembling voice in unison, whispered, "**YES**!" Later we would learn that Kimberly's lunch had been gently highjacked by Dad to help facilitate our conversation. She told us she was impressed by his non-pushy, polite manner, but could sense his loving urgency, which is why she agreed to represent him at such an inopportune time.

It felt like everything around us faded into the background in a quiet haze. We were surrounded by a deafening silence and felt embraced by his presence, similar to being wrapped in a warm blanket. Dad was there with us—not just his voice, but we saw enough of him to verify to our doubting minds that it really was him and he was there. As he shuffled from foot to foot, we would catch glimpses of him, a hand, his chin, his profile. It took a moment for our brains to relay the message that what we thought was happening was really happening.

Several paragraphs were spoken by our dad before either one of us consciously began to grasp the meaning behind them. It felt warm and safe to be near him again, and we breathed that into our hearts. We wanted to linger in the feeling part of the discourse, but our father quickly nudged us to engage intellectually as well.

The contrast between our emotions and his were stark. Where we were ecstatic, he was uncharacteristically somber. Perhaps if we had clearly seen his face immediately, we might have been comforted by his heart-moving smile or, for sure, the warmth of his pale blue eyes would have convinced us; but at first, all we received was the sound of his voice, deep and serious. The tone of his voice calmed us and coaxed us to put the jubilance that was bubbling up in us on hold, to stamp down our disbelief and allow the moment to simply happen. It was clear that he had an urgent message that he needed us to hear.

Sometimes, it was Kim's voice we heard, sometimes, our father's. Mostly we felt the exchange…in our souls. The words resonated within us. He knew us deeper and more truly than anyone ever had. Kim seemed to disappear into the background as Dad's urgency stole the spotlight. We felt the power of his love magnified with the love of Christ, and we just knew that this was not a ruse, not a hoax, this was *holy*. Our hands reached for our throats where we clutched the crucifix hanging there as a visible reminder of the invisible faith that ruled our lives.

So we stuffed our emotions into our socks, as best we could, and pushed ourselves—not always successfully—to focus on his words. We tried not to be distracted by reality or the sweet sound of his gravelly voice or Kim's oh so tentative rendering. Sometimes, we would hear his voice, and the meaning of his words would slide over us as we became distracted by the enormity of the occurrence. In those moments, Kim's words would bring us back with a clearer, restated version: "He's trying to say this…he's showing me that…"

The words he spoke to us on that first day were recorded by us immediately upon returning to the privacy and sanctity of our retreat room. My sister and I each wrote down specifics of what we heard and saw; then we shared the notes with each other, and the following is our accurate recollection.

Dads First Visit

September 12, 2009

I have waited here a long time for Mom. I love her very much.

I have chosen not to move on to other levels and places, because I love Mom and I want to be there for her. I am with her almost all the time now.

Dan and I have both passed on. We are not of the earth, but we can come back and forth. I am with your mom a lot lately.

At the mention of our deceased brother name, I stumblingly asked our first question, "Dan's there with you?"

Dad nodded and replied, *I'll go get him.*

Go get him? How was that possible? Before we could even form the questions, Dad's words reappeared through Kim.

Dan can't come because he is in training. He is deciding to come back again, either in our family or with another family. I can't tell you which, but I've seen it. Often, there is a 'knowing.' Dan won't remember. He'll move on.

His words pushed the breath out of us. What? Was he talking about reincarnation? Really? Come on Dad, we're Catholic! Mom would not approve of this. Seriously!

There was patience in Dad's voice as he tolerated my question about Dan, but it was clear that he had a more pressing agenda.

Before we could ask any other questions or sideline the conversation, he got right to the point.

There is one relationship in Mom's family with a problem. It is heavy on Mom's heart, and it holds her to the earth. It is really heavy on her heart lately. It's ridiculous!

His impatience was palpable. He was clearly worried and driven to express the importance of the message. At this point we were lost as to what he was really talking about. We felt his intensity, but were quietly trying to decipher his meaning.

There has to be forgiveness. Tell Mom to write a letter to her sister. It needs to say, "I'm sorry. Forgive me. I forgive you. Even if you don't receive this, I forgive you."

This has divided the family for a long time and caused strife between the families. It doesn't matter if it is received, if Mom writes it and mails it, it will release her. When you tell Mom this, she will believe it.

Egads, he wants us to tell Mom *that*? Mom's relationship with Aunt Sue Ellen had been none of our business. It's not something Mom's mentioned very often. We weren't exactly sure what the rift was, for heaven's sake. Forgiveness is such a personal thing and we didn't want to intrude. The Bible tells us to reconcile with others before approaching God, but is Dad insinuating that unresolved conflicts affect us in the afterlife? (Matthew 5:17–37). That would not be an easy conversation to have with our mom.

Tell Mom, "You're on the right path, don't worry, it's easy."

Then he abruptly changed the subject. *I am proud of you.* Naturally, we thought he meant us, Molly and me, so we puffed up a bit. He could apparently read our thoughts because he added, *No ALL of you.*

Okay, Dad, we get it. Molly and I are not your only focus. You are proud of all your children.

I loved phrases, look for phrases, it is me speaking to you. I will put writings in front of you. On the floor, in the newspaper...you've got some sayings written down already.

I had started a list of his sayings about ten years after his death, but had misplaced it. How did he know this? So I asked him where they were.

They are under some other things, in a drawer.

Later I regretted my trivial question which wasted precious minutes of our time together. However, I did find the list when I returned home in the bottom drawer of my nightstand, neatly tucked beneath books I have every intention of reading someday. Why did this matter? What was the significance of his statement? Of course, we knew he loved sayings, limericks, jokes, puns, and the like. Why would he waste precious seconds of his time with us to discuss this? He's the one who brought it up. The full revelation came much later at which time it would all make sense to us.

There is big love in our family, all love.

I am waiting for her.

Molly asked Dad if there are educational opportunities in heaven.

Yes, I continue to learn.

Another abrupt change in the conversation signaled that he had another purpose to communicate.

Christmas is important this year. Christmas is at Debi's.

Family Christmas had never been at my house before. It was only decided the day before on the phone as I was driving to the retreat center. How could he have known this unless he was listening in on my conversation?

Big, tall Christmas tree.

We have a fifteen-foot flocked tree, but hadn't put it up since his grandchildren were married and started homes of their own.

Presents laid out. You walk in the door, and it is warm. Table beautifully decorated with purple dishes. Gifts under the tree for Mom from me. There may not be many more holidays. I don't know the time. Don't worry, your mother will die a peaceful death.

My purple dishes had been purchased in the last few years, so he had never actually used them.

What gift did he have in mind for Mom? Our thoughts went astray so we didn't get that question specifically asked.

We asked if we prayed for Mom, thought about her and tried to reach out to her after she dies, if it would cause her any difficulties as she tried to move on.

No, it doesn't work that way.

His words grew faint as Kim tried to refocus the connection. We could feel the distance growing. We didn't want him to go, but didn't know how to get him to stay. It was clear that he had accomplished his task.

I jumped in with a last-ditch effort to prolong the exchange, to revisit the message with calmer countenance, "Dad, Dad can we talk to you tomorrow?" His voice did not hold the delight that we had expected, as he almost reluctantly replied, *Okay.*

And then he was gone, unceremoniously vanished. We should have asked when. We should have asked where. We should have asked a lot of important things, but we didn't. There would be another opportunity. We would be allowed another minute, maybe two, with him tomorrow.

The sounds and smells of the cafeteria clamored around us once again. We hugged Kim and each other. Leadenly, we placed our trays on the rack and exited the space. Surely, everyone around us must be in awe by what had just transpired; but as we glanced around, it was chatter as usual. No one had even noticed that the most significant miracle of our lives had just taken place. We had not sought this out, it came to us. Dad came to us.

Slowly, it registered with us that the messages had been private, intended only for us, but with the expectation that we would share his words with each other, with Mom, with our siblings. Beyond that, we could not commit. It's dangerous in the secular world to trust something so personal with people who might not understand, believe, accept. People who might pass judgement, point fingers, flail against his message. I thought about Blessed Mary and how difficult it must have been for her to face the clamor of the Jewish community when she conceived her baby out of wedlock and then again when her son died and rose from the dead. How challenging it must have been for the apostles to walk away from the life they knew and share a message that was not easily received by many. A message that could and probably would set them up to be taunted, ostracized or even killed.

As we cloistered ourselves in our room, we found ourselves shaking from the emotional, surreal encounter. To capture the experience and to keep the message pure, we each wrote down what we remembered from Dad's conversation. Then we compared our notes. There were many "Oh, I forgot he said that" or "Yes, that's the word he used." We compiled his words into one mutually sanctioned accounting. And there we sat on the bed, hugging each other, speechless.

Slowly, very slowly, we realized that we had an opportunity to consciously insert our own agenda into the conversation tomorrow. So we spent the remainder of the night compiling a list of questions, some foolish, some self-serving, some unanswerable. We were giddy with excitement when we finally dozed off to sleep as the night broke unceremoniously into the dawn.

The jarring of the alarm startled us, and we lay still for a moment, letting the events of yesterday percolate. Did it really happen? One look at Molly told me all I needed to know. A second look at the handwritten accounting of our dad's words confirmed it.

On this beautiful day with the sun gleaming through the window panes catching snippets of particles floating to their destination, we would speak with our father again. This time, we would be ready. This time, we would wield pen and paper and capture his words as they poured into our souls.

Dad's Last Visit

September 13, 2009

It was hard to go about our daily schedule knowing that a second visit with our dad was on the horizon. We watched for him, listened for him in every moment of the day. Would he keep his word to revisit us, or was it just a hastily uttered assurance to end the conversation? We couldn't be sure, but we knew our father to be a man of his word, so we trusted in that knowledge.

The moment came near the end of the day as we were entering the last session of the workshop. We were in the doorway poised to step into the room when we once again felt enveloped in a haze. The sights and sounds around us disappeared as we felt his warmth surround us. A hush fell over us, and we breathed in his love. We would have stood there forever had Kim not rescued us.

In her calm, loving, and collected manner, she nudged us out of the steady stream of conference attendees attempting to get around us to enter the small conference room. She pointed to a cozy sitting area in the hallway just outside the door. We were unaware of the conference congestion as they scuttled into the room arranging themselves, finishing up conversations, fetching last-minute water bottles. Their chirpy voices did not penetrate our thoughts. Did they notice us? Did we seem odd to them? Who knows? Who cares! We were engrossed in the words of our father.

The conversation with our dad was off to a jumbled start. The transition to the sofa had been cumbersome, and we missed his greeting, his first words. We sat for a minute, trying to collect our thoughts, to get settled, to encourage him to begin anew. There was an awkward pause, and we were fearful that we had ruined the moment, lost the connection, or defused the energy. We refocused our emotions and our petty human concerns and reached out with the first question on our hastily constructed list.

"Dad, what is heaven like?"

Heaven is not like there. It's lighter. There's no attachment to things. It feels free.

"What emotions are in heaven?"

The only sadness that is here is when we see people we love in pain.

It was as if we had distracted him from his purpose long enough. He seized the moment and spoke the words he wanted us to hear.

Tell Mom, Jesus is okay with reincarnation. Blessed Mother is too. She will believe you. Many of my friends have gone to where Dan is and on to other lifetimes or levels. You go when you're ready to look at possibilities. You're not aware of it in life.

It was an abrupt change of topic, and we wondered if he had been listening to our conversation last night in our room. The subject of reincarnation made us uncomfortable, so instead we changed the topic and asked a question from our list. "Have you seen Jesus and Blessed Mary?"

Yes. Yes. They are around a lot. Blessed Mother is not as stern looking as in the pictures.

Sometime in the past year or so, at one of our sister gatherings, Pam, Molly, and I were discussing a book we had read, *Out of Egypt*, by Anne Rice. We were lamenting how little is actually known about Jesus and his mother in the early days. An inordinate amount of artwork portrays her as sad, serious, somber, and yes, Dad, stern, rather than highlighting the joyful moments, which certainly must have been present in her mothering. Had Dad been listening to our conversation even then?

I am not an earthbound spirit. They stay there because they are connected to things, people. I'm waiting for Mom. In this level, I can still go there, not from the next.

There were noticeable changes in our dad; he saw the world differently. Sometimes, those differences were too great to overcome and reconcile into our understanding. During the years since his death, it was undeniable—our father had continued to grow and evolve just as we had. What a concept! Yet through it all, he remained the true essence of our dad.

People are still healing here. I helped Dan. He's in preparation now. Humans can't know what that's about, because he is on a different plane. You can get to a different level. We are both in the middle plane now. Dan is preparing for his new blueprint and is checking out future families. He is understanding his mission. Dan's dying brought our family closer together.

Hmmm, that is true. When our family lost Dan, we held fast to each other. We shared our grief, expanded our love, and bonded more tightly together. Could that be the reason he died? Is that a significant reason or just a pleasant consequence? Perhaps we are not meant to know the answers…in this world.

I remember the three boys together swinging each other around. Very happy.

Oh yes, the three brothers—Mike, Al, and Dan—had swung each other on that tire swing until they fell to the ground or threw up or both!

I have been connecting to Mom a lot. She is in pain now. Tell her, "It's EASY! You are on the right path."

Mom's right path had included so many faithful and holy contributions. Besides the usual attendance at weekly and often daily Mass, she prayed regularly throughout her day. She baked cookies, pies, and yeast rolls to deliver to the elderly and shut-ins in her area. Dad was probably also referring to her efforts to feed and clothe the less fortunate via St. Vincent's.

This Christmas should be a celebration of life, everyone's life. All the family together. I will be there. Sing songs. She knows that I loved Christmas so much. It will touch her heart. That will show her how safe it is. Jesus should be celebrated.

Hmmm, both messages sounded like a repeat of yesterday's words. Perhaps this is important. And why is that? What is he trying to tell us with such intensity?

I've met Jesus and Mary. Lots of beautiful beings. Wonderful, more than you could want or wish for. It's not scary.

We asked him, "What does Mom need from us?"

She's in a lot of pain now. You guys are very skilled in knowing what to do for that.

We are blessed with three medical professionals in our family, to answer her immediate needs. Was there more that we could and should be doing to help? Mom was so stoic it was sometimes difficult to tell and we didn't press for more specifics.

Like in my passing, what you all did for me.

Ah, we remembered how special that had been for us and obviously for our dad too, though we didn't know if he was even conscious enough to share it with us at the time of his passing. We remembered the singing and our cross necklaces placed on his chest. We remembered holding hands and graciously, lovingly passing him on to the next world, passing him into Jesus's arms and out of ours.

My sisters and I had been worrying about all of us being present when Mom passed. What if there wasn't time to get there? What if it happened when she was visiting my sisters out of state? How could Dad know this? How is it that he was so conscious of our concerns?

Your intention to be there is enough. Okay, but you may not all be present for Mom, maybe one or two of you. I'll be there for her.

It's funny how much we worry about making the last moments on earth special when an entire lifetime preceded that one, comparatively inconsequential moment.

Lily.

We aren't sure why he said this. It's not her favorite flower, and we are not aware that it holds any particular significance. We don't know anyone named Lily or Lilly if that's what he meant. We'll have to ask Mom about this. We didn't ask Dad to clarify because the very next words he sent us *were* important to us.

Mom's Rosary beads—worn, black or burgundy. You know, the ones she uses. Say the Rosary with her. It gives her comfort. Hold her hand.

I try to give you all messages in your sleep. You have to welcome them in. Send white, light, spirit love to each other to help in difficult times.

Really, our father had been trying to reach us in our dreams while we slept? Some days, I awoke thinking of him, feeling close to him, but had not particularly paid attention to the substance of my dreams. Could I connect with him there? Did he also mean that our prayers, our thoughts, our intentions could travel to the siblings in times of trouble, for support, for love? How powerful were our ruminations? Perhaps we should set and direct our intentions instead of lazily allowing our thoughts to tumble pell-mell through our conscious and unconscious minds.

I'm not proud to admit that the next question we asked was totally self-serving. We really wanted financial advice from Dad, but he clearly would not be bothered with hot stock tips or winning lottery numbers. We asked the question, but with his tone and cadence, he shut us down. Oops. He became clearly agitated and closed the subject.

*Money is not important. Money is **NOT** important. I spent too much time worrying about money. Love and family is all that matters. You can't take it with you.*

In this moment, he reached out, and we clearly saw his hand, rubbing the thumb across the fingers as if to symbolize greed. The motion reminded us of the days when we would count our restaurant tips on the floor of the living room, while complaining about our job. With glee on his face, Dad would rub his thumb to forefingers and proclaim, "Money, money, money!" As a father of teenagers, I see that he was trying to instill a work ethic and an appreciation for earning money. That was a far different message and meaning than the one he was delivering now. His final words on the subject were clear.

Let go.

He was chuckling, probably remembering, as we were, the numerous money lessons he taught us growing up. Is letting go part of the earthly journey or the heavenly one?

It was clear that he was leaving us now as we saw him turn from us and his presence dissipate. I called him back with one quick whimsical question that stopped him in his tracks. He swung around to face us one last time, and we saw all of him looking into our eyes. He dipped his head just enough to listen and register surprise...at our audacity? Our frivolousness? Our humanity?

Dad always loved a good game of penny-nickel poker with his buddies. So I dared to ask him, "Dad, is there poker in heaven?" Was the question sacrilegious? I was almost, almost too embarrassed to ask. His answer and the accompanying gesture tickles me to this day. We clearly saw his chin as Dad threw his head back and gave a huge belly laugh, so characteristic of him, and then uttered the last word we would ever hear from his lips.

YES!

And then he was gone. In that moment, we didn't know, couldn't understand that it was forever this time, really forever.

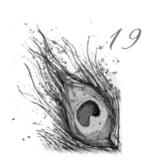

We Replied…and Complied

Soooooo, we have this information; now, what do we do with it? We have to talk to Mom, obviously. Siblings? Others? While the main message of forgiveness could and would be received by Mom and the family, this business about reincarnation would be a concrete stumbling block.

Dad treated this idea so matter-of-factly. Reincarnation is not a solidly held tenet of the Catholic faith and holds scant credence to its validity in our family and among anyone we know. It's not that it was abhorred, but that there were such precious few bits of evidence to support it, not in the Bible nor in Catholic doctrine. It's not preached from the pulpits. It's not mentioned in polite circles. It's too controversial too—out there. Everyone will think we are nuts or worse.

We pondered for a bit, and then just like that, we let it go. "It's not our deal, not our job." Everyone travels their own faith journey, and this was inexplicably ours. We experienced this, and our lives would be forever altered, our belief system expanded. If it touches others—our siblings, Mom, friends, readers—it is not for us to say. It will resonate as it is supposed to and speak to those who need to hear it. Nothing more, nothing less. It is all in the capable hands of God, not us. Our job was to tell Mom and those closest to us. Mom was the hardest, for sure. How mysterious and miraculous are the ways of the Spirit. Now to proceed.

Molly and I chose to share our experience, albeit hesitantly, nervously, with Mom. The first thing we did was call her. "Hey, Mom, we've had a change of plans. You know Molly was going to fly home right after the conference, but instead, we are driving home together to see you."

Of course, she was thrilled, but also a bit curious. Whether there was a nuance in my voice or simply the news of our unexpected visit, she knew something was up. Her mom radar was activated!

Molly and I talked strategies, discussed possible scenarios, but nothing felt comfortable or clear. Instead, we just prayed most of the trip, asking God to guide our thoughts and our words and to help us to speak from the heart. We were going to rock the world of our eighty-seven-year-old mother and wondered if she could handle the shock waves. We prayed for God to prepare Mom's heart to receive Dad's message. We prayed for the Holy Spirit to speak through us, to give us the right words in the right moment. We committed our abilities, limited and human, to Jesus and asked for his strength, guidance, and protection.

We couldn't keep our experience from her; after all, she was the reason Dad came to us at all. We knew he would never do anything to harm her, but what if we handled it wrong, messed it up, stumbled and babbled? We comforted each other with Dad's words, "She will believe."

When we pulled in the driveway, a host of memories flooded back to us. This old, two-story farmhouse was home for us. The house was small, three tiny bedrooms with only one bath, which the eight of us shared; but each room was filled with memories and love. Throughout all our growing-up years, we had always lived here; and now, only Mom remained.

When we arrived home, Mom met us at the door with conflicted emotions. Joy and uncertainty resided in the creases of her well-worn and well-loved expression. She just sensed that something suspicious lay behind our smiling faces. Had the Holy Spirit alerted her? Had Dad been nudging her?

She didn't have to live in ambiguity for long before Molly suggested our well-worn family signal for a private, significant conversation, "Can we talk to you in the bedroom?" Mom knew what that meant; privacy was needed for an important matter. With six kids, privacy and importance had to be signaled, or they would get squashed by the rambunctiousness of a large family living in a very small house. We had begun, and that was the most difficult part.

From there it flowed, we couldn't back out. We let God speak through us, and we shared our notes with her. Dad was right, the mention of Christmas won her over because she knew all too well that Dad loved Christmas. Mom was amazed, as we had been, that Dad already knew that the location for Christmas had been recently changed to my house for the first time and that I had new purple dishes. Her eyes twinkled with the message that he would have a present for her there. "Well, how will he accomplish that, and what 'thing' could ever measure up to the anticipation?" We were all at a loss and tried not to give in to the pressure that was building.

As Mom listened in awe, her tired green eyes closed with solemnity. She felt him near her, sensed his love ever alive, ever present. She accepted our words without a flicker of doubt. The message rang true and resonated in her heart, a heart that the Lord had prepared.

She bowed her head with regret when we reached the crux of Dad's words. Forgiveness. She knew she had languished in hurt and pettiness with Sue Ellen for far too many decades, burying jealousy, irritations, and thoughts of retaliation. Well, maybe not just thoughts; hadn't her actions at St. Vincent's recently been her way of getting even with her sister? While it felt good in the moment, the guilt had plagued her.

She felt ashamed. Her husband had reached his hand through the veil to help her wipe the scar from her heart.

There has to be forgiveness. Tell Mom to write a letter to her sister. It needs to say, "I'm sorry. Forgive me. I forgive you. Even if you don't receive this, I forgive you."

This has divided the family for a long time and caused strife between the families. It doesn't matter if it is received, if Mom writes it and mails it, it will release her.

Silently, she nodded her head. "I will do this. Forgiveness is so important that it brought him here, to warn me, to help me. Of course, I'll do this."

When we reached the money part, Mom huffed a bit. "Well, that's easy for him to say. He's forgotten that it takes money to survive down here," she bristled. "If I didn't have his prison pension and insurance, it would have been a mighty tight fourteen years without him." She was pragmatic to the end, even if Dad, from his new enlightened vantage point, couldn't recall the years of worrying how they would ever feed the children and keep the roof from leaking overhead.

The longing on Mom's face as she heard the words specific to our deceased brother, Dan, was palpable. It is clear that a parent never stops mourning the loss of a child, no matter how much time passes or how faithful the passing. She knew he was in heaven with Dad, joyfully living the afterlife, but it felt so meritorious to have her beliefs confirmed, her faith buoyed.

There was one word that Dad had uttered that meant nothing to Molly and me. Dad had mentioned the word *lily*. We were confident that Mom would be able to enlighten us, but she remained perplexed.

"I held lilies on my wedding day, but roses have always been my favorite."

We talked about it for several minutes when Mom settled the matter, "I'll just ask him when I get there."

"Okay, Mom," I said with a not-so-small lump in my throat. How could we ever bear to lose her too? Can't think about that now. Stay present, stay close to her. Enjoy this moment, here and now. And that's just what we did.

And the moments were enjoyable as we laughed and cried and shared each of Dad's words with reverence and love with the woman who had held his hand and his heart for fifty years.

We talked late into the night, late enough to see the quiet whispers of dawn breaking slowly across the farmland spreading out as far as the eye could see. Land that had been cleared and planted with the sweat from our father's brow. Land that provided the sustenance that kept our family together, healthy, alive, and filled with love.

We spent the night, or what was left of it, in our girlhood bedroom, all warm and snug and loved, in the very house that was once such a ramshackle mess that Mom was embarrassed to even think of allowing her precious children to be raised in such squalor. A thousand times I've wished to return to this cocoon, when times were hard, confusing, and lonely. It would be so comforting to just lose myself in a memory. But that was so very long ago, and this moment was not about my life, my memories, my experience—it was about hers.

While we were swaddled with the warm memories of our childhood upstairs, Mom sat alone downstairs. With pen in hand, she released herself from the accumulation of hard feelings toward her sister. She carefully wrote the words exactly as Ken had directed and sealed them in an envelope.

The rays from the breaking dawn were vibrant, with shards of yellow and magenta streaking the horizon. She tilted her head upward and felt the brisk air against her cheek as she offered up a prayer of thanksgiving, of love, of fidelity. The envelope addressed to Sue Ellen was reverently placed in the mailbox at the end of the gravel driveway. She stood staring at stars, so far away and watched their luster slip away as the dawn overshadowed them. God's presence was all around her. "Thank you for sending Kenny to me long ago and now. I will embrace every word. Please forgive my sins, Father." She closed her eyes and found comfort in God's promises and His forgiveness.

"Bear with each other and forgive one another if any of you has a grievance against someone. Forgive as the Lord forgave you" (Colossians 3:13).

We awoke as we had so many years ago to the aroma of freshly brewed coffee and bacon sizzling on the griddle. We were enchanted by the sweet scent of Mom's legendary yeast rolls, Dad's longtime favorite. We spoke very little that morning of the things that had transpired. We were spent.

Our farewell was heart-wrenching. We didn't want to leave, but our adult lives beckoned. How would we re-enter the world after having experienced such a connection? How would we explain it to our spouses, our siblings, our children...our friends, our neighbors, our Bible study group, you?

Mom's well-worn words of wisdom provided the answer we sought. "Don't borrow trouble." And so we didn't. With kisses and hugs and promises to talk soon, we went our separate ways, leaving Mom to her thoughts. She stood at the window, waving to us, with her faith intact and her heart overflowing with love. Her thoughts turned to her husband, whose tender words still echoed in her soul.

20

We Wouldn't Say So till We
Tried...to Gather

Where our plans for Christmas were tentative before, they were now driven...by our father's words, by our emotions, by the very real possibility that this would be our last Christmas with Mom. Dad had suggested that he would have a special gift waiting for Mom, and we knew that somehow, we needed to be his hands. Without guidance or advice, we pondered the meaning of his words. What special gift did he imagine for the woman who had shared fifty years with him and bore him six beautiful children, speaking, of course, with loads of bias. How could anything tangible left on earth compare to that?

We thought and we prayed and we scoured our notes for clues. Dad had mentioned that he would send us messages and sayings if we were only paying attention. And so we did, all of us. We watched for his presence in the mundane happenings of daily life. An old picture showing up on the floor of the closet, a newspaper article about John Deere tractors, a poem or a drawing, a tiny snip of carpet from the old house, Beemans gum, a guitar pick, a fish hook. Everyone in the family wrote notes of things they remembered, things that were important, and things merely whimsical or fun or sentimental. We tried to remember all of Dad's favorite limericks, poems, jokes and wrote them down. From all corners of the family, Dad's gift for Mom began to materialize.

All hands in the family working with one mission, together as if one body, it felt like the church. God calls on the talents and the gifts of each person to contribute to the whole. Preparing Mom's gift taught us to be more watchful for messages from heaven. We felt more connected, less alone, more inspired, as if God were winking at us. "See this, feel that. I made this for you to enjoy. Pay attention. I am with you always."

There was an undercurrent of urgency, and that sentiment, if not the message, was catapulted throughout the family ranks. One by one, every family member made arrangements to return to Michigan for this one special Christmas. Mom's five living children would be physically present, plus Dan and Dad in spirit. All the spouses would be in attendance with all the grandchildren. Even three of the four precious great-grandchildren (Melanie, Miranda, and Joseph), whom Dad had never physically met, would share in the family bonding. Jace, a great-grandson, was absent only because he was too young to travel and lived so far away. He was loved and missed!

It would be a full house for sure, not nearly enough bedrooms or refrigerators or bathrooms for the whole tribe, but we would manage. Mom and I cooked for days, easy meals that we could make in advance. She tired easily, and I worried that the festivities might prove too much for her. She had needed several blood transfusions to perk up her energy, and that worried us all. Pam Dickson, Pam Stanberry, and Molly Clark, our family medical experts, were monitoring her condition closely.

The preparations were underway. Some relatives flew in, others drove. One by one, they arrived, laden with extra pillows and blankets, gifts, festive food, and love—lots and lots of love.

Each adult brought a bundle of specially requested items to complete Dad's heartfelt Christmas present to Mom. They were placed in an intricately carved memory box with a gold-leaf-embossed lid that was beautifully wrapped and lovingly placed beneath the fifteen-foot-tall flocked Christmas tree that dominated the room, the tree that Dad had remembered and mentioned in his visit to us. A tree that had rested uselessly in the attic for years. It was too cumbersome, too complicated to get down and too messy to be practical without little children to enjoy it. But this Christmas was different. The house was alive with family, and the tree was the backdrop as the Dicksons gathered all together for the last time, although no one was really sure that it truly was the last time, until it was.

The logistics of the weekend fell together effortlessly with different family members stepping forward to get the masses fed. Others spearheaded the cleanup efforts and still others organized and directed the sleeping arrangements. While it was challenging, to be sure, there was not a harsh word spoken or a negative thought spawned. Peace reigned supreme, if only for the weekend, and that was enough.

After the main meal was consumed, I played the guitar, and we sang Christmas carols. The Bible reading of the birth of Christ set the tone and tenor for the evening's events, after which an important conversation was broached, tentatively, but with the inner confidence born from firsthand experience and steadfast faith in the power of love, both here and beyond.

Molly and I shared our experience with Dad as simply and as honestly as we could. We presented copies of our notes to each member of the family. An incredulous silence engulfed the room as the reality took root in the hearts and minds of all those present. Here and there, a tear was wiped until all of Dad's messages had been shared.

It was difficult, for sure, but in this space surrounded by everyone our dad and mom loved, it was safe. Safer, for sure, than my attempt to write this book and share it with the world.

Mom's cheeks flushed as she spoke up, "I sent the forgiveness letter to my sister the very night I heard the message, and she sent an identical one back to me. When I received it, I felt a pressure lift from my chest. I could breathe better. I was lighter. I called her immediately, and shared the news about Kenny's visits. We cried for what seemed like hours on the phone, neither of us wanted to hang up. We've been talking ever since. I never knew the importance of true forgiveness and how that feels, until Kenny emphasized it with his words. Remember this lesson in your life."

"For if you forgive other people when they sin against you, your heavenly Father will also forgive you. But if you do not forgive others their sins, your Father will not forgive your sins" (Matthew 6:14–15).

The pinnacle of our Dad's love was realized in the collection of memories that we had all gathered on his behalf, his final gift to her. The room fell silent when his gift was presented to Mom. "I can't imagine what else he can give me. Really, what else do I need? You are all here, and that is an answer to my prayers. I want you to know how much I love you and pray for you. That will never stop, ever."

The tears in her eyes were obscured by the glasses perched on her nose. She looked down through the lower half of the lenses to get a better view of the miracle she was holding, a final gift from her husband, dead now for fourteen long years.

As she unwrapped Dad's present, she noticed the lid that read, "**FAITH**—Every Good And Perfect Gift Is From Above."

When she lifted the lid, the package of Beemans gum caught her attention first. How he had loved to tease her about her gum-chewing habit. Family memories too precious to process instantly began to settle into her soul as she touched them one by one—a small cross, a snippet of carpeting from the old house, a prayer card, a lock of hair tied with a ribbon, a child's drawing, a label from a container of chocolate ice cream, a ring, pictures, Dad's pocket watch, poetry, jokes from the newspaper, a poker chip. It was a veritable fountain of memories, of life, of love. A weighty silence engulfed the room as each person marveled at the incredible gift. She wrinkled up her nose to hold back the tears while melancholy and nostalgia claimed her heart. She sat sedately, quietly allowing the feelings to swirl within her.

Dad had found a way to reach out to her from the grave. His words, his life, his experiences lay before her mirrored through the eyes of their children, grandchildren, and even great-grandchildren.

There were many more memories that they shared, of course, but these were the important ones, the ones that would go the distance and travel down through the generations, God willing. These were the memories that had taken root in the children; their legacy lived on.

Mom smiled for all that had taken place throughout their fifty years together. She smiled self-consciously, at the loving faces gathered in her honor. She smiled at the box filled with love that lay on her lap, waiting to be rediscovered. But most importantly, Mom sent a smile of thanks to God for allowing all this abundance.

Our Christmas ended too quickly as family members had lives to resume. Mom left with Molly to spend a month in Texas, followed by another month in Kansas with Pam. The Michigan winters were cold and unforgiving, and our mother appreciated the respite.

On the final leg of her journey in Wichita, with Pam there to help, Mom's fortitude dwindled. Weekly blood transfusions were required to barely maintain her life, a diminished existence bereft of the exuberance and joy that she had cherished all her days. She slept far too much and lost the strength to engage her daughter in chatty conversation, a hallmark of the Dickson tradition.

"She's becoming so weak," Pam mused. "How long can she continue?" These were Pam's thoughts as she focused on dressing for 6:30 a.m. Mass at St. Elizabeth Ann Seton Church after which, Mom would need to be returned to the house before Pam could head out for work. Mom loved to attend daily Mass whenever she felt strong enough. She had an intense appreciation of the Eucharist and wanted to frequently experience a deep connection with the Lord.

Pam hurried from her bedroom, calling, "Mom, are you ready?" She found Mom sitting in the living room with her shoulders slumped, her heavy coat draped over her thin shoulders, her pocketbook hanging across her chest. With a trembling voice, she spoke quietly, "I can't go today. I am so tired. I can't keep going on like this." Pam stopped in her tracks and reached for our mother's frail hands, barely breathing. "Mom, what are you saying?" Pam asked. Mom softly replied, "I am ready to go to heaven to be with Dad."

Mom's voice quivered as she spoke. "I want to see a priest. I need to have peace in this decision to continue with the transfusions or not." Pam swallowed her emotions and supported our mother's decision to explore her options.

Father Matt Marney, the local priest at St. Elizabeth Ann Seton, was summoned on a chilly Kansas weekday just after the last of the ice had fallen from the trees. The ground beneath was sprouting hints of green, which forecast the amplitude to follow. The sky was the deep vivid blue of spring, crisp and sparkling, sending out a gentle but nippy breeze to remind every living creature that winter had not entirely given up its grasp. In the warmth of Pam's home, however, with Pam busying herself in the next room, Mom found the answers she sought.

Fr. Marney was recently ordained, and the Spirit of Christ radiated from his countenance. His brown eyes focused intently as he engaged Mom in gentle conversation. He placed his young, strong hand on hers, and together they prayed. When Mom finally gathered the courage to ask the questions she was almost embarrassed to put to words, Fr. Marney was neither appalled nor unnerved. He lovingly explained that extreme measures to prolong life are never mandated by the church or by God. While suicide, of course, was not endorsed, any external medical intervention could be rejected. With this reassurance, Mom's conscience was put at ease. She declined further treatment.

Pam sat with her in silence after the priest left. "What can I do to help, Mom?"

"I want to receive daily Communion, but I can't make it to the church," Mom responded.

"Don't worry, Mom, I'll figure it out with Fr. Marney."

Without regard to his burgeoning pastoral obligations, Fr. Marney compassionately volunteered to visit Mom daily and bring her Communion himself. He likewise brought comfort, companionship, and counsel to her last days as she shared her motherly wisdom.

Mom called each of us children, explaining her decision to decline further treatment. "I want to go home to be with God. Kenny has waited there for fourteen long years. I'm ready. It's time."

While shock and disbelief registered with a thud, the final nod of selfless love was given by each of us to a mother who had loved, nurtured, and supported us through every step of our lives. Now it was our turn to support her decision even though it was so painful to endorse. We took turns traveling to see her, a final pilgrimage to spend one last weekend privately with the woman who had given us life and love and so much more.

When I first saw Mom on my last weekend, I was struck by how much her health had deteriorated in just a few months' time. She was pale, listless, and slept much of the time. I sat with her, held her hand, and prayed for the journey she would soon take without me, without any of us.

During one of her awake moments, she lovingly reminded me to read my poem at her funeral Mass. I blinked my assent, embarrassed that I had not remembered it. It seemed ages since Dad's passing; a lot had transpired in those fourteen years. The most incredible was watching my mother grow in confidence, poise, and faith. Out of necessity at first, she became more outgoing, even funnier. Our Dad's shadow, when he was alive, was larger than life, and Mom relished the shade. In his absence, she had evolved. "I guess life really does go on," I thought to myself as I sat at my mother's deathbed, grasping solace where there was precious little.

As she lay silently, listening to my fears, my concerns, my emotions, I was reminded of the countless times we'd spent the entire night talking. Her open invitation stood as a testament of her love, "You can talk, and I'll listen as long as you need me to listen about anything you want to talk about." Tears trickled down my cheeks. "I will miss you so much, Mom."

When my time was over, it was so hard to say good-bye; truthfully, it was hard for her too, but she solemnly, bravely derided, "Well, did you think I was going to live here forever?"

"I wanted you to, Mom, I wanted you to live with us forever," I sobbed.

Always the mother, Mom weakly smiled. "I can see that you think that is best for you, but this is what is best for me. It's time, Debzi D, it's time. I want you to know that when I get to heaven, the first thing I'm going to do is whisper into the ear of God about your retirement."

Our State Department of Education had been bantering about the idea of an early retirement incentive for seasoned educators, but no clear decision had been reached. At fifty-three, I wasn't even sure I wanted to retire *if* I qualified, but our mother was adamant.

"You have to do this, if you can. There is a big and wonderful world out there that you are missing because you work so many hours. The stress is wearing you down, shortening your life, eating at the joy you should be experiencing. You need to spend more time with those you love, because in the end, that's what really matters most."

The words, so laden with maternal devotion, took me by surprise, and I choked on my reply, "Oh no, Mom, if you get a chance to whisper into the ear of God, plead for something incredibly important like world peace or an end to sickness or strife or pain."

Mom's response came from the wellspring of motherly love where the welfare of her own precious children takes top priority. "Oh, Debi, there *is* nothing more important than you."

Her words fell solidly on my chest, where I stood humbled by my mother's devotion even in her last moments on earth. While I often felt like an only child basking in the total adulation of my parents, I realized, of course, that all my siblings felt the same. Mom had a list of prayers for each of us, shared on her deathbed, which she intended to deliver in person to the Almighty.

From then on, tears were shed in private. If our mother could be this brave, shouldn't we do the same? We didn't want to make this any harder on her or on us. None of us wanted to muddle what precious time we had with tears and lamentation.

When she was strong and alert enough, she shared new lessons or reinforced old ones with fresh insight, wisdom, and love. We listened more closely, coveting every last word, knowing it was really the last. "Somehow," she whispered quietly, "I managed to perform what I was meant to do. I've lived a good life and I want that for you."

When Molly made her pilgrimage to our Mother's bedside, she was cognizant of the fact that it was her final chance to share her heart with mom in physical form. Mom had prayed for each of us children every day and encouraged us to pursue our unique talents and dreams. Mom said, "I'm so proud of you, Molly. The therapy you do touches people in deep ways and heals them of their pain. Tell me your dreams, Molly. I'll continue to pray for you even after I die." Molly had tears in her eyes at the profound gift of a praying mother, and the impact that has on a child forever.

By the end of Al's visit, Mom's strength was visibly waning. Her thoughts were tight as she whispered, "Alan, I have a favor to ask you."

"Of course, Mom, anything."

"Holy communion is the most powerful gift Jesus has given us. I've been blessed here because Pam has made sure that I receive it almost every day as I wait for God to call me home, but there are six lonely shut-ins near the church who are not so lucky. When I'm there, I bring them communion after Sunday Mass. Will you do that for me until they are called to heaven?"

Al took a deep breath before responding, "Of course, I will." Impulsively he cringed as he mentally added the new task to his already stacked list of responsibilities. Work was time-consuming, and the home tasks never ended. His daughter, Daneel, was actively involved in so many school and social activities; their calendar screeched from the pace. Even the summer months were packed full as Daneel adored baseball and worked with a private pitching coach, in addition to the regularly scheduled practices and games at school.

Unexpectedly, Dad popped into Al's thoughts, which brought a warm, but short-lived grin to his somber lips. For not the first time, he wished that Dad were still alive. How excited he would have been to watch his granddaughter excel at baseball, his favorite sport. Did he know? Life really wasn't fair, and now Daneel was losing her "Gramma D" too. The full impact of that realization was crushing.

In the end, all of us children respected our mom's wishes and her wisdom. We followed her example and sent up a multitude of prayers. She had always been the family prayer horse.

"Mom, can you pray during my job interview?"

"Hey, Mom, the baby's been sick for a week, can you send up some prayers?"

"Can you add my neighbor to your prayer list?"

"I'm trying to buy a sealcoat business, the medicine isn't working, I might need surgery, we're having trouble, we're behind on the bills, there's a pain in my back, do you think I should...please pray." Now, it was our turn to surround her in prayer, and we did.

Our mother traveled quietly in her sleep on a late winter morning in 2010 to her heavenly home. Each of us children felt certain that our dad was waiting at the pearly gate as promised. She entered the kingdom of heaven where she rests, learns, and grows in wisdom while she waits for each of her precious children to join her. Naturally, we will, one day, in the not-so-distant future. Do we expect to live here forever? No, that's not the way of things. Sadly, it's just not. We children take comfort in the words of our father—forgive and love, that's the essence of life.

Et Cetera

Final Thoughts

About the Author

Gratitudes

Contributors

Thoughts to Ponder

Epilogue

Within short order, the State Department of Education must have received their marching orders from On-High, for miraculously, their early retirement stipulations aligned perfectly with my unique situation, and I accepted their offer. Thanks, Mom! Thanks, God!

Every good and joyous memory I've ever had in all my years has included my parents. They are a part of me, and I'm a part of them. A circle of love this strong can never be severed. We will love forever but just not here, and that's a very long time.

I'd like to say we were able to talk Dad into visiting us regularly for private tutoring sessions to get us through the rest of our lives, but that never materialized. Instead, we were granted just these two visits from him and none from Mom.

The lessons are clear: keep your heart on the Lord and only the Lord. Follow Him because He will never leave you or lead you astray. Love Him, love each other and forgive, forgive, forgive. Nothing else matters.

It is my belief that when Mom arrived in heaven, Dad took her hand and they moved on to the next level from which communication with us is not an option. Of course…it's entirely possible that he is just too busy catching up on all the news from Mom.

Afterword

Good prickled at me for months to get busy with it! I was scared. The task was daunting. What in heaven's name do I know about writing a book, even less about agents/editors/publishers? No one's going to believe me anyway. What a colossal waste of time, and besides, as the poem goes, "Somebody said that it couldn't be done."

But He was relentless. He would wake me up in the middle of the night with book thoughts and interject phrases and content ideas during my daily prayer times. His ministrations intruded on my waking tasks, interrupted telephone conversations, wreaked havoc on my concentration while driving or painting or playing with grandbabies. Try as I might, I just couldn't get away from it. Even at Church, I could not escape the needling. I prayed about it, felt confident in His answer, and did what we all do best when faced with a momentous task: I procrastinated, of course.

At just the precise moment when I needed inspiration the most, He sent this bible verse to me through a dear friend, Carol Lucas. She said she felt an uncanny push to share it with me, like God was nudging her.

The verse is from Isaiah 55:11:

> "So is my word that goes out from my mouth:
> It will not return to me empty, but will accomplish what I desire and achieve the purpose for which I sent it."

Finally, one Lent, I made it my offering to write for an hour every day. It surprised me every time that I could never keep the writing to an hour, as night after night disappeared behind the glow of my computer screen and turned into month after month.

I found courage in Mother Teresa's words, "In spite of all our defects, God is in love with us and keeps using us to light the light of love and compassion in the world."

The words flowed through me, unbidden and effortlessly. "With a bit of a grin on his chin," God had placed them there for me to discover and put on the page. For what purpose, that's not for me to say. I completed the task that He set before me. God's will be done.

So here it is, *The Words of Our Father*, for better or worse; it's entirely up to God now.

Meet Debi Dickson Wagner

Debi Dickson Wagner retired as an elementary principal from Ann Arbor Public Schools after thirty-four years in education, including a full-time position with the Michigan Department of Education. She has two grown sons, Justin and Barron Roberts, plus three stepchildren—Kyle, Seth, and Elizabeth Wagner. They all live in close proximity to her home in Adrian, Michigan. Debi winters with her husband, Richard, in Cape Coral, Florida. They are faithful parishioners in both locations, Holy Family Parish and St. Katharine Drexel.

In addition to writing, Debi enjoys exotic travel, scuba diving, painting, mosaic work and Euchre. Her grandchildren light up her life with simple, unembellished family fun; playing Aggravation, going for nature walks, and creating finger-painted masterpieces. She holds fast to her faith and encourages her children and grandchildren to do the same. She tries to live by her mother's words, "Love God and love each other!"

Personal Reflections

What do I believe? I believe that this life and the afterlife are more complex than we can comprehend. I don't possess, nor do I need to know, all of life's answers right now. I know this experience opened my eyes and awakened me to God's gentle whispering in my own heart. Through Him all things are possible, especially love and forgiveness in a world that struggles to embrace both.

Someday, I pray my dear grandchildren will want to read this book and talk with me about my experience. Conversations that transcend comprehension are not the easiest. I hope I find the wisdom to invite them to share in the wonder of God's love and to grasp the healing power of His forgiveness.

May this book bless you, my gentle reader, with joy, hope, harmony and a sense of triumphant celebration for the abundance of miracles and mysteries that surround all of our lives.

*"Some things are true...
whether we believe in them or not."*

(Spoken by the angel Seth, in the movie *City of Angels*)

Acknowledgements

I am forever indebted to Joseph Magnoli, the Covenant Books acquisition agent, and his team of readers for picking my manuscript for publication and to Bentley Thurlow, my publication assistant, for persevering with me through the long and tedious editing, re-editing and seemingly endless revisions.

Likewise, it was an honor and a pleasure to fine-tune the manuscript with the insightful assistance of the President of Operations, Denice Hunter. Your patience, promptness, cooperation, wisdom, professional advice, and steadfast attention to detail made all the difference! You were a joyful addition to my team. Thanks for standing faithfully beside me with such a positive attitude.

Additionally, I'm grateful to the editing and typesetting crew for your tenacity when our opinions differed. As always, you were right. Thanks for being gentle, kind and caring. The personal touch at Covenant Books has been a cozy fit for me and my book. Such a miracle!

The cover illustration rocks, thanks to my dear friend Norma Jean Sass' undeniable artistic talents. I had hoped for something colorful, happy, lighthearted, and fun, and it certainly is that and more. The pair of feathers reminds me of my parents; Dad flamboyant and larger than life, Mom nestled closely in his shadow, basking in his love, glowing with contentment. The cover alone makes me smile. A special thanks to Covenant's art department for allowing us to creatively depart from protocol. Bless you!

In particular, I offer bottomless gratitude to my family for your thoughtful and engaging perspective, especially my sister

Pam, the family historian, for your emulsifying feedback, research skills, and fact-checking talents. You were like my own private sous chef, always by my side, mincing words to just the right consistency, fetching this, foraging for that, dicing, blending, supporting, spreading on the wisdom, flavoring my manuscript to make it more nourishing and certainly yummier. I really 'kneaded' you! Similarly, my sister Molly was invaluable with your ruthless knack for synthesizing and slashing superfluous words, sometimes to my chagrin. I treasure you both and you are forever etched in my heart.

I offer loving appreciation to my longtime confidant and adopted sister, Melissa Elliott, who is a scrupulous and tenacious grammar guru. Thank you for pointing out all of my linguistic failings in the nicest possible way and for patiently and lovingly accepting all the times I totally ignored your advice.

Steve Gardner and Cindy Larson, my unofficial editors, offered excellent suggestions and challenged me to objectively evaluate my manuscript more expansively from a non-family perspective. Thank you for your palatable frankness laced with love and encouragement, shared at just the right times to spur me onward. Your perspectives helped renew my confidence that the final product would have a positive impact however God intended.

Our old family friend, Colleen Holland Rufenacht, an Ancestry aficionado, supported me by chasing down names, dates, places, and the minutia necessary to bring this story alive, even though many of the characters were not. You opened the door for prompt feedback from the Bean Creek Valley History Center in Fayette, Ohio, who were enormously cooperative.

I offer heartfelt appreciation for two special groups of women who comprise my favorite book clubs: Read 'Em and Eat in Michigan and Paradise Book Club in Florida. Your supportive words of encouragement and faithful prayers for me and this book were empowering. Thank you!

The development of this manuscript has brought me back in contact with some long-lost cousins, whom I cherish—Peggy

Irwin Parran, Lisa Dickson, the Murphy clan. All our parents must be so happy. We not only share genetics, but faith as well. Let's stay in touch!

Above all I give boundless thanks and praise to Almighty God, who never doubted my ability to finish the work, even when I stumbled, procrastinated, and pouted. He has proven once again that "all things turn to good to those who love the Lord" (Roman's 8:28).

ACKNOWLEDGEMENTS

Reference Section

Molly Clark PT, LMT
713-677-3535
Mollyclarktherapy.com

Molly Clark received her Physical Therapy degree from Grand Valley State University in 1989. She has extensive training in advanced healing skills with the Chikly Health Institute (CHI) and has taught this leading-edge curriculum worldwide for twenty years. Ms. Clark is a member of the International Alliance of Healthcare Practitioners. She listens to the innate wisdom of the body and works with it to bring health and healing on many levels. Her specialties include relieving chronic pain, fibromyalgia, spinal pain, and chronic head injuries (CTE). Her private practice is in Chattanooga, Tennessee.

Alaya Chikly
Chikly Health Institute (CHI)
480-999-0808 or 888-333-1055
Trainings@ChiklyInstitute.com

Alaya Chikly is the creator of a healing emotional experience, Heart Centered Therapy, that calls upon the wisdom of the heart to transform trauma without reliving it, held in the safety, love, and compassion of the heart.

As a young woman, Alaya traveled for twelve years overseas, looking for a deeper truth and understanding of life. She studied with teachers in Israel, Thailand, France, and India. She has a BA degree as well but proclaims that her education was not what gave her the resources to fulfill her mission, nor create her work and her classes. Instead, it was the gift of knowing that everything she needed to know was in her heart. The heart naturally understands how to unify and dissolve beliefs and mental constructs that may hold pain, confusion, and/or separation.

By clearing the limiting family and ancestral beliefs and, above all, the most damaging belief, "I am not loved," opened the gateway to inner wisdom and clarity. Her work restores trust in life and rejuvenates self-confidence. It restores the foundational love bonds of mother-father, the basis of all relationships. Once we identify who we are not, we are free to discover who we truly are.

Kimberly Ann Egberts M.S.
Spiritual Healer,
Spiral Healing Waves
207-653-8263
kimberlyannintuitive@gmail.com

Kimberly Ann Egberts has been working in the field of healing arts for over twenty years and is a member of the International Alliance of Health Practitioners. She is a spiritual healer, who uses her abilities to create profound change in her clients.

Ms. Egberts initially studied psychology and received a BA from SUNY at Stony Brook, New York. She received a masters degree from NOVA Southeastern University, Florida, in 1990 in the area of communication disorders and worked as a Speech-Language Pathologist.

She expanded her studies of gentle body and energy work with Chikly Health Institute, which led to an awakening of her intuitive nature and her ability to see beyond the physical form. Her journey, integrating healing arts and mediumship, began in 1990 and continues today. Kimberly is associated with Upledger

Institute, and is the founder of Spiral Healing Waves. She believes life is a journey of self-discovery and learning.

Norma Jean Sass
Artist
248-761-5885
sassynjs@gmail.com

Norma Jean Sass has a passion for art that takes her in many directions. Although she has always loved art, a demanding career and a family with three children and a Great Dane often left it out of reach. Now that she is retired and residing in Florida, she is free to explore sculpture, as well as watercolor, pastels, and acrylic mediums. Grandmother to seven and an avid animal lover, it is no wonder her favorite subjects are children and animals. She has won awards with her pet portraits. Contact Norma Jean by email if you would like a portrait of that special pet or person. She would enjoy sharing some of her work with you.

Alanah Lucas
Capture the Dream Photography
ctdphotographylee@gmail.com
239-634-5888
alanahlu@aol.com

Alanah Lucas received her first camera when she was eleven and has been snapping photos ever since. Her gallery experience includes pets, babies, families, special events, and even wildlife art. She has a creative flare that adds a level of artistic fun to the photo shoot. Her sessions include candid and posed photos, which beautifully captures the essence of each individual. Alanah's ready smile and comforting nature relaxes even the most reluctant subject.

Ms. Lucas began her photography career in sunny Florida, near a host of picturesque settings, such as Bowditch Point at Fort Myers Beach, which was the location for Debi Wagner's author photo. In addition to destination photo shoots, she also makes home visits. Her business has recently expanded to Sylva, North Carolina which provides an awe-inspiring cornucopia of scenery options to expand and enrich her portfolio.

Her companion business is graphic design, where she can turn your photos into art, cards, posters, etc. The commercial aspect includes photo layouts for print copies and other marketing tools to assist companies in promoting their business.

Colleen Rufenacht
419-388-3518
beancreekhistory@gmail.com

Colleen Rufenacht was instrumental in the success of the Country Music Round-up which operated from 1963 to 1979. Her musical talent served her well as co-owner of Grisier's Music store in Archbold, Ohio. With a team of dedicated historians, she helped to establish the Bean Creek Valley History Center in Fayette, Ohio, where she has served as president for five years. She currently teaches guitar lessons in Fayette, where she is on the board of the Fayette Opera House.

Biblical Support

God forgives us	I John 1:9, Romans 8:1
God loves us	John 3:16, John 3:34
We are not alone	Hebrews 13:5
No need to worry	I Peter 5:7
Love God	Deuteronomy 6:5
Love each other	John 15:9-17
Wisdom	I Corinthians 1:30
Grace	Psalm 91:15
Courage	II Timothy 1:7
Guidance	Proverbs 3:5-6
Faith	Hebrew 11
Hope	Psalm 38:15
Forgiveness	Colossians 3:13
	Ephesians 4:31-32
	Mark 11:25
	Romans 12:18-21
	Luke 6:35-36
	Proverbs 10:12
	Matthew 6:12

Questions and Topics
for Discussion

1. In chapter 7, Noreen uncharacteristically examines her own career path. What is her emotional response to the lack of possibilities? Was her career path predetermined, or did she choose it freely? How are things the same and different today for women?

2. What personal sacrifices did Ken make for his wife and children? In what ways do you think he behaved selfishly?

3. Discuss instances when Noreen exhibited personal strength or an independent nature. Who do you think was the most surprised by her actions?

4. The book is about the importance of forgiveness. Ken suggested one way for Noreen to allow forgiveness to enter into her relationship with her sister. What are other ways to bring about forgiveness? Who benefits most? Do you think our actions on Earth affect our experience in Heaven?

5. For the survival of the family, Leola returned to her brother for assistance. How do you think she felt? How did her brother feel? Were there other options available to her?

6. What was the impetus for Ken's return fourteen years after his death? Was he successful in his mission? How did his messages enhance the lives of his family?

7. Discuss Noreen's view of divorce, culturally and religiously, in the context of society in 1948. Do you think she would have had the courage to go through with it, if he continued drinking? How might they differ from her mother's views?

Her daughters? Her granddaughters? In your opinion, is divorce ever justified?

8. How did Noreen succeed in raising career-minded daughters from a farm wife's experience? What were her tactics? Who were her role models? Who were your role models and how did they influence your life? Were there negative influences or social pressures that likewise impacted your life choices?

9. How do you think you would react if messages were delivered to you from beyond this life?

10. What are your thoughts about Noreen's decision to allow her life to end?

11. Do you think Noreen approved of Ken's career choices—farming and prison guard—or did she just go along? Why or why not?

12. How do you think Noreen really felt about being left alone on her birthday each year? Was there a different way to resolve the birthday-versus-hunting dilemma?

13. Ken's information about reincarnation was a shock to the author and her family. Why did the sisters worry about sharing the messages with their mother? Were you surprised by her reaction? Do you think the sisters should have kept that information to themselves to protect their mom? Other family members? You?

14. Why was it easier for Noreen to forgive her mother-in-law, Leola, for snooping in her dresser drawer than it was for her to forgive her sister? How does timing play a role?

15. What are the hardest things to forgive?

16. The generation who experienced the Great Depression is known for their self-sacrifice. How has that changed in today's more secular world? Why?

17. Which of the characters do you most identify with and why?

18. It was difficult for the author to tell this story as most people would typically try to keep this type of experi-

ence private. Why is it difficult to discuss? Have you or anyone you've known had a supernatural experience? How does it feel to share it with others?

19. Losing a child is always difficult. Discuss some of the ways people deal with such a loss.

20. What historical fact about the dust bowl were you especially surprised to discover? The book describes several potential causes for the dust bowl. Can you think of others? How does that event compare and contrast with other natural disasters today such as woodland fires, hurricanes, flooding, drought, and extreme temperatures?

21. The Irwin fire was temporarily devastating, but turned out to be beneficial. Describe a time when something in your life felt catastrophic but worked out positively in the end.

22. Infertility is often a very personal and painful experience. Noreen fielded many inconsiderate comments by family, friends, and acquaintances. Describe a time in your life when questions that were too personal made you uncomfortable. How do you handle an unwanted inquisition?

23. In what ways did Ken and Noreen try to decrease the stigma and pressure around Dan's disability? Are there other things they could have done? How are things different and the same today?

24. Parents often feel responsible for their children long after they have left home. When is the appropriate time to let children lead their own lives?

25. Living through the death of a child and a spouse are both unimaginable. In what ways are they the same, and in what ways are they different? Describe the various coping strategies, both positive and negative, that you have witnessed or experienced.

26. Should the poker question have been asked of Ken? Why or why not? Were you surprised by his response?

27. Discuss the ways that Ken and Noreen completed each other. What did they need from each other? What was lacking and how did those needs get reconciled?
28. Describe ways that World War II changed the world. How was it the same and different from other wars, including Vietnam? How has war affected your family and friends?
29. What is the significance of the cover art as it pertains to the text? Do you feel it adequately reflects the contents of the book? Why or why not?
30. In chapter 7, Noreen vows to avoid negativity in her own life and to avoid wallowing at all costs? Why was that important to her? Give examples of times she succeeded and times she did not. Which experiences in your life sparked that characteristic? Discuss how life experiences shape our beliefs and our behaviors.

CPSIA information can be obtained
at www.ICGtesting.com
Printed in the USA
LVHW012213100721
692283LV00009B/391